PSYCHODYNAMIC, AFFECTIVE, AND BEHAVIORAL THEORIES TO PSYCHOTHERAPY

ABOUT THE AUTHOR

Dr. Marty Sapp is a professor of Educational Psychology at the University of Wisconsin-Milwaukee. He earned his Ed.D. in Educational Psychology at the University of Cincinnati, and his substantive areas of interests are cognitive-behavioral therapies, hypnosis, anxiety disorders, research methods and designs, measurement, statistics, and counseling theories and issues.

Dr. Sapp is a licensed psychologist and Fellow of the American Psychological Association. He is a distinguished alumnus of the University of Cincinnati College of Education, Criminal Justice, and Human Services and the recipient of the School of Education Research Award at the University of Wisconsin-Milwaukee, 2005. In addition, he has published 8 single-authored books and more than 55 refereed journal articles. Moreover, he is an editorial member of the *Journal of Rational-Emotive and Cognitive-Behavior Therapy* and the *International Journal of Clinical and Experimental Hypnosis.* Currently, he is Associate Editor, *Multicultural Learning and Teaching.* He has served on the following editorial boards: *The Counseling Psychologist, Journal of Counseling and Development, Multiple Voices for Ethnically Diverse Exceptional Learners, Cognitive and Behavioral Practice,* and *Journal of Mental Health Counseling.* Finally, he has served as a reviewer for the following journals: *Educational Foundations, Professional Psychology: Research and Practice, Measurement and Evaluation in Counseling and Development,* and *Journal of Cross Cultural Psychology.*

PSYCHODYNAMIC, AFFECTIVE, AND BEHAVIORAL THEORIES TO PSYCHOTHERAPY

By

MARTY SAPP

Professor
Department of Educational Psychology
(Counseling)
University of Wisconsin-Milwaukee

CHARLES C THOMAS • PUBLISHER, LTD.
Springfield • Illinois • U.S.A.

Published and Distributed Throughout the World by

CHARLES C THOMAS • PUBLISHER, LTD.
2600 South First Street
Springfield, Illinois 62704

ISBN 978-0-398-07895-9 (hard)
ISBN 978-0-398-07896-6 (paper)

Library of Congress Catalog Card Number: 2009020443

With THOMAS BOOKS *careful attention is given to all details of manufacturing and design. It is the Publisher's desire to present books that are satisfactory as to their physical qualities and artistic possibilities and appropriate for their particular use.* THOMAS BOOKS *will be true to those laws of quality that assure a good name and good will.*

Printed in the United States of America
SM-R-3

Library of Congress Cataloging-in-Publication Data

Sapp, Marty, 1958-
Psychodynamic, affective, and behavioral theories to psychotherapy / by Marty Sapp.
p. cm.
Includes bibliographical references and index.
ISBN 978-0-398-07895-9 (hard) -- ISBN 978-0-398-07896-6 (pbk.)
1. Psychodynamic psychotherapy. 2. Behavior therapy. 3. Cognitive therapy. 4. Psychotherapy. I. Title.

RC489.P72S27 2009
616.89'14–dc22

2009020443

To my students

PREFACE

Psychodynamic, Affective, and Behavioral Theories to Psychotherapy is designed for clinicians who are interested in the three major approaches to psychotherapy: psychodynamic, affective, and behavioral. In addition, graduate students in counseling psychology, clinical psychology, and related areas will find that these chapters with experiential exercises bring these theories to life. To facilitate the assimilation of material, key terms are in boldface, and many chapters have glossaries. Moreover, examination questions are provided at the end of each chapter and the *DSM-IV-TR* is covered. Theories of psychotherapy are defined as specific skills that a clinician or student can master. Specifically, theories of psychotherapy are broken down into three phases or levels: beginning (Level I); intermediate (Level II), and action (Level III). Theories that are Level I are appropriate for establishing a counseling relationship. Level II counseling skills further enhance this initial counseling relationship. Level III theories are action-oriented theories of psychotherapy that are designed to move a client toward change. Theories of psychotherapy are categorized into three phases and along three dimensions, psychodynamic, affective, and behavioral.

Theoretical eclecticism, haphazardly drawing from opposing theories, can lead to confusion and epistemological incompatibility. Technical eclecticism is the focus of this text, and this suggests using procedures and techniques from many theories without endorsing the individual theories. This writer believes that it is possible to be eclectic within a broad theoretical framework without randomly trying to integrate diametrically opposite theories. Many books on psychotherapy do not address counseling research, but this book will provide a basis for why various forms of psychotherapy are effective.

M. S.

ACKNOWLEDGMENTS

It took several individuals to bring this text into press. First, I would like to thank the students on my research team. Second, I offer thanks to the University of Wisconsin-Milwaukee School of Education word processing pool for typing this part of this manuscript. In closing, comments or discussions concerning this text are encouraged. My address is The University of Wisconsin-Milwaukee, Department of Educational Psychology, 2400 E. Hartford Avenue, Milwaukee, Wisconsin 53211. My telephone number is (414) 229-6247, my e-mail address is sapp@uwm.edu, and my fax number is (414) 229-4939.

CONTENTS

PSYCHODYNAMIC, AFFECTIVE, AND BEHAVIORAL THEORIES TO PSYCHOTHERAPY

Chapter 1

CHAPTER OVERVIEW

Chapter 1 presents definitions of counseling and psychotherapy and an overview of counseling and psychotherapy research. In addition, the notion of case conceptualization is presented.

Definitions of Counseling and Psychotherapy Counseling or psychotherapy are an interpersonal relationship between a professional who has at least a master's degree in the helping professions, such as counseling psychology, counselor education, social work, psychiatric nursing, and so on, in which services are provided to a client. By definition, a client is a person who is at least 18 years of age and is able to sign an informed consent agreement for counseling. Within the modern world of clients, there can be groups or organizations. Clients seek counseling for a variety of interpersonal issues, such as intrapersonal difficulties, job-related issues, drug and alcohol issues, marital and family concerns, sexual issues, eating disorders, issues of self-identity, difficulty maintaining relationships, and a host of other issues. Most state boards of counseling, social services, and nursing regulate counseling services.

Within this text, counseling and psychotherapy are used interchangeably, but within certain settings a professional may be identified as a school counselor or, for example within a hospital setting, as a psychotherapist. Moreover, within certain settings, such as state-certified mental health facilities, the title psychotherapist may be a protected title.

Counselor licensure and certification laws are designed to protect the public by preventing nonlicensed and noncertified people from practicing. Counselor licensure offers stronger legal sanctions than does counselor certification. More specifically, counselor licensure offers title protection – meaning individuals cannot call themselves counselors or psychotherapists – and practice protection. Practice protection prevents individuals who do not meet state requirements from practicing counseling. Many counselor licensures and certifications generally cover the following areas:

Individual counseling theories
Vocational psychology or career counseling theories
Essentials of counseling practice
Multicultural counseling
Counseling practicum and internship
Theories of learning and personality
Developmental psychology
Family therapy
Abnormal psychology
Legal and ethical issues
Measurement and evaluation
Research methods and techniques
Statistical methods
Psychodiagnostics
Biological bases of behavior

Finally, state licensure and certification for counseling require at least a master's degree in counseling or a related field and several hundred hours of counseling experience with appropriate supervision.

Readers should be aware that, in addition to state certifications, there are a variety of other certifications, such as certification in schools. State boards or departments of education establish standards for certification in schools. The Council for Accreditation of Counseling and Related Educational Programs (CACREP) sets educational standards for graduate counseling programs, and the Council on Rehabilitation Education (CORE) accredits graduate programs in rehabilitation counseling. The American Counseling Association (ACA) and the American Psychological Association (APA) are the two national organizations that regulate counseling. ACA and APA have a variety of divisions that deal with subjects from adult development and aging to mental health counseling. Readers can access ACA at http://www.counseling.org/ and APA at http://www.apa.org/.

Goals of Psychotherapy

Because counseling or psychotherapy differs in terms of clientele and settings, there are goals of counseling that transcend both. Specifically, some of the goals of counseling are self-exploration and changes in feelings, thought, and behaviors. Moreover, another goal of counseling is to help cope with personal or situational changes.

Psychotherapy Effectiveness

How do we know that psychotherapy is efficacious? Bergin and Garfield (1994) found that all forms of psychotherapy were efficacious, but they differ in terms of effect sizes. Unlike statistical null hypothesis testing, which attempts to reject or fail to reject the null hypothesis (the population means are equal), effect sizes measure the degree of effectiveness and practical significance or the degree to which the null hypothesis may be false. Bergin and Garfield used meta-analysis, a technique that averages effect sizes across several studies, to show that psychotherapy was efficacious. When psychotherapy groups are compared to control groups, psychotherapy has an average *d* effect size of .70 (Sapp, 1997a, 1999, 2002, 2004a, 2006a, b). Moreover, patients receiving psychotherapy are better off than 79% of patients not receiving treatment. Kirsch (1990) and Kirsch and Lynn (1999) believe that psychotherapy is mostly an expectancy manipulation, or placebo effect. The theories of expectancies come from a group of behavioral theories called social learning theories, and these theories add social psychological and cognitive perspectives to aspects of behaviorism.

The Effect Sizes *r* and *d* and Their Confidence Intervals

The effect size *r* is a correlation coefficient, and unlike reliability, is an unsquared measure. The effect size *r* is the relationship or association between an independent variable, denoted by *x*, and a dependent variable, denoted by *y*. Moreover, the effect size *r* can be the correlation of a pretest or covariate of *a* before hypnosis measure and a posttest hypnosis measure.

Effect sizes allow researchers to determine if a relationship has practical significance. Traditional statistical tests such as *t*-test, *F*-test, chi square, and so on only allow one to determine if a relationship is significantly greater than zero. In other words, traditional statistical tests permit one to reject or fail to reject the null hypothesis, no treatment effect, or the population means are not significantly different, but effect sizes allow one to determine the degree of effect a treatment has within a population, or the degree in which the null hypothesis may be false (Sapp, 1997a).

The r effect size, also called Pearson Product–Moment Correlation, measures a linear relationship between two variables. Quasi-interval data or higher are assumed with the r effect size. Quasi-intervals are obtained from data when equal differences among measurements represent the same or equal amount of difference. For example, the difference between an 8 and a 9 on the Stanford Hypnotic Susceptibility Scale, Form C (SHSS:C) is an equal distance of one point, and most standardized hypnotizability scales are quasi-interval data. Moreover, psychological tests are quasi-intervals.

The Pearson r is another name for the effect size r, and it communicates two bits of information. First, it gives the magnitude of the relationship between two linearly related variables. The larger the size of the correlation, the greater the magnitude; however, the maximum magnitude the effect size r coefficient can have is $+1.00$ or -1.00. Second, the effect size r tells us the direction of the relationship. For example, an r effect size of $+1.00$ indicates a perfect, positive relationship between two hypnotizability measures. For example, as the independent hypnotizability variable increases, the corresponding dependent hypnotizability variable increases. In contrast, an r of -1.00 indicates a perfect negative relationship between the independent and dependent hypnotizability variables with a perfect negative r effect size. As the independent hypnotizability variable increases, the corresponding dependent hypnotizability variable decreases. The reader should note that it is arbitrary which variable is called independent or dependent, because the effect size r is a symmetrical correlation. This means that the correlation of X and Y equals the correlation of Y and X, and this is referred to as the symmetrical distribution assumption of the effect size r. Another interesting fact about the effect size r is that the more variability that exists within X and Y, the greater the correlation. It is also assumed that X and Y have equal skewness and kurtosis. In addition, the effect size r assumes linearity, and when the relationship between X and Y is not linear, the correlation η or the correlation ratio is the appropriate effect size.

Verbally, the formula for the *r* effect size is the mean of the product of *z*-scores. In other words, we find the *z*-scores for all *X* and *Y* scores and then multiply every *X* and *Y* pair and we add the product (multiplication) of every corresponding *X* and *Y* *z*-score and divide by the total number of pairs. This simple formula is expressed as:

$$r = \frac{\sum Z_x Z_y}{N}$$

Here, Z_x is every *X* value minus the mean of the *X* values divided by the standard deviation of the *X* values. Similarly, Z_y is every *Y* value minus the mean of the *Y* values divided by the standard deviation of the *Y* values. Z_x and Z_y are analogous to standard deviation and are referred to as moments, hence the name Pearson Product–Moment Correlation. The reader should note that a moment is a measure of variability like the standard deviation.

A practical example will help clarify the effect size *r*. Let us suppose that four students were measured on two hypnotizability scales denoted by *X* and *Y*. Even though four pairs would not permit any real conclusion, this example will help to clarify the *r* effect size:

Students	X	Y
1	8	9
2	7	6
3	5	0
4	4	7

The following are the Statistical Package for the Social Sciences (SPSS) and Statistical Analysis Software (SAS) commands for calculating the effect size *r*:

SPSS

```
Title "Pearson r".
Data List/X 1-2 Y 4-5 .
Begin Data .
8 9
7 6
5 0
4 7
End Data.
List .
```

SAS

```
data pearson;
input x y @@;
lines;
8 9 7 6
5 0 4 7
Proc corr;
proc print;
```

```
Correlations Variables =
X Y/
  Print = twotail/
  Statistics = all/.
```

The *r* for this example is .471, and it is close to what Rosenthal (1984) called a large effect size ($r = .50$).

The following are the formulas for η^2, η, and a sample data set:

$$\eta^2 = \frac{\text{between sum of squares}}{\text{total sum of squares}}$$

$$\eta = \left(\frac{\text{between sum of squares}}{\text{total sum of squares}}\right)^{1/2}$$

Participants	Group ID	Dependent Variable
1	1	53
2	1	54
3	1	52
4	1	55
5	1	54
6	2	53
7	2	56
8	2	57
9	2	55
10	3	57
11	3	56
12	3	54
13	3	58
14	3	59
15	3	58
16	4	62
17	4	62
18	4	61
19	4	60
20	4	56

The SPSS control lines for η^2 are the following:

```
UNIANOVA
 VAR00002 BY VAR00001
 /METHOD = SSTYPE(3)
 /INTERCEPT = INCLUDE
 /PRINT = ETASQ OPOWER HOMOGENEITY
 /CRITERIA = ALPHA(.05)
 /DESIGN = VAR00001 .
```

The following are selected output from SPSS, and they include the Levene's Test of Equality of Error Variances and Tests of Between-Subject Effects:

Levene's Test of Equality of Error Variances[a]

Dependent Variable: VAR00002

F	*df* 1	*df* 2	Sig.
.564	3	16	.646*

* Is the homogeneity of variance test, and it is tenable.

Tests the null hypothesis that the error variance of the dependent variable is equal across groups.

Tests of Between-Subjects Effects

Dependent Variable: VAR00002

Source	Type III Sum of Squares	*df*	Mean Square	*F*	Sig.	Partial η^2
Corrected Model	118.050	3	39.350	11.500	.000	.683**
Intercept	62569.717	1	62569.717	18285.214	.000	.999
VAR0001	118.050	3	39.350	11.500	.000	.683
Error	54.750	16	3.422			
Total	64244.000	20				
Corrected Total	172.800	19				

** Is η^2 and equals .683.

One can verify η^2 by substituting into the following formula:

$$\eta^2 = \frac{\text{between sum of squares}}{\text{total sum of squares}}$$

$$= \frac{118.050}{172.800}$$

$$= .683$$

Cohen's *d* Effect Sizes

The *d* effect sizes are analogues to *t*-tests, and these effect sizes are called standardized mean differences (Cohen, 1977).

Readers may remember that one can use a one-sample *t*-test to compare a sample mean to a population mean. For example, let us assume that we had the grade point averages of twenty-one high school students randomly chosen from a high school, and let us assume that we know the population mean grade point average for every student at the high school was 3.1. The following are these data for the twenty-one high school students:

Student	GPA
1	2.9
2	2.7
3	2.8
4	3.0
5	2.6
6	2.9
7	3.1
8	2.9
9	3.0
10	2.7
11	2.9
12	3.0
13	2.8
14	3.1
15	2.9
16	2.7
17	3.2
18	2.8
19	2.8
20	3.1
21	3.0

The following are the SPSS control lines:

```
T-Test
  /TESTVAL = 3.1
  /MISSING = ANALYSIS
  /VARIABLES = VAR00001
  /CRITERIA = CI(.95)
```

The following output from this analysis includes the following headings: One-Sample Statistics and One-Sample Test.

One-Sample Statistics

	N	Mean	Std. Deviation	Std. Error Mean
VAR00001	21	2.9000	.15811	.03450

One-Sample Test

	Test Value = 3.1					
					95% Confidence Interval of the Difference	
	T	*df*	Sig. (2-tailed)	Mean Difference*	Lower	Upper
VAR00001	-5.797	20	.000	-.20000	-.2720	-.1280

Cohen's *d* for one sample case is the following:

$$\begin{aligned} d &= \frac{\text{mean difference}}{\text{standard deviation}} \\ &= \frac{-.20}{.15811} \\ &= -1.265 \end{aligned}$$

For a two-group situation, suppose we have the following means and standard deviations:

Group Size	Mean	Standard Deviation
Treatment Group	82.5	3.5355
Control Group	78.0	7.0711

The effect size can be calculated in a variety of ways, but two will be illustrated. First, it can be the difference between means divided by the control group standard deviation.

$$d = \frac{82.5 - 78.0}{7.0711} = \frac{4.5}{7.0711} = .64$$

Second, the *d* effect size can be expressed as the differences between means divided by the pooled standard deviation. Readers may remember that the formula for the pooled standard deviation is the following:

$$\text{pooled} = \left[\frac{(N_1 - 1)s_1^2 + (N_2 - 1)S_2^2}{N_1 + N_2 - 2}\right]^{\frac{1}{2}}$$

$$= 5.59$$

$$\text{Therefore, } d = \frac{82.50 - 78.00}{5.59} = .81$$

Readers may notice a difference between the two effect sizes. This is the nature of effect sizes, and one has to operationally define a *d* effect size and consistently apply the same definition and formula throughout a study (Sapp, 2006c).

In summary, Cohen (1977) defined the most basic effect measure, the statistic that is synthesized, as an analog to the *t*-tests for two means, and this is one of the commonly reported ones in the literature. Specifically, for a two-group situation, he defined the *d* effect size as the differences between two population means divided by the standard deviation of either population, because homogeneity or equality of variances is assumed. The *d* effect size has the general formula

$$d = \frac{\mu_1 - \mu_2}{\sigma}$$

μ_1 = the treatment group
μ_2 = the control group
σ = common population standard deviation

Suppose μ_1 equals the population mean, and in this case we are using it to represent the treatment group population mean of 1.0. Let us assume that μ_2, the population mean for the control group, equals .2, and, finally, σ equals 1.00. By substitution,

$$d = \frac{1.0 - .2}{1} = .8$$

Again, according to Cohen's definition, this is a large effect size.

The effect size for paired samples *t*-test follow the same logic as the ones for the one-sample and two-sample cases. Suppose ten students were pretested, given hypnotic suggestions designed to impact career choice, and posttested on the Strong-Campbell Interest Inventory.

The purpose of the study was that students were given hypnosis as a means to affect career choice after the pretest. This design can be depicted as the following:

Pretest	Hypnosis	Posttest
50		65
51		56
45		32
53		30
55		51
47		53
46		50
61		47
55		47
53		44

The SPSS control lines for this design are the following:

```
T-Test
  PAIRS = VAR000001 WITH VAR00002 (PAIRED)
  /CRITERIA = CI(.95)
  /MISSING = ANALYSIS.
```

Selected output from this analysis follows and it includes the following headings: Paired Samples Test, Paired Samples Test, Paired Samples Statistics, and Paired Samples Correlations.

Paired Samples Test

	Paired Differences					t
				95% Confidence Interval of the Difference		
	Mean	Std. Deviation	Std. Error Mean	Lower	Upper	
Pair 1 VAR00001 – VAR00002	2.10000**	9.38616***	2.96816	-4.61445	8.81445	.708*

**See* next page.

	Df	Sig. (2-tailed)
Pair 1 VAR00001 – VAR00002	9	.497

Paired Samples Statistics

	Mean	*N*	Std. Deviation	Std. Error Mean
Pair 1 VAR00001	51.6000	10	4.88080	1.54344
VAR00002	49.5000	10	8.47545	2.68017

Paired Samples Correlations

		N	Correlation	Sig.
Pair 1	VAR00001 & VAR00002	10	.091	.802

*In the first Paired Samples Test, statistical significance was not achieved, but the *d* effect size is the following: Mean of Differences Scores 2.1 divided by the standard deviation (9.38616), and the *d* effect size equals

$$d = \frac{\overline{D}}{S_D} = \frac{2.1}{9.38616} = .22$$

This represents a small effect size.

Cohen (1977) provided the following rough guidelines of *d* equals .2 as a small effect size, .5 as a medium effect size, and .8 as a large effect size measure; however, one needs to determine the importance of an effect size by consulting the professional literature (Wolf, 1986).

The *d* effect size can suggest that a treatment is harmful, or it may suggest that a control group is outperforming a treatment group. This can happen when the effect size measure is negative. Rosenthal (1984) provided the following rough guidelines for effect size *r*. For values of *r*, .1 is considered a small effect size, .3 a medium effect size, and .5 a large effect size. As Sapp (1997, 1999, 2002a, 2006c) noted, arithmetic operations cannot be performed on *r* because as the population correlation coefficient gets further and further from zero, the distribution of *r* becomes skewed. Therefore, Fisher (1928) developed a transformation of *r* called *Zr* or Z_r. The following is the formula for *Zr*.

$$Z_r = \frac{1}{2}\log_e\left[\frac{1+r}{1-r}\right]$$

Meta-Analysis

During the twenty-first century, after hearing about meta-analysis, many clinicians and researchers assumed that it would provide the ultimate truth or answer. The reader, however, will shortly see that there are a variety of techniques for performing meta-analyses, and there are several schools of thought on how values can be calculated.

Hence, there are a variety of effect size measures. **Meta-analysis** is a quantitative method for synthesizing the literature, and this technique is not new. For example, Cohen (1977) was one of the first researchers to describe meta-analysis and a related technique called power analysis. The reader should note that the *r* effect size and the *d* effect size can be added across several studies to provide an overall effect called a meta-analysis.

There are three concepts related to hypothesis testing; they are Type I error, Type II error, and power. **Type I error** is the level of significance chosen by a clinician or researcher to test the significance of a given statistical test. Type I error is the probability of wrongly rejecting the null hypothesis (no treatment effect) or the probability of rejecting the null hypothesis when it is true (Stevens, 1999). In effect, with Type I error one is saying that the groups differ, when in fact they do not. **Type II error** is the probability of accepting the null hypothesis when it is false. For example, we are saying the groups do not differ when in fact they do. The reader should note that Type I and Type II errors are inversely related; that is, as one controls Type I error, Type II error increases, and as one controls Type II error, Type I error increases. Now, power is the probability within statistical or hypothesis testing of rejecting the null hypothesis when it is false; in essence, **power** is the probability of making a correct decision. As Sapp (1997, 2002, 2006c, 2008) noted, Type II error and power are related because power equals one minus Type II errors; therefore, if a clinician or researcher chooses a small alpha level, Type II error increases and power decreases. In fact, it may not be wise to choose an extremely small alpha level such as .01 or .001, since these values tend to reduce statistical power and inflate Type II error. In summary, meta-analysis and its statistics, called effect size measures, allow a clinician or researcher to determine the degree of effect a treatment has within a population, and it determines the degree to which the null hypothesis may be false.

Hedges (1982) argued that the *d* effect size is biased, and he provided a formula to find a weight *d*. This formula is accurate when both the experimental and the control group sample sizes are greater than ten and the effect size is less than 1.5.

$$\bar{d} = \frac{\Sigma wd}{\Sigma w}$$

d is the unweighted effect size measure, and *w* is the reciprocal of the estimated variance of *d* for each study to be aggregated within the meta-analysis.

When the experimental and control groups have approximately equal numbers of participants greater than ten, Hedges (1982) provided the following formula for *w*:

$$w = \frac{2N}{8 + d^2}$$

Where *d* is the unweighted effect size, and *N* is the combined sample size for the treatment and control groups.

Suppose for our example that we calculated an uncorrected or biased *d* of .8, and the combined sample size for the treatment group and control group was 80. Substituting in the formula for *w*,

$$w = \frac{2(80)}{8 + .8^2} = \frac{160}{8.64} = 18.52$$

Now, if we substituted into the $\overline{d}$ formula,

$$\overline{d} = \frac{18.52(.8)}{18.52} = \frac{14.816}{18.52} = .80$$

Even though within this example the $\overline{d}$ and *d* are almost equal, when several studies are involved *d* is a weight average of *d*. Wolf (1986) provides the following values of *d*, *W*, and *N* for four fictional studies:

Study	*N*	*d*	*W*
1	82	.60	19.6
2	62	–.50	15.0
3	202	.43	49.4
4	22	.75	5.1

The mean of the unweighted or biased *d*

$$d = \frac{.60 + (-.50) + .43 + .75}{4} = .32$$

Now, the weight *d* is the following:

$$- \quad (19.6)(.60) + (15.0)(-.50) + (49.4)(.43) + (5.1)(.75)$$

$$d = \frac{}{19.6 + 15.0 + 49.4 + 5.1} = .39$$

The reader should notice that the unbiased or weighted *d* of .39 is slightly larger than the unweighted *d* of .32. This emphasizes the point that when the sample sizes are greater than ten participants, the two values are close (Green & Hall, 1984). Weighted effect sizes are referred to as corrected effect sizes and unweighted effect sizes are called uncorrected effect sizes.

As previously stated, Rosenthal (1984) described another effect size that he prefers, which is the Pearson Product–Moment Correlation coefficient. One can transform a Cohen's *d* to an *r* using the following formula:

$$r = d/(d^2 + 1/pq)^{1/2}$$

Where *p* is the proportion of the participants of the first of the two groups compared, and *q* (1 – *p*) is the proportion of participants in the second group that is being compared. Rosenthal (1984) provided the following rough guidelines for effect size *r*. For values of *r*, .1 is considered a small effect size, .3 a medium effect size, and .5 a large effect size. As Sapp (1997a, 2002a, 2006c, 2008) noted, arithmetic operations cannot be performed on *r* because as the population correlation coefficient gets further and further from zero, the distribution of *r* becomes skewed. Therefore, as mentioned earlier Fisher (1928) developed a transformation of *r* called *Zr* or Z_r. The following is the formula for Z_r:

$$Z_r = \frac{1}{2}\log_e\left[\frac{1 + r}{1 - r}\right]$$

Like values of effect *d* can be corrected; the same can occur with the effect size *r*. Suppose we calculated an *r* value of .6 with an *N* of eleven. First, *r* is divided by 2(*N* – 1), which is the estimated bias.

$$\text{estimated bias} = \frac{.6}{2(10)} = \frac{.6}{20} = .03$$

Now, this bias is removed from Z_r, which is .693 for an *r* of .60; therefore, we correct or subtract .03 from .693 (Z_r). Corrected $Z_r = .693 - .03 = .663$, which is associated with an *r* of .580. If we repeat the cal culation for the value of *r* equals .580 and Z_r equals .693, estimated bias equals

$$\frac{.580}{2(11 - 1)} = \frac{.580}{20} = .029$$

$$.693 - .029 = .664$$

The value Z_r of .664 is associated with an r of .580. Notice that the corrected r of .580 differs from the uncorrected r of .60. Now, it should be apparent to the reader that effect sizes can be corrected or uncorrected or biased.

Before leaving the topic of meta-analysis, I would like to use an example from Rosenthal and Rosnow (1984) to illustrate how a moderate effect size of r can have important practical significance. Rosenthal and Rosnow compared the results of a treatment and a control group. The dependent variable was whether the patients lived or died. Rosenthal and Rosnow presented the following table:

	Treatment Outcome		
	Alive	Dead	Total
Treatment Group	66	34	100
Control Group	34	66	100
Total	100	100	200

Because this example involves a frequency or contingency table for dichotomous dependent variable (alive versus dead), chi square is the correct test statistic, and

$$\text{chi square} = \frac{021}{E1} + \frac{022}{E2} + \frac{023}{E3} + \frac{02}{E4} - N$$

$$\text{where } E = \frac{R(C)}{N}$$

$$R = \text{the row total}$$

$$C = \text{column total}$$

$$N = \text{the number of participants}$$

Es are needed for the following cells:

Row 1, Column 1

$$(1,1) = \frac{100(100)}{200} = 50$$

Row 1, Column 2

$$(1,2) = \frac{100(100)}{200} = 50$$

Row 2, Column 1

$$(2,1) = \frac{100(100)}{200} = 50$$

Row 2, Column 2

$$(2,2) = \frac{100(100)}{200} = 50$$

$$\text{chi square} = \frac{(66)^2}{50} + \frac{(34)^2}{50} + \frac{(34)^2}{50} + \frac{(66)^2}{50} - 200$$

$$= \frac{4356 + 1156 + 1156 + 4356}{50} - 200$$

$$= 20.48$$

Now, Cramer's phi, a Pearson Product–Moment Correlation for dichotomous dependent variables, is the following:

$$\text{Cramer's phi} = \left[\frac{\text{chi square}}{N(K - 1)}\right]^{\frac{1}{2}}$$

where K = smaller of rows or columns
N = the number of participants

$$\text{Cramer's phi} = \left[\frac{20.48}{200(2 - 1)}\right]^{\frac{1}{2}}$$

$$= [.1024]^{\frac{1}{2}}$$

$$= .32$$

Alternatively, Glass and Hopkins (1996) defined this correlation as

$$\text{Cramer's phi} = \frac{bc - ad}{[(a + c)(b + d)(a + b)(c + d)]^{\frac{1}{2}}}$$

Rearranging our table, a, b, c, d would be as follows:

$$a = 66 \qquad b = 34$$

$$c = 34 \qquad d = 66$$

Now,

$$\text{Cramer's phi} = \frac{34(34) - 66(66)}{[(100)(100)(100)(100)]^{\frac{1}{2}}} = -.32$$

We referred to the Cramer's phi of .32 as a moderate effect size, and if we square this Cramer's phi, the variance explained is 10.24%. However, survival rate is increased from 34% to 66%; therefore, effect sizes must be interpreted within the substantive research area. Finally, for a detailed discussion of meta-analysis and effect size measure, see Rosenthal and Rosnow (1984), Wolf (1986), Rosenthal (1984), and Hunter and Schmidt (1990).

Confidence Intervals Around Effect Size *r*

Unfortunately, the sampling distribution of the population Pearson product-moment correlation is skewed when the value is other than zero, and when the value is zero it is symmetrical and almost normal. Moreover, the degree of skewness of the sampling distribution of the population correlation is also a function of sample size (Sapp, 2004a, b).

For example, when the population correlation coefficient is not zero and the sample size is small, there is greater skewness within the sampling distribution. Since the sampling distribution of the population correlation coefficient is not a normal distribution, the statistician R. A. Fisher developed a logarithmic transformation of r with tables that can be found in Sapp (2006c). Suppose a researcher found that the items of two hypnotizability scales had a correlation of .30, how would one construct a 95% confidence interval? First, using Table 2.7 from Sapp (1997a), we find the Fisher's z transformation of .30, which is .31. Next, we calculate the standard error which is 1 divided by the square root of the number of cases minus 3. If we assume that the number of cases is 25, the standard error is .21. The 95% confidence interval is the following: .31 plus or minus 1.96(.21), with the lower confidence limit of –.10 and the upper limit .72, but we have to transform the Fisher's z back to regular r, which becomes –.10 for the lower limit and .62 for the upper limit. The 99% confidence interval can be found by substituting 2.58 for 1.96 and following the same steps. The reader should notice that the confidence interval, –.10, .62 contains zero; therefore, the population coefficient does not differ significantly from zero. The reader should notice that when zero is in a confidence interval, statistical significance is not obtained.

Cohen (1977) was one of the first researchers to describe effect sizes and a related area called power analysis. Power is the probability of rejecting a false null hypothesis (population means are equal). Even though there are a variety of effect sizes, two are commonly used within meta-analysis: the correlation, which was discussed within the section on confidence intervals around validity, and the *d* effect size. The Pearson Product–Moment Correlation or Pearson *r* is familiar to readers, and Rosenthal (1984) defined a value of *r* of .1 as a small effect size, and a value of .3 as a medium effect size, and a value of .5 as a large effect size. Rosenthal is clear that these are rough rules of thumb and effect sizes have to be evaluated within a substantive area. Cohen (1977) defined the *d* effect size as the difference between two means divided by the standard deviation or some form of variability.

Even though there are over forty different effect sizes, the effect sizes *r* and *d* are commonly reported one in the literature. Confidence intervals around correlations are the same process described by Sapp (2004a). Confidence intervals around *d* effect sizes require, like coefficient alpha, noncentralized distributions. In addition, readers who are interested in the software for these distributions can consult Bird (2002), Smithson (2003), and Cummings and Finch (2005). Actually, Professor Geoff Cummings, at La Trobe University in Australia, has developed software that runs under the program Excel®, and it can be downloaded from the following website: http://www.latrobe.edu.au/psy/esci. This writer prefers Cummings' software, but later within this chapter the control lines for SAS version 8 will be presented for calculating confidence intervals around *d*.

Table 1–1 has the 95% confidence intervals for the highest average *d* effect sizes for the various forms of psychotherapy along with the power values, and these intervals were calculated with software found in Smithson (2003). As previously stated, SAS version 8 can also calculate these intervals. For example, clearly short-term dynamic therapy and reality therapy both have lower power values than the other therapies. Stevens 2002, 1999 defined power values greater than .70 as adequate and values greater than .90 as excellent. Both short-term dynamic therapy and reality therapy have lower power values because of their small sample sizes. Power is not usually an issue with sample sizes of about 100. The readers should also notice that short-term dynamic therapy and reality therapy both have zeros within their confidence intervals that suggest the null hypothesis was not rejected and negative values within these intervals also suggest that both therapies can produce negative effects or harm; however, clearly any form of psychotherapy can produce negative effects, especially treatments with large effect sizes.

In summary, both short-dynamic therapy and reality therapy have confidence intervals that include zero, and confidence intervals around *d* provide more information than the single point estimate of *d* (Radtke, Sapp, Farrell, 1997).

Cognitive-behavioral therapy had a lower limit of .4677 (about a medium effect size and an upper limit of .6614, again a value reflecting a medium effect size). Hypnotherapy had a lower limit of .8025 (large effect size) and an upper limit of 1.0163 (large effect size).

Dynamic/humanistic therapy, person-centered therapy, and Gestalt therapy all had lower confidence intervals that are within the lower ranges, with dynamic/humanistic therapy with a lower limit of .0648, which is the lowest of the humanistic therapies.

In terms of cognitive-behavioral therapies with upper limits of values that are .80 or larger, only hypnotherapy, covert-behavioral therapy, modeling, and reality therapy had upper limits with high *d* effect sizes using confidence intervals.

These confidence intervals suggest that true population parameters vary from the *d* effect size point estimates. Most forms of cognitive-behavioral therapies have upper confidence intervals within the medium effect size ranges and not the larger ranges as suggested by the point estimates of *d*.

Using SAS Version 8 for Calculating the *d* Effect Size Confidence Intervals

Calculating confidence intervals for *d* effect sizes involves complex distributions called noncentralized distributions (Steiger & Fouladi, 1997). These distributions do not assume that the null hypothesis is true. Kline (2004) stated that the families of central distribution *t*, *F*, and chi square are special cases of noncentralized distributions. The

Table 1–1.
Confidence Intervals for Highest Effect Sizes for Various Forms of Psychotherapy with Power Values

Therapy Orientation	Effect size *d*	Estimated *t*-values	95% Confidence Interval for *d*	Power values	Number of studies
Short-Term Dynamic	.71	1.81	–.0451, .7483	.41	26
Psychodynamic	.69	7.52	.2523, .4374	1.00	475
Dynamic Eclectic	.89	9.69	.3505, .5392	1.00	474
Adlerian	.71	6.87	.2502, .4589	1.00	375
Dynamic/Humanistic	.40	2.93	.0648, .3354	.83	214
Person-Centered	.63	6.10	.2111, .4185	1.00	375
Gestalt	.64	6.97	.2274, .4118	1.00	475
Transactional Analysis	.67	7.30	.2424, .4272	1.00	475
Behavioral	1.06	7.75	.3861, .6723	1.00	214
Hypnotherapy	1.82	19.83	.8025, 1.0163	1.00	475
Systematic Desensitization	1.05	11.44	.4287, .6206	1.00	475
Implosive	.68	7.41	.2474, .4323	1.00	475
Behavior Modification	.73	7.95	.2717, .4575	1.00	475
Cognitive-Behavioral	1.13	12.31	.4677, .6614	1.00	475
Cognitive	1.00	7.31	.3571, .6413	1.00	214
Self-Control	1.01	7.39	.3624, .6469	1.00	214
Biofeedback	.91	6.66	.3140, .5956	1.00	214
Covert-Behavioral	1.52	11.12	.6072, .9116	1.00	214
Flooding	1.12	8.19	.4151, .7034	1.00	214
Relaxation	.90	6.58	.3087, .5899	1.00	214
Reinforcement	.97	7.09	.3424, .6258	1.00	214
Modeling	1.43	10.46	.5642, .8645	1.00	214
Reality	.75	1.72	–.0722, .8083	.38	21

d: population effect size for the *t*-test for independent two groups and $t = (\sqrt{N}/2)d$ and $d = 2t/\sqrt{N}$
According to Stevens (2002), power >.70 is adequate and >.90 is excellent.

reader should note that central distributions *t*, *F*, and chi square assume that the null hypothesis is true, and they are used for null hypothesis significance testing (NHST). In addition, they are used to determine critical values for test statistics.

Kline (2004) stated that the central *t* distributions are defined by one parameter, the degrees of freedom; however, as previously stated, the noncentralized distributions are defined by two parameters, the degrees of freedom and the noncentrality parameters. When the centrality parameter equals zero for a *t*-test, the resulting distribution is the symmetrical centralized *t* distribution. Cummings and Finch (2005) noted that as the noncentrality parameter becomes positive, the noncentral *t* distribution becomes more positively skewed. In contrast, when the noncentrality parameter becomes increasingly negative, the noncentral *t* distribution becomes negatively skewed.

SAS version 8 can easily calculate noncentrality interval estimations through an iterative interval estimation process. Kline (2004) provided the SAS control lines to compute an exact 95% confidence interval for the *d* effect size for two groups of participants, and the following are these control lines:

SAS Control Lines to Compute an Exact 95% Confidence Interval for Effect Size *d* for Two Groups of Participants

```
data noncentral_ci_for_delta;
/*two-group design*/
/*data*/
t=3.10;
df=58
n1=30
n2=30
/*lower, upper bounds for ncp*/
ncp_lower=tnonct (t, df, .975);
ncp_upper=tnonct (t, df, .025);
/*lower, upper bounds for delta*/
delta_lower=ncp_lower*sqrt ((n1+n2)/(n1*n2));
delta_upper=ncp_upper*sqrt ((n1+n2)/(n1*n2));
output;
run;
proc print;
run;
```

Note: The only changes in the control lines for a 99% confidence interval is (*t*, *df*, .995) and (*t*, *df*, .005).

Output

Obs	*t*	*df*	*n*1	*n*2	ncp_lower	ncp_upper	delta_lower	delta_upper
1	3.1	58	30	30	1.04844	5.12684	0.27071	1.32374

The reader should notice that one has to transform *d* into *t*. As noted at the bottom of Table 1–1, $t = (\sqrt{N/2})d$. If we assume that $d = .8$, then $t = 3.10$. In addition, one has to find the degrees of freedom which is *n*1 equals 30 plus *n*2 equals 30 minus 2 or 58. Within the output section, delta_lower is the lower confidence limit, which is .27071, and delta_upper is the upper confidence limit, which is 1.32374.

The following are the SAS control lines for completing an exact confidence interval for the effect size d with one group of participants.

SAS Control Lines to Compute an Exact 95% Confidence Interval for Effect Size *d* for One Group of Participants

```
data noncentral_ci_for_delta;
/*One-group design*/
/*data*/
t = 1.81;
df = 25
n = 26
/*lower, upper bounds for ncp*/
ncp_lower=tnonct (t, df, .975);
ncp_upper=tnonct (t, df, .025);
/*lower, upper bounds for delta*/
delta_lower=ncp_lower/sqrt(df+1);
delta_upper=ncp_upper/sqrt(df+1);
output;
run;
proc print;
run;
```

Note: Inserting (*t*, *df*, .995) and (*t*, *df*, .005) will provide a 99% confidence interval.

Output

Obs	*t*	*df*	*n*	ncp_lower	ncp_upper	delta_lower	delta_upper
1	1.81	25	26	-0.22946	3.81558	-0.045001	0.74830

The reader should notice that these are the control lines used to obtain the results for short-term dynamic therapy, where $t = 1.81$ and the number of studies was 26; therefore, the degrees of freedom (*df*) equals the number of studies minus 1 or 25. Again, delta_lower is the lower limit, which is -0.045001, and delta_upper is the upper limit, which is 0.74830.

Discussion

The *r* and *d* effect sizes, along with their confidence intervals, are necessary to improve counseling research. Many counseling researchers know how to calculate the *r* effect size and put confidence intervals around this value, but the computer software SAS version 8 can calculate confidence intervals for the *d* effect size. As previously stated by Sapp (2004a), counseling researchers need to report reliability measures for all items used within studies and confidence intervals around reliabilities. In a similar vein, confidence intervals are also required for validity indices used within counseling research (Sapp, 2002a). If counseling researchers start routinely reporting effect sizes within studies, it will aid with meta-analytical thinking and improve the area.

Summary of Meta-Analysis

As previously stated, meta-analysis is a numerical way of summarizing the literature within a given area (Sapp, 2004c; 2006c). Statistics called effect sizes allow researchers to determine if a form of counseling has an effect size greater than zero; hence zero would indicate that a treatment did not have an effect; however, with effect sizes, there are over 40 different effect size measures (Sapp, 2004c; Thompson, 2003). Versions of the *r* and *d* size are the most common. As the reader may know, *r* is a correlation coefficient and is the relationship between an independent variable and a dependent variable. Cohen (1977) defined the *d* effect size as the difference between two population means divided by the standard deviation of either population, provided that the homogeneity of variances assumption is tenable using the Levene's test from the statistical software package called SPSS.

There are several issues with the *d* effect size. For example, the population standard deviation can be from the control group posttest measure, or it could be the pretest population standard deviation for the control group, or it could involve pooling or weighting standard deviations from each group.

The *r* effect size can be converted into a Fisher's *z*, averaged and converted back into *r*. This averaged *r* value is a meta-analytic value or the measure of the effects of all the *r* values used for the calculation. Like the *r* effect, *d* effect sizes from several studies can be averaged, and the result is an overall effect for a series of *d* values.

Readers tend to confuse effect sizes with statistical significance testing, which attempts to reject the null hypothesis (the population means are equal). In contrast, meta-analysis and its effect sizes measure the degree to which the null hypothesis may be false. Essentially, meta-analysis allows one to determine practical significance.

Cohen (1988) defined *d* as the difference between means divided by the population standard deviation of each group. The formulas are as follows:

$$d = \frac{M1 - M2}{\sigma}$$

$$\text{where } \sigma = \sqrt{\left[\frac{\Sigma\,(X - M)2}{N}\right]}$$

where *X* is the raw score, *M* is the mean, and *N* is the number of cases.

$$d = \frac{M_1 - M_2}{\sigma \text{ pooled}}$$

$$\sigma \text{ pooled} = \sqrt{\left[\frac{\sigma_1^2 + \sigma_2^2}{2}\right]}$$

$$d = \frac{2t}{\sqrt{(df)}} \text{ or}$$

$$d = \frac{t(n_1 + n_2)}{[\sqrt{(df)}\ \sqrt{(n_1 n_2)}]}$$

$$d = \frac{2r}{\sqrt{(1 - r^2)}}$$

Cohen (1988) also defined *d* as the percentage of nonoverlap of the treatment group scores with those of the untreated group. For example, the following shows various effect sizes and percentage of nonoverlap.

Cohen's standard	*d* Effect Size	Percentage of Nonoverlap
	4.0	97.7
	3.8	97.0
	3.6	96.3
	3.4	95.3
	3.2	94.2
	3.0	92.8
	2.8	91.2
	2.6	89.3
	2.4	87.0
	2.2	84.3
	2.0	81.1
	1.9	79.4
	1.8	77.4
	1.7	75.4
	1.6	73.1
	1.5	70.7
	1.4	68.1
	1.3	65.3
	1.2	62.2
	1.1	58.9
	1.0	55.4
	.9	51.6
Large	**.8**	**47.4**
	.7	43.0
	.6	38.2
Medium	**.5**	**33.0**
	.4	27.4
	.3	21.3
Small	**.2**	**14.7**
	.1	7.7
	0	0

An effect size of zero indicates that the distribution of scores of the treatment group overlap completely with the distribution of the control group. Cohen (1977) provided the following rough guidelines for interpreting the *d* effect size: ***d* = .2 small effect size, *d* = .5 medium effect size, and *d* = .8 large effect size**. Wolf (1986) cautions against blindly interpreting effect sizes as small, medium, and large because one must interpret effect sizes within a given professional area. The *r* effect size and *d* effect size are related in the following manner:

$$r = \frac{d}{\sqrt{d^2 + 4}}$$

The following is the relationship between *r* and *d*:

	d effect size	*r* effect size
	4.0	.894
	3.8	.885
	3.6	.874
	3.4	.862
	3.2	.848
	3.0	.832
	2.8	.814
	2.6	.793
	2.4	.768
	2.2	.740
	2.0	.707
	1.9	.689
	1.8	.669
	1.7	.648
	1.6	.625
	1.5	.600
	1.4	.573
	1.3	.545
	1.2	.514
	1.1	.482
	1.0	.447
	.9	.410
Large	**.8**	**.371**
	.7	.330
	.6	.287
Medium	**.5**	**.243**
	.4	.196
	.3	.148
Small	**.2**	**.100**
	.1	.050
	0	0

Rosenthal (1984) described the effect size *r*. Like Cohen (1977) with the *d* effect sizes, Rosenthal provided rough guidelines for *r*: .1 small effect size, .3 medium effect size, and .5 large effect size.

The *r* effect size, also called the Pearson correlation coefficient, is biased when applied to independent samples. Essentially, the effect size *r* tends to be sample specific and biased with small sample sizes and small population effect sizes. Wang and Thompson (2007) recommended that the Ezekiel *r* squared correction and Smith *r* squared correction for controlling such bias. If *r* squared equaled .01 with a sample size of ten, the Ezekiel *r* squared correction and Smith Pearson *r* squared correction are the following:

Ezekiel

$$1 - [(n - 1) / (n - p - 1)] [1 - R^2]$$
$$1 - [(10 - 1) / (10 - 1 - 1)] [1 - 0.01]$$
$$1 - [9 / 8] [0.99]$$
$$1 - [1.12] [0.99]$$
$$1 - 1.11$$
$$\mathbf{= -0.11}$$

Smith

$$1 - [n / (n - p)] (1 - R^2)$$
$$1 - [10 / (10 - 1)] (1 - 0.01)$$
$$1 - [10 / 9] (0.99)$$
$$1 - [1.11] (0.99)$$
$$1 - 1.1$$
$$\mathbf{= -0.10}$$

R^2 equals the Pearson *r* squared, *p* equals the number of predictors.

In summary, the effect size *r* tends to be sample specific and not cross-validated; that is, it tends to shrink in value when applied to independent samples. Finally, both correction formulas showed how the effect size *r* tends to be biased.

Multivariate Measure of Effect

The term multivariate can be a confusing term, but in one sense it involves examining several variables simultaneously. Within a regression context, it is the relationship between two or more predictors (independent variables) and a dependent variable. From a multivariate regression context, it involves the relationship between two or more predictors and two or more dependent variables. Within the correlational multivariate methods, these include path analysis, factor analysis, principal components analysis, canonical correlation, and predictive discriminant analysis (Sapp, Obiakor, Gregas, & Scholze, 2007).

When two or more groups of participants are measured on several dependent variables, this is also a multivariate analysis of variance (MANOVA), a multivariate extension of ANOVA. In addition, multivariate statistics include multivariate analysis of covariance (MANCOVA), a multivariate generalization of ANCOVA; step-down analysis, a multivariate test procedure that focuses on the ordering of dependent variables through a series of analyses of covariance; descriptive discriminant analysis, a multivariate technique that determines group membership; and log linear analysis, an extension of the chi square test to three or more variables. In summary, if participants are measured on two or more dependent variables, a multivariate situation exists.

Why are multivariate statistics important? First, they control type I error, but with many univariate tests it cannot be easily estimated. Second, univariate statistics do not take into account the correlations among variables. Finally, multivariate statistics are more powerful than univariate statistics.

Hotelling's T^2

Hotelling's T^2 is the squared multivariate generalization of the *t*-test. The univariate *t*-test is the following:

$$t = \frac{\overline{y}_1 - \overline{y}_2}{\sqrt{\frac{(n_1 - 1)s_1^2 + (n_2 - 1)s_2^2}{n_1 + n_2 - 2}\left(\frac{1}{n_1} + \frac{1}{n_2}\right)}} \qquad (1)$$

Hotelling's T^2 is the following:

$$T^2 = \frac{n_1 n_2}{n_1 + n_2}\left(\overline{y}_1 - \overline{y}_2\right)' S^{-1}\left(\overline{y}_1 - \overline{y}_2\right) \qquad (2)$$

where $\left(\overline{y}_1 - \overline{y}_2\right)'$ is the transpose of vector of means, S- the sample covariance matrix, S^{-1} the matrix analogue of division is inversion, $\left(\overline{y}_1 - \overline{y}_2\right)$ the vectors of means.

The connection between Hotelling's T^2 and F is the following:

$$F = \frac{n_1 + n_2 - p - 1}{(n_1 + n_2 - 2)p} T^2 \qquad (3)$$

Formula (3) shows that T^2 provides an F distribution with p and $(N - P - 1)$ degrees of freedom. The p is the number of dependent variables, and N equals the sample size. Essentially, T^2 is the comparison of between variability divided by within variability. The univariate d and Mahalanobis distance (D^2) are the following:

univariate $$d = \frac{\overline{y_1} - \overline{y_2}}{s} \qquad (4)$$

multivariate $$D^2 = (\overline{y_1} - \overline{y_2})' S^{-1} (\overline{y_1} - \overline{y_2}) \qquad (5)$$

D^2 is also the following formulas:

$$\left[\frac{n_1 + n_2}{n_1 n_2}\right] T^2 \qquad (6)$$

$$\frac{1}{1 - r^2}\left[\frac{(x_{i1} - \overline{x_1})^2}{s_1^2} + \frac{(x_{i2} - \overline{x_2})^2}{s_2^2} - \frac{2r(x_{i1} - \overline{x_1})(x_{i2} - \overline{x_2})}{s_1 s_2}\right] \qquad (7)$$

Formula (7) shows that D^2 takes into account the interconnection of variables, and T^2 is the following:

$$\left[\frac{n_1 n_2}{n_1 + n_2}\right] D^2 \qquad (8)$$

Unlike univariate statistics, Mahalanobis distance takes into account the intercorrelation of variables.

Let us consider a two-group Hotelling's T^2 problem. Suppose two forms of treatment – person-centered and rational emotive behavior therapy (REBT) hypnosis – are used to reduce state anxiety and trait anxiety in college students. There are three participants in the person-centered group and six in the REBT hypnosis group. State and trait anxiety has a mean of 50 and a standard deviation of 10. The following are the fictitious data:

Person-Centered		REBT	
State Anxiety	Trait Anxiety	State Anxiety	Trait Anxiety
51	53	54	56
53	57	56	58
52	52	56	58
		55	60
		55	60
		54	66

The following are the SPSS codes for these data:

```
Title 'Two-Group Manova'.
Data list free/gp dep1 dep2.
1 51 53
1 53 57
1 52 52
2 54 56
2 56 58
2 55 60
2 55 60
2 54 66
End data.
Manova dep1 dep2 by gp(1,2)/
  Print=cellinfo(means)/.
```

The following selected output from SPSS has the results of Hotelling's T^2:

EFFECT .. gp
Multivariate Tests of Significance ($S = 1$, $M = 0$, $N = 2$)

Test Name	Value	Exact F. Hypoth.	*df*	Error *df*	Sig. of *f*
Pillais	.80855	12.66972	2.00	6.00	.007
Hotellings	**4.22324**	12.66972	2.00	6.00	.007
Wilks	.19145	12.66972	2.00	6.00	.007
Roys	.80855				

Note. . F statistics are exact.

EFFECT . . gp (Cont.)
Univariate F-tests with (1,7) D. F.

Variable	Hypoth. SS	Error SS	Hypoth. MS	Error MS	*f*	Sig. of *f*
dep1	18.00000	6.00000	18.00000	.85714	21.00000	.003
dep2	64.22222	73.33333	64.22222	10.47619	6.13030	.042

$$D^2 = \frac{N\ (T^2)}{n_1 n_2} = \frac{9\ (4.22)}{18} = 2.11$$

and this is a large effect size.

Unlike univariate statistics, Mahalanobis distance takes into account the intercorrelation of variables. D^2 is used within a regression context to locate outliers on predictors, and a large value suggests an outlier on a predictor.

Stevens (1980) provided power values for D^2, and he found for values of $D^2 < .64$ and $n < 25$, power is usually poor ($< .45$) and seldom adequate $> .70$. Usually, studies will report T^2 and using formula (3) one can find D^2. In summary, Mahalanobis distance, or D^2, is the multivariate analogue of the univariate *d* effect size. Stevens (2002) provided the following guidelines for interpreting D^2: .25 is small effect, .5 is medium effect, and > 1 is large effect.

Mahalanobis distance is a multivariate measure of effect, and it is a multivariate measure of distance. For example, large values of D^2 indicate large effect sizes. To summarize:

$$D_1^2 = \left(Xi - \overline{X}\right)' S^{-1} \left(Xi - \overline{X}\right)'$$

D^2 is defined in terms of the covariance matrix of S. *Xi* equals the vector of the data for case *i*, and $\overline{X}$ is the vector of means, or what statisticians call the centroid for predictors within the regression context. In closing, D^2 is essential for improving research, and it can be helpful in locating outliers and influential data points in regression analysis (Stevens, 1984).

Psychotherapy Effectiveness*

How do we know that psychotherapy is effective? Bergin and Garfield (1994) found that all forms of psychotherapy were effective. However, various forms of psychotherapy differ in terms of effect sizes. Bergin and Garfield used **meta-analysis**, a technique that summarizes the effect sizes of several studies. When psychotherapy groups are compared to control groups, psychotherapy has an overall ***d* effect size** of .70 (Sapp, 1997a, 1999, 2004c). In addition, clients undergoing psychotherapy are better off than the 79% of clients receiving no treat-

* The material in this section was adapted from Sapp (2004a).

ment. Some theorists, such as Kirsch (1990) and Kirsch and Lynn (1999), believe that psychotherapy is mostly a **placebo effect** or an **expectancy effect**, and they base their position partially on automaticity theory.

Kirsch and Lynn's (1999) notion of **expectancy** comes from a group of behavioral theories called **social learning theories**. For example, Miller and Dollard, Rotter, and Bandura developed social learning theories (Sapp, 1997a). Neal Miller and John Dollard (1941) were the first theorists to use the term **social learning theories**. They took tenets from Clark Hull's theory of learning and extended it to reflect social and cognitive perspectives. Hull believed that **drives** (reinforcement) energized all behavior; however, they do not direct behavior. He stated that there were two types of drives: primary and secondary. **Primary drives** are physiological needs such as food, clothing, and shelter; in contrast, **secondary drives** are associated, or acquire reinforcement value by being associated, with primary drives. For example, money, diamonds, pearls, and stocks are some examples of secondary drives. **Cues** determine how people respond to drives. For example, if one were having dinner at a prestigious restaurant and did not know which fork to use while eating, one could observe others and determine from the social cues which fork to use. According to Miller and Dollard's social learning theory, social cues are learned through a trial-and-error method. In essence, Miller and Dollard proposed a drive reduction theory in that reinforcement involves drive reduction. It is worth noting that Miller and Dollard were among the first theorists to attempt to combine psychoanalytic theory with behavioral theory, and their notion of drive reduction has the same meaning as it does within Freud's theory. Finally, Miller and Dollard's theory influenced the theories of Rotter and Bandura.

Rotter's (1966) social learning theory was the second development within the area of social learning. Rotter included more of a cognitive emphasis with his theory. Rotter's theory has four basic constructs: behavior potential, reinforcement value, expectancy, and psychological situation.

Behavioral potential is the potential for behavior, and it is the probability that a given behavior will occur in a situation, if it is reinforced. Reinforcement value is a client's preference for one reinforcer over another, and expectancy is a belief that a certain behavior will produce a certain reinforcer (Sapp, 1997a). The psychological situation is the context in which behavior occurs. Rotter's theory can be summarized as behavior potential equals function of (expectancy and reinforcement value). This formula states that behavior potential is a function of the interaction of expectancy and reinforcement value; therefore, a client's subjective perception, not external reality, determines his or her behavior potential. Finally, Rotter stated that behavior has to be interpreted within the social context of the client, and one does not want to give too much influence to dispositional factors.

Bandura's social learning theory was the third development within the area of social learning. Even though Bandura started his career as a traditional behaviorist, he found that operant and classical conditioning could not explain complex behaviors. He found that clients who had requisite skills for certain behaviors could extend their repertoire of skills by observing a therapist perform specific behaviors. What is interesting about Bandura's notion of observational learning, learning by observing, is that the public assumes that modeling will occur if there is a model. There is an important ingredient for successful modeling, however; the client has to accept the model. This point is often missed by popular psychology books and individuals within the media.

In summary, Bandura's theory is a social-cognitive-behavioral one, and he stated that behavior is determined by the complex interaction of personal, behavioral, and situational factor **reciprocal determinism**. Moreover, reciprocal determinism explains why clients think, feel, and do the things that they do.

Recently, Kirsch and Lynn (1998) and Wegner and Wheatley (1999) presented a **sociocognitive theory of automaticity**. According to Bargh and Barndollar (1996), the following four conditions are necessary and sufficient for cognitive processes or behavioral actions to be **automatic** (Bargh and Gollwitzer, 1994):

1. The cognitive process of behavioral action is outside the client's awareness.
2. The cognitive process or behavioral action cannot be prevented; therefore, the cognitive process or behavioral action is uncontrollable or unstoppable.
3. The cognitive process or behavioral action does not require cognitive resources to become initiated; that is, the client does not have to think about the cognitive process or behavioral action for it to be initiated.

4. The cognitive process or behavioral action does not require volitional effort to become initiated; therefore, the cognitive process or behavioral action is unintentional or nonvolitional.

Kirsch and Lynn's (1998) theory was influenced by several social cognitive theorists (Bargh, 1994; Bargh & Barndollar, 1996; Bargh & Gollwitzer, 1994; Dixon, Bruent & Laurence, 1990; Dixon & Laurence, 1992; Libet, 1985; Lynn, 1992; Lynn & Rhue, 1994) and Kirsch's (1990, 1997) response expectancy theory. Kirsch and Lynn proposed that all routinized behaviors are automatic. The reader may be aware that theories such as classical conditioning describe responding as automatic (Pitsch, Sapp & McNeely, 2001). For example, if a puff of air (unconditioned stimulus) is blown into one's face, the automatic response is to blink (unconditioned response). Moreover, sudden loud noise tends to produce automatic startle responses. In addition, Van Den Hout and Merckelbach (1991) presented a persuasive argument that clients are genetically prepared to respond to certain conditioned responses and that classical conditioning is not just the simplistic cue to responses but clients' anticipations about the probable relationship between stimuli (Sapp, 1997a). In summary, this neo-Pavlovian theory states that clients can respond to automatic and intentional responses.

Kirsch and Lynn's (1998) theory is also influenced by Norman and Shallice's (1986) model. Norman and Shallice stated that all behavior is initiated automatically, and this happens through hierarchically organized interactive sensory motor **schemata**. Readers may remember that Bartlett (1932) and Piaget (1926) were the first to describe the concept called schemata. Schemata comprise four interconnected concepts: cognitive structure, cognitive propositions, cognitive operations, and cognitive products (Granvold, 1994). **Cognitive structure** is how information is mentally stored in the brain or mind; cognitive propositions are the content stored with cognitive structures. Cognitive operations select, encode, and retrieve information. Cognitive products are the results of information processing, and they are self-cognitions, self-judgments, self-expectations, and self-conclusions. Finally, schemata serve as the basis for attributing actions as automatic.

According to Norman and Shallice (1986), two complementary systems control the initiation of actions. The lower system is called **contention scheduling**, and it handles routine actions and does not require attentional or conscious control or effort. The **supervisory**

attentional systems control novel tasks and nonroutinized behaviors (Woody & Farvolden, 1998).

Clearly, with Norman and Shallice's (1986) two-tier model, volition is connected with the supervisory system, and this model is similar to Hilgard's (1994) **neodissociation model of nonvolitional hypnotic responding**. Hilgard explains automatic hypnotic responding through a **dissociation theory**. Actually, before Hilgard developed his theory, Jean Marie Charcot (1825–1893) and his student, Pierre Janet (1859–1947) presented a dissociation theory of hypnosis. They believed that dissociation was more likely to happen when a client was exposed to extreme psychological stress or trauma. According to their theory, when clients experience extreme stress or trauma, there is a tendency for ideas and behavioral patterns that normally associate to become dissociated or separated. Hilgard's (1994) theory differs from Charcot's and Janet's in that he presented an incomplete theory of dissociation among cognitive systems, and his theory is based on cognitive psychology. Specifically, his theory has the following assumptions: (1) there is a central processing unit, called the executive ego, that evaluates activities, and (2) the executive ego has several hierarchical subsystems below it that govern cognitive functions. Hilgard suggested that automaticity within hypnosis is the result of a combination of dissociation among the executive ego and the cognitive subsystems and the erection of an amnesic or communications barrier among the dissociated parts. Woody and Farvolden (1998) modified Hilgard's theory, and they presented a dissociated control theory of hypnotic automaticity. They did not, however, believe that automatic hypnotic responding was the result of an amnesic barrier, rather they believed it was the result of hypnosis weakening control of the frontal lobe brain functions, which results in a dissociation of brain functions (Woody and Sadler, 1998).

Kirsch and Lynn (1998) argued that **response expectancies** determine clients' subjective feelings of automaticity and that response expectancies are self-confirming and tend to generate the subjective and physiological substrates of automaticity. To illustrate, Kirsch (1999; 2000) found that the placebo-induced expectancies could produce changes in asthma, anxiety, depression, panic, sexual arousal, tension, heart rate, blood pressure, dermatitis, and bronchial constriction. In essence, according to Kirsch and Lynn (1999), automaticity is the result of response expectancies; therefore, when a client expects to experience automaticity, he or she can modify his or her expectancy for that response and it can occur as a result of response expectancy modification.

Kirsch and Lynn's (1998) position on automaticity theory explains one facet of automaticity, especially within the area of hypnosis. For example, within the area of hypnosis, Barber (1999, 2000) describes positively set clients as having positive motivations to perform well in experiences during hypnosis and have positive expectancies. Moreover, these clients are able to think with and imagine the suggested phenomena. In essence, these clients are conforming, trusting, and imaginative (Sapp, 2000; Spiegel & Connery, 1982). However, Barber described two other types of clients: amnesic prone and fantasy prone. Barrett (1990, 1996) found that certain clients had amnesia for hypnosis, and these clients had amnesia during their daily lives. Barber described these clients as amnesic prone. Moreover, Barber described a third type of hypnotic client that he termed fantasy prone that, unlike the positively set clients and amnesic-prone clients, have a long history of make-believe and fantasy, vivid memories dating back to the age of 3, and the ability to use their minds to affect their bodies. In summary, the fantasy-prone clients have well-developed fantasies, and they use their fantasies to live interesting lives.

In conclusion, Kirsch and Lynn's (1995a, 1998) theory is too simplistic to explain all the features or mechanisms of automaticity. This is due to the fact that automaticity is a multivariate construct as opposed to a univariate or a common factor construct like some response expectancies. Automaticity includes, but is not limited by, suggestions, dissociation, fantasy proneness, and response expectancies. As Pashler (1998) pointed out, automaticity is a theory, not a fact; Kirsch and Lynn, however, appear to assume that it is a fact. Finally, research will determine if theories of automaticity will provide empirical data that complement theories of counseling and psychotherapy.

Lambert and Bergin (1994) found that the average *d* effect size for placebo control groups was .42, which is a small effect size. Kirsch and Lynn (1999) even argued that antidepressant medications are placebos. The concept of placebo comes from expectancy theory, or the notion that expectations lead to change. Clearly, there is a placebo component to medications as well as psychotherapy; however, Hamburg (2000) voiced disagreement with this position. He reported methodological problems with placebo-control trials. For example, placebo-control trials of antidepressant medications are biased against antidepressants. Moreover, participants vary greatly in such studies, and drug effects are reduced or canceled out completely because of participants' individual differences. Hamburg concluded that the most effective antidepressants produce response rates of 60% and that participants who are the most likely to respond are those with moderate-to-severe depression. If Kirsch and Lynn's (1999) thesis about placebos were correct, if one could increase the response expectancies of clients with moderate-to-severe depression, then depression would decrease as a result of the placebo effect. Finally, there are fairly conclusive data that certain forms of hypnosis are correlated with changes in brain functions that are independent of placebo effects (Woody & Bowers, 1998).

Confidence Intervals Around Reliability

Thompson (2002) has made a number of recommendations for social sciences research. First, he recommended that researchers put confidence intervals around reliabilities like coefficient alpha. Readers may remember, as Sapp (2002a) stated, that reliability is a function of test items and reliability measures the consistency of test items. Thompson defined a confidence interval as an interval among an infinitely large set of intervals for a given parameter in which 95% of the intervals would capture the population parameter.

Confidence intervals around reliability indices require a noncentral distribution, which allows one to a perform power analysis, or the probability of rejecting a false null hypothesis (no treatment effect). Fortunately, SPSS can calculate noncentral distribution for reliabilities, and, unlike centralized distributions, which have a mean of zero, noncentralized distributions have a mean of some hypothesized value and are skewed (Bird, 2002).

Fan and Thompson (2001) provided the following SPSS code for reliability confidence intervals:

```
Reliability variables = v1 to v3/
        scale(TOTAL) = v1 to v3/
        statistics = corr cov/summary = means var total/
        icc = model(random) type(consistency) cin = 95 testval = .70/
        model = alpha.
```

The following are the complete control lines on SPSS for the example from Fan and Thompson:

```
Title 'Crocker2.sps********'.
Data list free /person item score
Begin data.
1 2 1
7 4 6
3 1 1
3 2 5
7 4 4
7 4 6
5 3 4
3 2 2
2 1 1
0 1 2
end data.
list.
reliability variables item score/
        scale(Total) = item score/
        statistics = corr cov/summary = means var total/
        model = alpha.
```

The following are the results from this analysis:

Intraclass Correlation Coefficient

Two-Way Random Effect Model (Consistency Definition):

People and Measure Effect Random

Single Measure Intraclass Correlation = .7473*
95.00% C.I.: Lower = .4414 Upper = .9222
F – 1.2340 DF = (9, 18.0) Sig. = .3351 (Test Value = .7000)

Average Measure Intraclass Correlation = . 8987
95.00% C.I.: Lower = .7033 Upper = .9726
F = 2.9617 DF = (9, 18.0) Sig. = .0239 (Test Value = .7000)

*Notice that the same estimator is used whether the interaction effect is present or not.
Reliability Coefficients: 3 items
Alpha = .8987 Standardized item alpha = .9417

The reader should notice several things from the output from SPSS. First, coefficient alpha is .8987. The 95% confidence interval is .7033,

.9726. The lower limit of value of the confidence interval is .7033, and the upper limit or value for the 95% confidence interval is .9726. Moreover, testing the hypothesized value for coefficient alpha of .7000 against the calculated value of coefficient alpha of .8987 did differ significantly because F equals 2.9617 and the probability level is .0239. It is recommended that the reader run this analysis with sample data in order to get the intuitive feel for interpreting the computer output.

In addition, Thompson has challenged the use of statistical significance testing within the social sciences; Sapp (1997a, 2002a) stressed the same point. Readers should be aware that statistical significance only allows one to determine if a relationship is significantly greater than zero. It does not ensure replicability, nor does it control for threats to internal validity (Sapp, 1999).

Internal validity is the judgment applied by a researcher to determine if an independent variable caused a change on a dependent variable. Theoretically, random assignment or randomly assigning participants to groups initially controls for all threats to internal validity.

Moreover, Thompson (2002), like Sapp, recommended that researchers provide effect size measures and reliability indices for their data. In addition, he recommended confidence intervals for effect size measures. Unfortunately, this process is an iterative one that involves noncentral distributions, and readers who are interested in SPSS programs for calculating such intervals can consult Bird (2002) and Smithson (2001). Professor Geoff Cummings, at La Trobe University in Australia, has developed software that runs under the Excel program and that can be downloaded for a nominal fee from the following website: http://www.latrobe.edu.au/psy/esci.

In summary, Thompson suggested that researchers provide effect size measures for their data and that they calculate reliability indices for their data. Thompson is suggesting that researchers think meta-analytically and not in the mindless way of applying statistical tests of significance.

Effect Size Measures for Traditional Cognitive-Behavioral Therapies

Cognitive-behavioral therapies are eclectic groups of techniques that combine strategies from cognitive and behavioral psychology. Albert Ellis is the grandfather of cognitive-behavioral therapy within the area of clinical psychology; Aaron T. Beck is a prominent figure for cognitive therapy within the area of psychiatry. Traditional forms of cognitive-behavioral therapies developed from academic psychology or were embraced by academic psychology.

Table 1–2.
Highest Average Effect Size Measures for Traditional Cognitive-Behavioral Orientations

Orientation	Effect size *d*	Effect size *r*	Number of studies
Behavioral Therapy	1.06	.48	214
Hypnotherapy	1.82	.68	475
Systematic Desensitization	1.05	.47	475
Implosive Therapy	.68	.33	475
Behavior Modification	.73	.35	475
Cognitive-Behavioral Therapy	1.13	.50	475
Cognitive Therapy	1.00	.46	214
Self-Control Strategies	1.01	.46	214
Biofeedback	.91	.42	214
Covert-Behavioral	1.52	.61	214
Flooding	1.12	.50	214
Relaxation Therapy	.90	.42	214
Reinforcement	.97	.45	214
Modeling	1.43	.59	214

In contrast, **nontraditional forms of behavioral therapies** did not develop from academic psychology, and they were not embraced by academic psychology. Effect sizes for the traditional cognitive-behavioral orientations are found in Table 1 2. **Behavioral therapy** is a collection of techniques to change behavior. **Hypnotherapy** is the therapeutic use of hypnosis to change behavior. Hypnosis parallels guided imagery, biofeedback, and progressive relaxation. In essence, it is a therapeutic process between a therapist and a client in that the client receives suggestions that have physiological effects. Hypnosis can lead to behavior change, and there are several approaches or styles of hypnosis.

Systematic desensitization is an imagination technique that pairs relaxation with anxiety-evoking stimuli. Implosive therapy is also an imagination-based technique that is similar to flooding but uses psychoanalytic connotations with the imagery scenes. Behavior modification is the use of behavioral techniques to modify or change behavior.

Cognitive-behavioral therapy is a blend of cognitive and behavioral psychology, and those who use it feel that a client's problems are the result of faulty belief systems. Cognitive therapy is a form of cognitive-behavioral therapy that was developed by Beck. The goal is to change clients' cognitive distortions. Self-control strategies are procedures that the client implements himself or herself, such as self-monitoring, self-reinforcement, self-punishment, bibliotherapy, self-hypnosis, and so on. Biofeedback is the use of computers and other technologies to provide clients with feedback about physiological processes, such as blood pressure, heart rate, body temperature, and so on. Covert behavioral therapy is an imagination technique that uses aversive stimuli to desensitize clients to anxiety. Flooding is an imagination or in vivo real life–based technique that leads to the extinction of unlearning of behaviors.

Table 1–3.
Highest Average Effect Size Measures for Nontraditional Cognitive-Behavioral Orientations

Orientation	Effect size *d*	Effect size *r*	Number of studies
Adlerian	.71	.34	375
Transactional Analysis	.67	.33	475
Reality Therapy	.75	.35	21

Relaxation therapy is the use of progressive relaxation or muscle-tension exercises or guided imagery to produce relaxation. **Reinforcement** is a procedure that leads to an increase in behavior. Finally, modeling is a social learning technique that uses models to model and change certain behavior. Table 1–2 has the highest average effect size measures for the traditional cognitive-behavioral orientations. The reader should notice that cognitive-behavioral therapy has a *d* effect size of 1.13, which is a large effect size. There are 475 studies to support this statistic. Hypnotherapy has a *d* effect size of 1.82–again a large effect size measure. Moreover, cognitive therapy has a large *d* effect size measure of 1.00, with 214 studies to support the overall effect. Of the traditional cognitive-behavioral techniques, implosive therapy has a medium effect size of .68. In contrast, flooding, a technique that is similar to implosive therapy, has a large *d* effect size of

1.12. One of the appeals of cognitive-behavioral therapy is that most of the techniques have large effect sizes.

Effect sizes for the following nontraditional cognitive-behavioral orientations are found in Table 1–3. Adlerian therapy is a precursor to traditional cognitive-behavioral approaches to psychotherapy. This is a cognitive-behavioral and analytic form of psychotherapy. Most of the theories discussed in this text were influenced by Adlerian psychotherapy. **Transactional analysis** is a nonacademic form of cognitive-behavioral therapy that did not develop from academic or traditional forms of behavior therapy. Generally, with this form of psychotherapy one will not see references to classical and operant conditioning but an analysis of a client's ego states, which is a behavioral way to operationally defining Freud's constructs of the personality: id, ego, and superego. However, transactional analysis refers to these constructs as the child, adult, and parent ego states. Unlike Freud's psychoanalysis, transactional analysis is a humanistic-existential form of psychotherapy that stresses that clients can choose and change even when experiencing strong environmental and social forces. **Reality therapy** also did not develop from academic psychology, and it has aspects of humanistic existential therapy and behavior modification. **Choice theory**, a recent development within reality therapy, teaches clients that they create their reality with their own brains or minds. Moreover, clients are taught to take personal responsibility for their behavior or actions, and clients are taught to take action in order for changes to occur.

Table 1–3 has the highest average effect size measures for nontraditional cognitive-behavioral therapies. For the nontraditional cognitive-behavioral therapies, or therapies that did not develop from academic psychology, Adlerian therapy has a *d* effect of .71, which is indicative of a medium effect size. This statistic was based on 375 studies. Transactional analysis, another nontraditional form of cognitive-behavior therapy, has a *d* effect size of .67, another medium effect size measure. Finally, reality therapy has a *d* effect size of .75, which rounded, is approximately .80 – indicative of a large effect size. However, there are only 21 studies used for this effect size.

Table 1–4 has 95% confidence intervals for highest average *d* effect sizes for various forms of psychotherapy along with their power values. These confidence intervals were calculated with software found in Smithson (2003). This table provides more information than Tables

1–2 and 1–3. For example, it is clear that short-term dynamic therapy and reality therapy both have low power values. Stevens (2002) defined power values greater than .70 as adequate and values greater than .90 as excellent. The reason short-term dynamic therapy and reality therapy have low power values is because of their small sample sizes. With a sample size of about 100, normally power is not an issue. The reader should also notice that short-term dynamic and reality therapy both have zero included within their confidence intervals,

Table 1–4.
Confidence Intervals for Highest Effect Sizes for Various Forms of Psychotherapy with Power Values

Orientation	Effect size *d*	Estimated *t*-values	95% Confidence Interval for *d*	Power values	Number of studies
Short-Term Dynamic Therapy	.71	1.81	–.0451, .7483	.41	26
Psychodynamic	.69	7.52	.2523, .4374	1.00	475
Dynamic Eclectic	.89	9.69	.3505, .5392	1.00	474
Adlerian	.71	6.87	.2502, .4589	1.00	375
Dynamic/Humanistic	.40	2.93	.0648, .3354	.83	214
Person-Centered	.63	6.10	.2111, .4185	1.00	375
Gestalt	.64	6.97	.2274, .4118	1.00	475
Transactional Analysis	.67	7.30	.2424, .4272	1.00	475
Behavioral Therapy	1.06	7.75	.3861, .6723	1.00	214
Hypnotherapy	1.82	19.83	.8025, 1.0163	1.00	475
Systematic Desensitization	1.05	11.44	.4287, .6206	1.00	475
Implosive Therapy	.68	7.41	.2474, .4323	1.00	475
Behavior Modification	.73	7.95	.2717, .4575	1.00	475
Cognitive-Behavioral Therapy	1.13	12.31	.4677, .6614	1.00	475
Cognitive Therapy	1.00	7.31	.3571, .6413	1.00	214
Self-Control Strategies	1.01	7.39	.3624, .6469	1.00	214
Biofeedback	.91	6.66	.3140, .5956	1.00	214
Covert-Behavioral	1.52	11.12	.6072, .9116	1.00	214
Flooding	1.12	8.19	.4151, .7034	1.00	214
Relaxation Therapy	.90	6.58	.3087, .5899	1.00	214
Reinforcement	.97	7.09	.3424, .6258	1.00	214
Modeling	1.43	10.46	.5642, .8645	1.00	214
Reality Therapy	.75	1.72	–.0722, .8083	.38	21

d = population effect size for the *t*-test for independent two groups and $t = \left(\sqrt{\frac{N}{2}}\right)d$ and $d = \frac{2t}{\sqrt{N}}$

According to Stevens (2002), power > .70 is adequate and > .90 is excellent.

which suggests that the null hypothesis was not rejected, and the negative values within these intervals also suggest that both therapies can produce negative effects or harm. However, any form of psychotherapy clearly can produce negative effects, especially treatments with high effect sizes.

To summarize, both short-term dynamic therapy and reality therapy have confidence intervals that include zero, and the confidence intervals around *d* provide more information than the single point estimates of *d*.

Cognitive-behavioral therapy had a lower limit of .4677 (about a medium effect size) and an upper limit of .6614, again a value that reflects a medium effect size.

Hypnotherapy had a lower limit of .8025 a large effect size and an upper limit of 1.0163, again a large effect size.

Dynamic/humanistic therapy, person-centered therapy, and Gestalt therapy all had lower confidence limits in the lower ranges, with dynamic/humanistic therapy having a lower limit of .0648, which is the lowest for the humanistic therapies.

In terms of cognitive-behavioral therapies with upper limits with values of .8 or greater, only hypnotherapy, covert-behavioral, modeling, and reality therapy had upper limits with high *d* effect sizes using confidence intervals.

Clearly, Table 1–4 provides more information about effect sizes for various forms of psychotherapy and values of *d* are more meaningful when the upper of lower limits of population parameters are estimated. To reiterate, in general, cognitive-behavioral therapies tend to have large *d* effect size values, but confidence intervals suggest that true population parameters vary from the *d* point estimates and most forms of cognitive-behavioral therapies have upper confidence limits within the medium effect size ranges.

Summary

There are many factors that determine the effectiveness of a given form of treatment. Smith, Glass, and Miller (1980) found that any form of counseling was more effective, on average, than was using untreated control groups. This suggests that all forms of psychotherapy have effects sizes greater than zero, because zero would indicate no effect. Smith and colleagues also found that group therapy is just as effective as individual therapy. Sapp (1999) reported that some of the factors that influence the outcome of psychotherapy are client-therapist factors, client factors, therapist factors, and treatment factors (Frank, 1986).

A good client-therapist treatment alliance is correlated with positive treatment gains (Gendlin, 1986; Marziali, Marmar & Krupnick, 1981). Moreover, higher levels of intelligence are correlated with better therapy outcomes. In addition, marital status is correlated with therapy outcome. For example, psychological problems are highest among separated and divorced individuals, followed by single persons and widows and widowers (Bootzin, Bower, Zajonc & Hall, 1986).

In terms of therapist factors, the more experience a therapist has, the greater the chances are that a client will not drop out of therapy and will experience positive outcomes.

Finally, as Paul (1967) pointed out, what treatment and by whom and under what conditions is effective for which kinds of clients with what kinds of specific concerns is an important question for psychotherapy outcome research.

Glossary of Key Terms

Automaticity: The theory that states that at the moment of activation all behavior is automatic, or does not require thought.
Behavioral therapy: Theories that are based on changing behavior or things that people do.
Classical conditioning: A theory of learning that is emphasized by some forms of behavioral therapy. The term conditioning means learning, and classical conditioning is the conditioning of reflexes.
Cognitive-behavioral therapies: Therapies that work on changing thoughts and behaviors.
Drives: A term used by the psychologist Hull (1952) as a synonym for reinforcement.
Expectancy: A term employed by social learning theorists to note that expectancies influence behavior.
Effect size: A quantitative method of measuring the effects of counseling or psychotherapy.
Meta-analysis: A quantitative method of summarizing the effect sizes of several quantitative studies.

Neodissociation: A theory of hypnosis that states that hypnosis is an altered state of consciousness.
Nontraditional forms of behavioral therapies: These are forms of behavioral therapy that did not develop from academic departments of psychology.
Null hypnosis: A statistical hypothesis that states that there is no treatment effect.
Placebo effect: A term from social learning theory that emphasizes the influence of expectations on behavior.
Practical significance: The significance of studies based on effect sizes.
Statistical significance: The rejection of the null hypothesis (no treatment effect) and the assumption of the alternative hypothesis (there is a treatment effect).
***r* effect size**: The correlation measure of effects, with ranges between −1.0 and +1.0, including zero. Zero would suggest no effect.
Traditional forms of cognitive-behavioral therapies: Cognitive-behavioral therapies that developed from academic forms of cognitive-behavioral therapy.

Review Questions

1. How do psychologists know that cognitive-behavioral therapies actually make a difference?
2. What is meta-analysis, and how does it differ from a traditional narrative literature review?
3. Compare and contrast the univariate effect size with the multivariate effect size.
4. What is the difference between cognitive-behavioral theories of counseling and nontraditional cognitive-behavioral approaches?
5. What are social learning theories, and what have they offered to psychotherapy effectiveness?
6. What is the sociocognitive theory of automaticity?
7. What is the Norman and Shallice's (1986) theory of automaticity?
8. Briefly describe the neodissociation model of nonvolitional hypnotic responding.
9. Describe schemata theory.

10. Compare and contrast the univariate effect size with the multivariate effect size.
11. When social learning theorists state that all forms of psychotherapy are just placebo effects, how do the data by Lambert and Bergin (1994) challenge this assumption?
12. Are there any problems in stating that one form of cognitive-behavioral therapy is consistently superior to others?

Chapter 2

CRITERIA FOR CRITIQUING TRADITIONAL AND NONTRADITIONAL COGNITIVE-BEHAVIORAL THEORIES OF COUNSELING

The goals of psychotherapy are to describe and predict the behavior of clients. Clinicians often forget that a theory is a systematic way of describing why clients do what they do. Moreover, a **theory** is an overall framework for understanding clients. In addition, theories are made up of constructs or concepts that can be operationally defined, or defined in measurement terms. A theory connects constructs through unifying themes. Without theories, the area of psychotherapy would consist of isolated parts without a common thread. Another reason theories are important is that they permit researchers to test hypotheses and to revise or change hypotheses. In summary, theories are important for the science of psychology and for the practice of psychology.

Sapp (1997a) and Ryckman (1989) provided the following seven criteria for evaluating theories of psychotherapy: comprehensiveness, precision and testability, parsimony, empirical validity, heuristic value, applied value, and multicultural application and limitations.

A **comprehensive** cognitive-behavioral theory would have to explain human development from birth through death. Many of these theories do not adequately explain how clients or why clients become disturbed. In summary, a comprehensive cognitive-behavioral theory must account for a wide range of data.

Precision and Testability

Precision refers to the operational definition of variables. For example, within social sciences methodology, independent variables and dependent variables are often used to explain the relationship between variables. A variable is any factor that can change.

For example, any form of cognitive-behavioral therapy would be a variable, or more specifically an independent variable. Within psychotherapy, **independent variables** are forms of psychotherapy or forms of treatment. They have at least two levels: one can give the therapy or not give it. **Dependent variables** are the results of the measures for independent variables. They are the presumed effect, whereas the independent variables, moderator control, and suppressor influence the dependent variables. **Moderator variables** moderate the relationship between an independent variable and a dependent variable. For example, motivation and level of intelligence are important variables to consider within the area of psychotherapy.

Control variables are held constant, within a research context, so they do not affect the results. For example, if a researcher were investigating reducing anxiety, he or she would want to hold constant anxiety; that is, find clients with high levels.

Suppressor variables are independent variables that suppress or obscure the relationship among interdependent variables because they are correlated with other independent variables but uncorrelated with the dependent variables. Within a regression context, a statistical technique deals with predicting variables. Pedhazur (1997) described their counterintuitive concept with the following example: Suppose three variables have correlations as follows:

$$r12 = .3 \qquad r13 = .0 \qquad r23 = .5$$

If variable 1 is the dependent variable, clearly it is not correlated with variable 3. However, variables 2 and 3 have a correlation of .3. Nevertheless, variables 1 and 3 are not correlated; hence, the correlation between these two variables is 0. Now, the semipartial correlation also called the part correlation can be denoted as $r1(2.3)$. This notion says that variable 3 has been partialed out from variable 2 but not from variable 1; in other words, this is the correlation between variables 1 and 2 with variable 3 held constant from variable 2 and not variable 1. The semipartial correlation is as follows:

$$r_{1(2.3)} = \frac{.3 - (.0)(.5)}{(1 - .5)^{\frac{1}{2}}} = \frac{.3}{(.5)^{\frac{1}{2}}} = \frac{.3}{.707} = .42$$

The reader should notice that the correlation between variables 1 and 2 increases from .3 to .35 when variable 3 has been partialed out from variable 2 but not from variable 1. In addition, Stevens (2002) provided the following example to illustrate a suppressor variables:

$$r_{yx1} = .60 \quad r_{yx2} = .0 \quad r_{x1x2} = .50$$

Note that *y* is the dependent variable and x_1 and x_2 are predictors of *y* or independent variables. The formula for the semipartial correlation is the following:

$$r_{y1.2(S)} = \frac{r_{yx1} - r_{yx2}r_{x1x2}}{(1 - r_{x1x2})^{\frac{1}{2}}} = .693$$

Again, the reader should notice an increase in predictive power of predictor $1(x_1)$ from .60 to .693. It is not uncommon for suppressor variables to have a negative regression coefficient, and a regression coefficient is a number that shows how values of an independent variable or predictor variable are connected with values of a dependent variable or criterion. This value is a part of what is called a regression equation. The formula for a regression equation is as follows:

$$y' = a + bx + e$$

where y' is the predict dependent variable, *x* is the independent variable, *a* is the *y* intercept, *e* is the error term, and *b* is the regression coefficient or slope. In summary, when several variables are intercorrelated and negative regression coefficients exist, their variables may be suppressor variable.

Lancaster (1999) cited the earliest study of suppressor variables or effects, which occurred during World War II as an attempt to predict pilot success. Researchers used mechanical, numerical, spatial, and verbal abilities to predict pilot success. Interestingly, when verbal ability was added to a regression equation, an equation to predict pilot success, the accuracy of the overall model increased. Nevertheless, verbal ability had almost a zero correlation with pilot ability and was a suppressor variable. Why did verbal ability increase the utility of the overall regression model? First, verbal ability was required to read the instructions and needed to take the paper and pencil tests. Second, verbal ability removed the measurement artifact variance from the mechanical, numerical, and spatial ability scores (Thompson, 1992). Finally, Lancaster (1999) provided the following concrete example of suppression and how the squared multiple correlation R^2 increases to 1.0, perfect prediction. Lancaster described a two predictor case; that is, two predicts x_1 and x_2 and one dependent variable denoted by y. The correlation of y with predictor one (x_1) was –.707106, the correlation of y with the second predictor (x_2) was 0, and the correlation of the two predictors was –.707106. He provided the following formula for finding the beta weight (β):

$$\beta = \frac{[r_{yx1} - (r_{yx2})(r_{x1x2})]}{1 - r_{x1x2}^{2}}$$

The β, or beta weight, for the first predict is the following:

$$\beta_1 = \frac{[(.707106-(0)(-0.707106)]}{1 - (-0.707106)^2}$$

$$= \frac{[(.707106-(0)(-0.707106)]}{1 - .49999}$$

$$= \frac{.707106}{.50001}$$

$$= 1.41$$

The beta weight for the second predict (β_2) is as follows:

$$\beta_2 = \frac{[r_{yx2} - (r_{yx1})(r_{x1x2})]}{1 - r_{x1x2}^{2}}$$

$$= \frac{[0 - (.707106)(-0.707106)]}{1 - .49999}$$

$$= \frac{[0 - (-.5)]}{.5}$$

$$= 1.0$$

He provided the formula for the multiple correlated squared (R^2) as the following:

$$R^2 = (\beta_1)(r_{yx1}) + (\beta_2)(r_{yx2})$$

$$R^2 = 1.42\ (.707106) + (1.0)\ (0)$$

$$= 1.0 \text{ (rounded to one decimal place).}$$

In summary, suppressor variables are not easy to detect. With regression research it is important to study the following: zero order correlations, which are correlations of each *X* variable with each *Y* variable; standardized beta weights or coefficients, or beta weights with a common mean; and standard deviation, structured coefficients that are the correlations of a predictor with a dependent variable divided by the multiple regression equation (Sapp, 2002a; Thompson, 1992; Vogt, 1999). In closing, suppressor variables are elusive but important variables within research.

The reader should notice that the semipartial correlation crystallizes the relationship between variables 1 and 2. Within a multiple regression context (two or more predictors for a criterion), simple correlations cannot determine the usefulness of correlations. Even when a researcher conducts a randomized study, it is possible that intervening variables could affect the results. Unlike independent variables and dependent variables, **intervening variables** are theoretical variables that cannot be seen, measured, or manipulated.

Once a clinician or researcher is aware of these variables, it is possible to operationally define them and turn them into moderating variables. For example, with cognitive-behavioral therapies, learning is an important factor to consider. However, learning is a theoretical construct or intervening variable that can be operationally defined into a moderating variable.

To summarize, **precision** is the relationship between independent variables and dependent variables, and testability is the testing of hypotheses of a theory based on some criterion that can be verified.

Parsimony is the notion that the best theories are concise or economical or have few concepts. For example, theories that include unnecessary concepts lead clinicians and researchers far afield. In conclusion, clinicians and researchers prefer theories that only use the number of concepts that are necessary to describe the phenomenon that is under investigation.

Empirical validity is related to precision and testability. Empirical validity suggests that a theory is based on hypotheses that can be verified using data such as observations or questionnaires. The notion of validity is complex within the area of counseling psychology and psychotherapy. Unlike what many clinicians and researchers believe, **validity** is a measure that is the function of test items – not instruments (Sapp, 2002a). Specifically, **validity** is simply that the test items measure what they are supposed to measure. There are many forms of validity, and the interested reader can refer to Sapp (2002a) for a detailed discussion. The simplest way to determine validity is to correlate the items from two instruments, and the result is a validity coefficient. Sapp (2002a) stated that structural equation modeling is the most effective way to explore the validity of test items. Specifically, **structural equations modeling** is based on testing the hypothesis that a sample covariance or correlations matrix differs from a population covariance of correlation matrix. The reader should note that the concept of validity is a complex issue, and within psychology certain instruments are assumed to be valid and are given a stamp of approval. Test items from instruments, however, are seldom valid under all conditions. This is especially the case in terms of various cultural groups (Herrnstein & Murray, 1994).

Heuristic value suggests that a given theory has stimulated other theorists, clinicians, and researchers to conduct studies or investigations. Inadequate theories can also stimulate researchers to conduct studies; however, heuristic theories tend to lead to fruitful areas of investigations. For example, the new technique called eye movement desensitization-reprocessing (EMDR), a desensitization procedure developed by psychologist Francine Shapiro to treat traumas, has stimulated many researchers to try to determine the mechanism underlying this new technique (Sapp, 1997a).

Applied value means that a theory can be applied within a clinical setting to solve clients' problems. Each clinician has to determine if a given theory is useful within his or her environment or clinical setting. For example, a clinician has to determine if techniques from a given theory can be applied within his or her setting. Within multicultural settings, the concept of applied value becomes more complex in that various cultural groups differ in how they may respond to techniques of psychotherapy.

Because the United States is a multicultural country, cognitive-behavioral theories must be evaluated with a multicultural context. Unfortunately, many traditional theories of counseling such as psychoanalysis were based on upper-class white clients. Cognitive-behavioral theories of counseling can be tested for multicultural applications by asking which cultural groups, such as African American, Hispanic, Asian, Native American, and so on, could benefit from a specific form of cognitive-behavioral therapy. Moreover, another question is what are the limitations of specific cognitive-behavioral therapies to various minority groups? A clinician must deliberate with regard to the utility of cognitive-behavioral therapies to minority groups.

In summary, it is doubtful that any one cognitive-behavioral therapy will have high ratings with all of the criteria; however, these criteria do provide a framework for evaluating cognitive-behavioral theories of counseling. It is important for clinicians to keep these criteria in mind when reading the theories that follow in the succeeding chapters.

Multicultural Counseling

Axelson (1993) pointed out that the goal of **multicultural counseling** is to include all the cultures that make up the United States, and this includes gay, bisexual, and transgender groups as well. Many readers may not be aware that **social class** is a factor that must be considered when counseling clients. For example, the **middle class social stratum** is the core class structure in the United States. Some values and aspects of the middle class are hard work, competition, and self-expression. In addition, the middle class has certain language, values, behaviors, lifestyles, and core values associated with it. **Culture** is a social personality structure. As Axelson stated, it involves language, sanctions, values, gender identity, family constellation, ethnic and racial identity, and acculturation. Moreover, culture can be seen as a social structure, social system, and social organization. Likewise, culture is defined by rules that guide social structures like marriage, patriarchy, matriarchy, nuclear family, and extended family. The APA ethical principles endorse the concept of multicultural counseling, and multicultural competence has been endorsed by this organization. Finally, any practitioner working within the United States needs to know about multicultural counseling and the various cultural groups within the United States. It is common knowledge that race is a myth, and yet we pretend that it exists within the United States as a means to stratify and discriminate against others within our society. The interested reader can consult Graves (2004) for a thorough discussion of the race myth.

Major Cultural Groups Within the United States

Many Americans are not aware of their own cultural identity. There are few Americans who are not immigrants to the United States. Within the racial group that identifies itself as white, there are subgroups, such as Anglo-Saxons, who comprise English, Celts, Welsh, Scots, northern Ireland Irish, Swedes, Norwegians, Danes, Finns, Germans, Dutch, and Appalachians. White ethnic groups include southern and eastern Europe, Irish, Italians, Sicilians, Poles, Austrians, Hungarians, Czechs, Greeks, Portuguese, Russians, and Yugoslavs. Jews, Mormons, and Amish are considered socioreligious ethnic groups. Blacks include Africans, African Americans, West Indians, and Haitians. The term Spanish/Hispanic is confusing in the United States because it includes individuals from Mexico, Puerto Rico, Cuba, Spain, Central America, and South America. Spanish/Hispanic individuals within their countries have racial categories, but once they come to the United States they are put into one racial category. Perhaps Latino or Latina is an alternative term to Hispanic. There are about 263 tribes of Native Americans within the United States, and the Navajo tribe is the largest group. Interestingly, Eskimos and Aleuts are considered to be Native Americans. Finally, the Asian/Middle Eastern category includes people from Asia as well as those from the Middle East, such as Iranians, Egyptians, Turks, and Pakistani. The following groups will be discussed in the next section: Anglo-Saxon Americans, white ethnic Americans, black Americans, Native Americans, Hispanic Americans, and Asian Americans.

Sapp (1997a) stated that Anglo-Saxon Americans formed the foundations for many of America's values, and they were the first group to migrate to America. When one thinks about values such as competition, individualism, and hard work, these values can be traced back to the Anglo-Saxons. These individuals came primarily from England and Germany. The early white Americans were Protestants, and sometimes they are referred to as white Anglo-Saxon Protestants (WASPs).

It was not until the period of between 1820 and 1929 that northern and western Europeans such as the Swedes, Danes, Norwegians, Finns, Dutch, and Germans emigrated to the United States. Germans were the largest group, followed by the Italians.

Appalachian Americans are individuals who now live in the Appalachian Mountains, which include parts of Georgia, Alabama,

Kentucky, Maryland, Mississippi, New York, North Carolina, South Carolina, Tennessee, Virginia, and West Virginia. Most Appalachian Americans are white. Before the 1950s, coal mines offered a means of employment for Appalachian Americans, but during the 1950s, when coal mines closed, the economic structure for these people collapsed. Unlike Anglo-Saxon Americans, Appalachian Americans did not want, nor did they seek, governmental or bureaucratic structures. Their basic values were dependence on family members and a simple lifestyle.

White ethnic Americans include individuals from southern and eastern Europe, which includes Austria, Hungary, Czechoslovakia, Greece, southern Italy, Sicily, Poland, Spain, Portugal, Russia, and Yugoslavia. Between 1880 and 1920 these groups arrived in America in large numbers, and they were primarily Catholic (Axelson, 1993).

According to Axelson, between 1880 and 1910, more than 4 million Italians from southern Italy and Sicily entered America. This group valued family and the expense of individual achievement, and few Italians entered college. Unfortunately, Axelson stated that this was one of the most illiterate ethnic groups to come to America.

Most Polish Americans came to the United States between 1880 and 1920, and similar to the Italians, they were indigent and illiterate and lacked political power. Michigan, Illinois, Indiana, and Pennsylvania have many Polish descendants, but some hide their identity by learning English and Americanizing their last names.

Jewish Americans were the last white ethnic group to come to the United States, and unlike Italian Americans and Polish Americans, many were professionals and used educational achievement to combat anti-Semitic practices during the early part of the twentieth century.

Most of the Africans who came to the United States were slaves, although a few were indentured servants. Axelson described the history of three groups of blacks in America: (1) freed blacks, (2) emancipated slaves, and (3) blacks from the West Indies. It may be hard for some readers to imagine, but blacks and whites were legally segregated until about the 1960s. There were separate restaurants, hotels, swimming pools, and so on, for blacks and whites. One benefit of segregation was that blacks were able to establish economically sound communities, and this laid the foundation for what is now the black middle class. Blacks immigrating from the West Indies make up about 1% of the total black population in the United States, and the first generation was poor and settled in the Harlem area of New York City. The second generation of West Indians were upwardly mobile, but the Haitians, the newest black immigrants, are extremely poor and may not be accepted by African Americans or white Americans.

It was not until 1865 that the *United States Constitution* abolished slavery (thirteenth Amendment), and it was not until 1868 that equal protection was provided to everyone under the law (fourteenth Amendment). The fifteenth Amendment of 1870 provided all persons the right to vote. As alluded to earlier, however, it was not until the 1960s that the United States started desegregating America. Even with a few amendments to the *United States Constitution*, African Americans were held under subservience by a variety of tactics, for example, the rise in many vigilante and hate groups such as the Ku Klux Klan. These groups used extreme tactics to control African Americans, such as lynching and *expost facto* racial segregation (Marger, 2000, 2003). Actually, segregation originated in the north as a means of disenfranchising African Americans and as a means of keeping them within their places. Even during the twenty-first century, African Americans appear to be affected by the aftermath of slavery, racial prejudice, and social discrimination.

For example, Herrnstein and Murray (1994) have argued that IQ differences between blacks and whites are due to genetic factors. Specifically, Herrnstein and Murray have perpetuated racial, ethnic, and gender stereotypes about intelligence (Sapp, 2002a). Many Americans are not aware that African Americans are divided into at least three strata: middle class, made up of white-collar and skilled blue-collar individuals; working class, consisting of semiskilled individuals; and the lower class, consisting of unskilled workers. Most of the attention within the United States focuses on lower class African Americans and the problems of high poverty rates, high welfare rates, and low educational attainment. Moreover, there are a host of problems such as high rates of teenage pregnancies, high crime rates, and extremely high dropout rates from schools, and so on. Clearly, when individuals refer to the "inner city" and "central city," the reference is often to African Americans at the lower stratum of American society.

A more recent act of possible racial prejudice was the death in 2001 of an African American police officer who was shot and killed by fellow police officers while he was off duty. In Providence, Rhode Island, Patrolman Cornell Young was mistakenly shot and killed when, while off duty, he tried to break up a fight at a local restaurant. Patrolman Young pulled his gun when he saw another man brandishing a gun. Apparently, the patrolman thought that the on-duty police officers recognized him. Unfortunately, the officers did not recognize him, and they fatally shot him in the head, stomach, and chest. What is even more striking about this case is that the patrolman's father was a high-ranking officer within the Providence police force. This stirred controversy because critics believed that Young was killed because he was African American. This notion that there is built-in and automatic discrimination will be addressed later within this chapter, when evidence is presented that supports the idea that prejudice may lie within the brain.

Many other minorities often forget that Native Americans are ethnic minorities within the United States. Like African Americans, this is a very diverse group and it also has had several synonyms, such as American Indians, Native Americans, Original Americans, and Native People. When Europeans came to America, they thought America was India, and they referred to Native Americans as "Indians." Native Americans were exterminated because early European explorers wanted their land, and these early explorers and settlers used various measures to take the land. For example, the exposure to European diseases, wars, starvation, moving Native Americans to reservations, and attempts at assimilating Native Americans within white American culture almost eliminated this minority group from the United States. The Indian Removal Act of 1830 had the devastating effect of destroying Native American culture by the federal government. This act relocated Native Americans to reservations. Unfortunately, life on reservations has also been devastating for Native Americans. For example, on reservations, unemployment often exceeds 30%; poverty affects about one half of the residents; alcoholism and school drop-out rates are high (Axelson, 1990, 1993; Marger, 2000, 2003; Sapp, 1997a). The Indian Gaming Regulatory Act of 1988 provided Native Americans with a means toward economic development with legalized gambling. Finally, even with the new gaming laws, most Native Americans still experience high rates of unemployment and poverty.

Hispanic or Latin Americans are increasingly becoming the largest minority group within the United States (see Table 2–1 with the U.S. Census data). Actually, about one out of every four persons in the United States is a minority. Latinos are persons from Latin, Central, and South America. Like African Americans and Native Americans, Latin Americans are a very diverse group. The common denominator among these groups is the Spanish language. Marger (2000, 2003) argued that Latin Americans are an “in-between” status minority. They are an ethnic group that is between European American groups and African Americans. Mexican Americans are a racially diverse group, and, within Mexico, racial distinctions are often more a function of social class and cultural differences than of physical characteristics. In addition, Puerto Ricans are also an in-between racial group with African, European, and Indian ancestry. Puerto Ricans cover the entire spectrum, and, like Mexican Americans, racial classifications are often a function of social class and culture. Within the United States, Cubans are the least racially diverse group; most Cubans are seen as “white.” Even the pattern of discrimination directed toward Latin Americans has not been as severe as those patterns directed toward African Americans and Native Americans. Overall, Latin Americans remain poor and are at the bottom rung of the ladder of American socioeconomic strata. Cuban Americans appear to have more social access than do Mexican Americans, and Puerto Rican Americans appear to be at the lowest socioeconomic level.

Like African Americans, Native Americans, and Latin Americans, Asian Americans are a very diverse group (Marger, 2000; Sapp, 1997a; Sue and Sue, 1990). This group includes Chinese, Filipinos, Japanese, Asian Indians, Koreans, Vietnamese, Cambodians, Hmong, and Laotians. In fact, Asian Americans in some ways are more diverse than even Latin Americans, in that a common language, not a common religion, is shared. Currently, within the United States, Chinese, Filipinos, and Asian Indians are the largest Asian groups. Marger (2000, 2003) and Sue and Sue (1990) both have argued that Asian Americans are not model minorities, but they are often used as a standard for other minority groups. However, in reality, Asian Americans experience high poverty rates and various forms of discriminations like other minority groups.

The Hmong are the most recent Asian group to enter the United States. As many as 160,000 Hmong are within the United States, and they tend to be concentrated in Wisconsin, Minnesota, and California. Like other Asian groups, they speak a variety of dialects. Moreover, there are Hmong in China, Thailand, and Laos. Hmong have been persecuted by communists in Thailand. Their culture is agrarian, with

Table 2-1. U.S. Census Data

Subject	Number	Percent
RACE		
Total population	**281,421,906**	100
One race	274,595,678	97.6
White	211,460,626	75.1
Black or African American	34,658,190	12.3
American Indian and Alaska Native	2,475,956	0.9
American Indian	1,865,118	0.7
Alaska Native	97,876	0
Both American Indian and Alaska Native	1,002	0
American Indian or Alaska Native, not specified	511,960	0.2
Asian	10,242,998	3.6
Asian Indian	1,678,765	0.6
Chinese	2,432,585	0.9
Filipino	1,850,314	0.7
Japanese	796,700	0.3
Korean	1,076,872	0.4
Vietnamese	1,122,528	0.4
Other Asian category	1,061,646	0.4
Two or more Asian categories	223,588	0.1
Native Hawaiian and Other Pacific Islander	398,835	0.1
Native Hawaiian	140,652	0
Samoan	91,029	0
Guamanian or Chamorro	58,240	0
Other Pacific Islander category	99,996	0
Two or more Native Hawaiian or Other Pacific Islander categories	8,918	0
Some other race	15,359,073	5.5
Two or more races	6,826,228	2.4
Two races including Some other race	3,001,558	1.1
Two races excluding Some other race, and three or more races	3,824,670	1.4
Two races excluding Some other race	3,366,517	1.2
Three or more races	458,153	0.2
HISPANIC OR LATINO		
Total population	**281,421,906**	100
Hispanic or Latino (of any race)	35,305,818	12.5
Mexican	20,640,711	7.3
Puerto Rican	3,406,178	1.2
Cuban	1,241,685	0.4
Other Hispanic or Latino	10,017,244	3.6
Not Hispanic or Latino	246,116,088	87.5
RACE AND HISPANIC OR LATINO		
Total population	**281,421,906**	100
One race	274,595,678	97.6
Hispanic or Latino	33,081,736	11.8
Not Hispanic or Latino	241,513,942	85.8
Two or more races	6,826,228	2.4
Hispanic or Latino	2,224,082	0.8
Not Hispanic or Latino	4,602,146	1.6

religious beliefs based on animism, which includes shamanism and other supernatural philosophies. As a people, the Hmong are refugees, and many of the Hmong within the United States are refugees from Laos. After the Vietnam War, the North Vietnamese government attempted to exterminate the Hmong because they had helped the CIA fight wars in Laos.

In summary, Asian Americans are diverse groups, and they have experienced racial discrimination just like other minority groups. Marger (2000) concluded that within the United States, the ideology reflects Anglo cultural preferences and that the American hierarchy consists of three tiers: white Protestants of various national origins at the top; white Catholics and Jews of various nationality, along with Asian Americans in the middle; and Latin Americans, African Americans, and American Indians at the bottom part of the hierarchy.

Racial Prejudice Hidden Within the Brain

As previously discussed, African American Patrolman Young was killed by fellow officers in Providence, Rhode Island. Why would officers kill one of their own? Is prejudice located somewhere within the brain? Is prejudice an automatic response to social and cultural pressures? Dasgupta, McGhee, Greenwald, and Banaji (2000) and Nosek and Banaji (2003) using the Implicit Association Test (IAT), a reaction time measure to black and white faces, found a strong automatic positive evaluation of white Americans and a consistently negative evaluation of African Americans. What is very interesting about this study is that about 50% of the African Americans also had a negative evaluation of other African Americans. These researchers showed that once a person learns certain stereotypes through associations to various cultural groups, these associations tend to bias an individual toward certain social groups (Baldwin, Critelli, Stevens & Russell, 1986).

For example, an individual may be consciously tolerant toward minority groups but, due to the automatic response to social and cultural cues, respond in a very prejudiced way that is essentially automatic and nonconscious. For example, the African American Patrolman who was gunned down was probably killed because he was a black police officer responding to an off-duty call. Clearly, the officers who shot him did not react in a conscious way, but there are many cultural and social stereotypes that are associated with blacks, especially black males in America. Apparently these officers reacted in the way that they were conditioned culturally to do within the United States, and they responded with extreme fear and overreaction. Because research shows that there is an automatic preference for white faces, clearly the opposite is also true: there is an automatic negative reaction to black faces. Anderson and Phelps (2000) showed that the amygdala of the brain is associated with the processing of emotional properties that we assign to social groups within the United States. Cultural influences affect people at all levels, which includes the brain. Nevertheless, what is not known is what IAT research will show or predict in the real world. For example, does it matter if a police officer has a high IAT score? Is a police officer with a high IAT score more likely to shoot someone who is black than is a police officer with a low IAT score?

These questions have not been researched, and readers who are interested in completing the IAT may do so at the following website: buster.cs.yale.edu/implicit/ or at www.tolerance.org/hidden_bias/index.html.

In closing, Nosek and Banaji (2003) have demonstrated that, on the average, there is an implicit preference for whites over blacks, younger individuals over older individuals, and males over females. This research suggests that there is automaticity in responding to stereotypes and that there may be dissociation between implicit and explicit social attitudes, and this may explain why Patrolman Young was killed by other police officers. In summary, automaticity, dissociation, and the amygdala combined with social stereotypes offer some explanations for racial prejudice. Readers interested in a through critique of the IAT can consult Blanton and Jaccard (2006).

Glossary of Key Terms

Dependent variables: The measurement variable or the variable that changes as a result of the independent or treatment variable.
Empirical validity: The validation of a study through observations and other forms of data. The term validity means that items of a test measure what they purport to measure, and empirical suggests that qualitative and quantitative are employed.
Independent variables: Independent variables are variables that have at least two levels, and, within psychotherapy, these are the treat-

ments. There are a variety of independent variables, such as control, moderator, suppressor, and so on. Theoretically, independent variables can or should cause a change on the dependent or measurement variable.

Multicultural counseling: A term that emphasizes all the cultures that make up a nation.

Review Questions

1. What are the goals of psychotherapy?
2. Describe how the criteria can be used to critique any scientific theory.
3. Describe the term multicultural counseling.
4. Describe the major cultural groups within the United States.
5. When some cognitive-behavioral theorists say that all problems are a matter of perception, how does this concept fail to address discrimination, homophobia, culture, sexism, and racism?
6. In terms of culture, what is the assumed hierarchy within the United States?
7. What are the implications that racial prejudice may be hidden within the brain?
8. Perform a Google search and see if biologists view race as myth or social construction.

Chapter 3

TRADITIONAL PSYCHOANALYSIS AND OTHER PROMINENT PSYCHOANALYSES

Schools of Psychology

One major inaccuracy about schools of psychology is that Freud created the first school of psychology. Actually, **Wilhelm Wundt**, a German psychologist, started psychology in 1879 in Leipzig, Germany. His school of psychology was called structuralism. Wundt used **introspection**, a method that subjectively analyzed images, sensations, and feelings, to analyze conscious experiences. Moreover, between 1920 and 1930, **functionalism**, the second school of psychology, was founded by an American psychologist, William James. James broadened psychology to include child development, animal behavior, abnormal behavior, religion, and so on. The third school of psychology started around 1910 with Max Wertheimer, a German psychologist. Wertheimer founded **Gestalt psychology**, which means whole or pattern. Gestalt psychology was in conflict with structuralism, which wanted to study the elements of conscious experiences. The Gestalt psychologists thought that the whole was greater than the sum of the parts and objected to the **structuralists** who wanted to break human experiences into parts. Even though it is apparent that Frits Perls borrowed techniques from Gestalt psychology in order to develop his Gestalt psychotherapy, the two terms are not synonymous because Gestalt psychology was an experimental form of psychology and Gestalt psychotherapy is an applied form of psychotherapy (Sapp, 1997a).

Brief History of Psychoanalysis

Sigmund Freud was born in 1856 in what is now part of the Czech Republic, but he lived most of his adult life in Vienna. He and his family escaped the Nazis in 1938 and moved to London where he suffered from advanced jaw cancer (Milton, Polmear & Fabricius, 2004). Freud started his career as a neurologist in private practice, and during medical school he spent most of his time studying physiology and neuroanatomy with Ernst Brücke. Brücke, influenced by Hermann von Helmholtz, believed that all living things could be reduced to physics and chemistry.

Freud, like Brücke, Helmholtz, and others, based his theory on the early neuronal theory of the 1800s. This theory stated that energy could move from one neuron to another. Freud theorized that at birth a certain area of the mind called the psyche, was sealed off and contained psychic energy that could move though the body. This notion was the basis for his famous psychosexual stages of development, which was based on the movement of energy from the mouth, anus, and genitals. There are many misconceptions and inaccurate beliefs about Freud and psychoanalysis. First, Freud was not a psychologist; he was a psychiatrist. He did not invent the concept of the unconscious. Actually, Gustav Theodor Fechner (1801–1887) found that a relationship existed between the mind and the body by demonstrating that the amount of sensation one feels, or the conscious experience, depends on the amount of stimulation experienced or received, or the unconscious experience. Essentially, Fechner showed that the unconscious sensations of threshold existed by using a method of psychology called psychophysics.

The reader, who may consider that Freud started psychotherapy, only needs to consult Corsini and Wedding (2008), who pointed out that several individuals conducted psychotherapy before Freud developed his psychoanalysis. For example, Joseph Breuer developed a talking cure before Freud developed psychoanalysis, and Franz Anton Mesmer (1734–1815), an Austrian physician, practiced hypnosis before Freud was born (Wallace, 1993).

The Seduction Hypothesis

The seduction hypothesis or seduction theory is a thorny issue within the analytic camp. Masson (1984) was critical of how Freud developed the Oedipus and Electra complexes. Through archival data, Masson found that Freud had a long communication with Wilhelm Fliess, in which Freud discussed his belief that many of his adult female clients were sexually abused as adults and by adults as children. Freud's notion that children were molested sexually was referred to as **Freud's seduction theory**. Masson claimed that because of the Victorian era Freud modified his seduction theory or **hypothesis** by reporting that children's reports of sexual activity with their parents were just simply unconscious fantasies. Therefore, Masson proposed that Freud created both the Oedipus complex and the Electra complex to diffuse the impact of the sexual molestation that his female clients were reporting. Finally, because Luborsky, O'Reilly-Landry, and Arlow (2008) have assumed that these allegations by Masson cannot be substantiated, they believed that Freud would have not changed the seduction hypothesis to avoid extreme social pressure.

A Few Key Historical Figures of Psychoanalysis

Sandor Ferenczi (1873–1933)

Ferenczi was a Hungarian who was interested in the role of environmental trauma on psychotherapy.

Karl Abraham (1877–1925)

Abraham was a German psychoanalyst, and he was the second analyst of Melanie Klein. She further developed his notions of primitive and psychotic processes.

Ernest Jones (1879–1958)

Jones was Freud's official biographer, and he helped bring Freud to safety during the Nazi period.

Melanie Klein (1882–1960)

Klein had her first analysis with Ferenczi, and, like Anna Freud, she worked with children. Klein expanded on Freud's death instinct.

Anna Freud (1885–1982)

Anna Freud moved to London with her father during 1938, and, unlike her father, she psychoanalyzed children. Like her father, she endorsed his structural theory of the mind. However, with children who were separated from their parents during the Second World War, she emphasized attachment therapy and a focus on the development of strong adult attachment figures.

James Strachey (1887–1967)

Strachey and his wife Alix provided a fascinating view into the world of psychoanalysis when she underwent analysis with Berlin in 1924 to 1925. James Strachey was one of the main translators of Freud's work into English.

Ronald Fairbairn (1889–1964)

Fairbairn was a key figure who moved beyond Freud's drive theory and, along with others, developed object relations theory. In contrast to the discharge of drives, object relations theorists see clients as relationship seeking. Fairbairn developed the concept of schizoid mode of thinking to describe the internal work of clients, but, unlike Freud, he did not view the internal world of clients as innate fantasy but as a substitute for unfulfilled relationships within the external social world.

Heinz Hartmann (1894–1970)

Hartmann, Kris, and Loewenstein developed ego psychology, a school of psychoanalysis that dominated the North American scene until the 1980s. In contrast to Freud, Hartmann stressed ego development and ego defenses and how it adapts to reality.

Donald Winnicott (1896–1971)

Even though he was deeply influenced by Klein, Winnicott developed his own theory of infant and child development, and he gave more weight to environmental influences than Klein did. Winnicott is known for developing the notions of transitional objects and transitional space (Winnicott, 1958, 1965).

Michael Balint (1896–1970)

Balint was interested in integrating psychoanalysis with other disciplines, and he worked with deeply disturbed clients. He coined the term basic fault to refer to deep layers of dissociated psychic deprivation (Milton, Polmear & Fabricius, 2004).

Otto Fenichel (1897–1946)

Fenichel attempted to systematize classical psychoanalytic theory and, unlike other figures, was not interested in deviating much from Freud.

Wilfried Bion (1879–1974)

Bion worked with psychotic clients and presented seminal work about the mental processes of psychotic clients. He extended Klein's theory by stressing how the individual's personality, internal fantasy world, and environment interacted (Bion, 1967).

Marion Milner (1900–1998)

Milner (1987) has a collection of work that has contributed to the aesthetics and creativity of freeing the unconscious. Interestingly, during her training she was analyzed by Winnicott.

John Bowlby (1907–1990)

Bowlby was trained by the British society of psychoanalysts and was one of the first to bridge the connection between psychoanalysis and ethology. His work on attachment provided support for object relations theories. Bowlby (1980) stressed the importance of attachment among mothers and their children.

Herbert Rosenfeld (1910–1986)

Rosenfeld was analyzed by Klein, Segal, and Bion, and he made extension to the Kleinian view of understanding psychosis from a psychoanalytic perspective (Rosenfeld, 1987).

Betty Joseph (b. 1917)

Joseph (1989) had a background in social work, and her orientation was influenced by her work with mothers and babies. She extended the work of Klein.

Hanna Segal (b. 1918)

Segal was born and medically trained in Poland but fled to Britain during the Nazi invasion. Very similarly to Bion and Rosenfeld, she contributed to theories of psychosis and extended Klein's tradition (Segal, 1981).

Heinz Kohut (1923–1981)

Kohut was the founder of the American school of self psychology that challenged the American school of ego psychology. Self psychology stressed psychological deficits rather than conflicts as the core issues for clients. Moreover, Kohut's work bordered with Winnicott and others. Unlike some other psychodynamic schools, Kohut stressed the needs of parents, and he saw resentment and regression as secondary responses to trauma, not primary responses (Kohut, 1977).

Harold Stewart (1924-2005)

Interestingly, Stewart, trained as a physician, explored the therapeutic uses of hypnosis. He contributed to dream interpretation, the concept of transference, and the treatment of regressed clients.

Joseph Sandler (1927–1998)

Sandler (1987), as an international figure, was one of the first psychoanalysts to achieve academic recognition in Europe. Sandler tried to bridge the gap between drive theories and object relations theories.

Traditional Psychoanalysis

Traditional psychoanalysis is a drive-oriented theory that reified three intrapsychic personality structures: id, ego, and superego. The reader can view Table 3–1 and see that there are several personality theories and theorists. The id is unconscious and drive oriented toward pleasure and aggression. In addition, the id is associated with primary process mentation. The ego is preconscious and conscious, and it is connected with secondary process mentation. The superego is located within the ego, and it can dip into the id and determine which aspects of the id can be admitted into the terrain of the ego (Corsini & Wedding, 2008). In summary, traditional psychoanalysis is based on a tripartite model of energy and drives.

As previously stated, traditional psychoanalysis is based on the early neuronal theory of the 1800s, and this theory stated that energy could move from one neuron to another. Freud adapted this movement of energy motif to the psyche. Freud theorized that at birth a certain area of the mind is sealed and contains psychic energy that can move throughout the body (i.e. psychosexual stages of development) and affect the personality as defense mechanisms.

Table 3–1
Partial List of Various Personality Theories

Abelson, R. P.	Least effort
Adler, Alfred	Individual psychology
Allport, G. W.	Personalism
Angyll, Andreas	Organismic theory
Assiogoli, Roberto	Psychosynthesis
Bandura, Albert	Social learning theory
Beck, Aaron	Cognitive therapy
Berne, Eric	Transactional analysis
Binswanger, Ludwig	Daseinsanalysis
Blake, R. R.	Grid theory
Boss, Medard	Daseinsanalysis
Branden, Nathaniel	Biocentrism
Buhler, Charlotte	Humanistic psychology
Buhler, Karl	Funktionslust
Burrow, Trigant	Phyloanalysis
Cattell, Raymond B.	Multivariate experimental theory
Combs, Arthur	Phenomenology
Dollard, John	Learning theory
Ellis, Albert	Rational-emotive behavior theory
Erikson, Erik	Developmental theory
Eysenck, Hans	Factor theory
Feldenkreis, Moishe	Body awareness
Festinger, Leon	Cognitive dissonance
Fisher, Seymour	Body image theory
Frankl, Viktor	Logotherapy
Freud, Sigmund	Psychoanalysis

Table 3–1 *(continued)*

Fromm, Erich	Humanistic psychoanalysis
Gendlin, Eugene	Experiential theory
Glasser, William	Reality theory
Goldstein, Kurt	Organismic theory
Greenwald, Harold	Direct decision theory
Guilford, J. P.	Factor theory
Harvey, O. J.	Conceptual systems
Heider, F.	Balance theory
Holland, John	Career development
Horney, Karen	Sociopsychological theory
Hubbard, H. Ron	Scientology
Jackins, Harvey	Reevaluation counseling
Jackson, Don	Systems theory
Janov, Arthur	Primal theory
Jourard, Sydney	Transparency theory
Jung, Carl	Analytical psychology
Kelly, Charles	Neo-Reichian theory
Kelly, George A.	Personal constructs
Kohlber, Lawrence	Moral development theory
Kohut, Heinz	Self psychology
Korsybski, Alfred	General semantics
Krumboltz, John	Social learning
Lazarus, Arnold	Multimodal behavior therapy
Lecky, P.	Self-consistency
Lewin, Kurt	Topological psychology
Linehan, Marsha	Dialectical behavior therapy
Low, A. A.	Semantic theory
Lowen, Alexander	Bio-energetics
Maltz, Albert	Psychocybernetics
Maslow, Abraham	Self-actualization
May, Rollo	Existentialism
Mead, G. H.	Social interaction
Meichenbaum, Donald	Stress inoculation training
Meyer, Adolf	Psychobiological theory
Miller, Neal	Learning theory
Moreno, J. L.	Sociometry
Mowrer, O. H.	Two-factor theory
Murray, H. A.	Need-press theory
Murphy, Gardner	Biosocial theory
Osgood, Charles	Congruity theory
Perls, Frederick	Gestalt therapy theory
Piaget, Jean	Developmental theory
Rank, Otto	Will theory
Reich, Wilhelm	Character analysis
Roe, Anne	Relational approach to careers
Rogers, Carl	Person-centered theory
Rolf, Ida	Structural integration theory
Rotter, Julian	Social learning
Sapp, Marty	Cognitive-behavioral theories

Table 3–1 *(continued)*

Sarbin, Theodore	Role theory
Schultz, William	Open encounter
Shapiro, Francine	Eye-movement desensitization and reprocessing (EMDR)
Sheldon, William H.	Morphological theory
Sifneos, Peter	Short-term psychodynamic
Skinner, B. F.	Operant conditioning
Snygg, Donald	Phenomenology
Sullivan, H. S.	Interpersonal theory
Super, Donald E.	Career theory
Thorne, Frederick	Eclecticism
Thurstone, L. L.	Experimental theory
Van Kaam, Adrian	Transpersonal psychology
Walters, Bernard	Observational learning
Watson, John B.	Neobehaviorism
Werner, Heinz	Developmental psychology
Wolpe, Joseph	Behavior therapy

Note: Adapted from Corsini (1977).

Table 3–2
Continuum of Defense Mechanisms

1. Dissociation
2. Rationalization
3. Regression
4. Repression
5. Suppression
6. Displacement
7. Compensation
8. Conversion reaction
9. Emotional insulation
10. Intellectualization or isolation
11. Idealization
12. Reaction formation or overcompensation
13. Identification
14. Undoing
15. Substitution
16. Introjection
17. Fantasy
18. Projection
19. Flight into reality
20. Incorporation
21. Sublimation
22. Denial
23. Aggression
24. Sympathism or sympathy seeking
25. Avoidance

Table 3–2 has a list of various defense mechanisms. Some of the more elaborate mechanisms are dissociation, regression, repression, rationalization, and reaction formation. Some of the more primitive defense mechanisms are denial, aggression, and avoidance.

Phases of Freud's Psychoanalysis

Freud's psychoanalysis has three phases, and the term psychoanalysis is used in three distinct ways. First, let us describe the term psychoanalysis. It is a theory that loosely describes the structure of the mind, the development of personality, and psychopathology. Second, it is a technique used to treat a range of psychological difficulties. Third, psychoanalysis is a method of scientific investigation, that is, Freud based psychoanalysis on a clinical observation called case study methodology. In addition, Freud based psychoanalysis on chemistry, physics, and the emerging theory of neurons of the 1800s (Sapp, 1997a).

From its inception, psychoanalysis was viewed as a method of uncovering psychopathological memories and a shift in mentation from nonadaptive patterns to adaptive ones. Furthermore, psychoanalysis has been associated with several mechanisms related to hypnosis such as repression, regression, automaticity, and dissociation.

During the first phase of psychoanalysis, Freud found that his clients were capable of mentation that was not immediately accessible to conscious awareness. Many behaviors are nonconscious and automatic, especially hypnotically induced responses. Hypnotically induced behaviors feel automatic to the client. In other words, these responses require few cognitive resources. Hence, humans can perform several behaviors – cooking while talking on the phone or driving and talking – because the human brain requires few mental resources for many human behaviors. In essence, during the first phase of psychoanalysis, Freud found that his clients were capable of nonconscious processes, which he referred to as unconscious activities.

Actually, during Freud's earlier theorizing about hypnosis, he viewed hypnosis as the lack of communication between conscious and unconscious mentation. Freud thought that repression was the mechanism that allowed clients to forget or push ideas out of consciousness. The "splitting off," or dissociation of mental processes, is often symbolically translated into psychophysiological symptoms (hysteria).

Freud viewed disorders such as hysteria as being based on a psychological mechanism and not a neurological one (Leiper & Maltby, 2004).

In summary, during phase one of psychoanalysis, Freud found that the central aspect of human mentation was unconscious thoughts that could be accessed through slips of the tongue, jokes, dreams, fantasies, hypnosis, free association, and so on.

The second phase of psychoanalysis started with Freud's discarding hypnosis and replacing it with free association. Freud would have a client lie supine on a couch, and with the client in front of him, he would instruct his client to say freely anything that came into conscious awareness, without the use of censorship.

Freud found that free association allowed clients to voluntarily suspend conscious censorship and permitted the emergence of repressed or unconscious materials, and he believed that psychoanalysis accounted for transference and resistance within clients. Because Freud wanted a theory that was uniquely his own, he moved away from hypnosis, which was viewed as a mode of therapy, and toward psychoanalysis and developed his own specific techniques such as dream analysis, free association, and so on.

During the third phase of psychoanalysis, Freud elaborated on his notion of dream analysis and primary and secondary processes. Primary processes are nonlogical or id-associated mentation, and they are connected with the pleasure principle. Moreover, primary processes can be found in dreams, poetry, myth and magic, and the ultimate form of primary process: psychosis. Secondary processes are governed by the laws of logic and are associated with the ego and the reality principle. In 1923, Freud wrote *The Ego and the Id.* This consolidated the concepts of primary and secondary processes.

During the latter part of the third phase of psychoanalysis, other analysts such as Jung (1875–1961), Adler (1870–1937), Horney (1885–1952), Sullivan (1892–1949), and Erikson (1902–1992) modified Freud's psychoanalysis (Sapp, 1997a).

Clinically, why is Freud's theory of psychoanalysis important? First, Freud's psychoanalysis has been integrated into American culture and language. For example, it is common for many Americans to search for historical causes (from the past) of their current behaviors.

Second, the intrapsychic nature of Freud's theory that psychic energy is sealed within the client's psyche and can move to the mouth, anus, and genitals is interesting; however, this notion of psychic energy provides a complex scheme for understanding some of the nonconscious mechanisms of human behavior. Clearly, Freud's original theory was incorrect; however, he was correct when he theorized that much of behavior is nonconscious and automatic. To illustrate, clients may have reasons for their behaviors (nonconscious and automatic) that are not immediately accessible to consciousness.

The major error with Freud's theory was not the emphasis he gave to sex and aggression, but his faulty interpretation of the developing theories of chemistry and physics. Being technically eclectic, the current writer can use procedures and techniques from Freud's psychoanalysis, which can be helpful to clients, without subscribing to the faulty aspects of the theory. Within the broad range of psychoanalytic theories, such as those of Jung, Sullivan, and Erikson, there are many epistemologically incompatible constructs. This is why the theoretical integration of these theories is impossible.

Phases of Traditional Psychoanalysis

Luborsky, O'Reilly-Landry, and Arlow (2008) outlined the following four overlapping phases of traditional psychoanalysis:

1. Opening Phase
2. Development of Transference
3. Working Through
4. Resolution of Transference

Opening Phase

During this phase, the therapist obtains the client's case history. He or she encourages the client to free associate or say whatever comes to mind, that is, the therapist assumes the role of a "blank screen" and allows free association to occur. Moreover, the therapist notes all free-associated material and uses that to understand a client's unconscious processes. This phase of therapy lasts from three to six months.

Development of Transference

This phase overlaps with the previous phase, and it – along with working through – represents the major portion of therapy. Possibly, transference was Freud's most important discovery. By analyzing transference, the client can distinguish fact from fantasy. Finally, analysis of transference develops into working through.

Working Through

Working through is a continuation of the development of transference. During this phase, transference is analyzed repeatedly. Each analysis produces insight. Working through tends to stimulate earlier childhood memories and leads to resolution of the transference phase.

Resolution of Transference

Resolution of transference is the termination treatment. Once the client understands the meaning of transference, the therapist can establish a date for termination of treatment. Although the analyst attempts to resolve the client's unconscious attachment to him or her, the client usually fears termination because the client enjoys the dependent relationship fostered through therapy. Also, additional repressed memories may surface during this period. Toward the end of therapy, the client may reveal fantasies of becoming an omnipotent being. The more transference and wish-fulfillment fantasies that can be resolved, the smaller the chances of relapse.

Case Conceptualization

Case conceptualization is the way professionals formulate their cases about clients. Essentially, this is a way to integrate information about clients that helps explain current, past, and future behaviors (Day, 2008). Readers can consult interviewing textbooks such as Ivey (2002); Cormier, Nurius, and Osborn (2009); and Stevens and Morris (1995). Day (2008) listed the following six basic content areas that are part of case conceptualization:

1. Descriptive background information such as age, gender, and cultural background
2. Presenting problem, or the reason the client is seeking assistance
3. Relevant history such as past events that contribute to the pre-

senting problem

4. Interpersonal style, such as how the client presents himself or herself, and this can include such descriptions as active, passive, aggressive, resistant, pleasant, abrupt, distant, and so on
5. Environment factors, such as indigence, fame, wealth, exposure to environmental toxins
6. Personality dynamics such as factors that seem to motivate clients

Diagnostic and Statistical Manual of Mental Disorders (DSM-IV-TR)

The *Diagnostic and Statistical Manual of Mental Disorders* (Fourth edition, Text revision) (*DSM-IV-TR*) is the manual used by psychologists, psychiatrists, social workers, counselors, and psychotherapists to diagnose patients and clients in order to receive reimbursement from insurance companies. The *DSM-IV-TR* is used to make a multiaxial diagnosis, one using five axes (*DSM-IV-TR*, 2000, pp. 27–38).

Axis I is used for the presenting problem or the reason a client came in for therapy. Several diagnoses can be made on this axis, such as the following:

Anxiety disorders – disorders marked by feelings of stress, tension, and worry.

Dissociative disorders – disorders within which one or more parts of mental processes become separated and dissociation of memory, identity, and perception is used to cope with stress.

Mood disorders – disorders involving disturbances in mood such as major depressive disorder, dysthymic disorder, bipolar disorders I and II, cyclothymic disorders, and others.

Eating disorders – disorders in relation to the consumption of food, which includes anorexia nervosa, bulimia and others.

Sleep disorders – sleep difficulties that occur before sleep such as insomnia or during sleep such as sleep apnea.

Sexual and identity disorders – physical and psychological disorders that affect coitus or the way a client views maleness or femaleness.

Delirium, dementia, and amnesia and other cognitive disorders – delirium is a disturbance of consciousness and a change in cognition. Dementia is a disorder that presents as multiple cognitive deficits such as memory, and amnesia is an impairment in memory with-

out other cognitive impairments.
Substance-related disorders – disorders related to drug and alcohol abuse.
Schizophrenia and other psychotic disorders – schizophrenia is a psychotic disorder associated with delusions, inappropriate behaviors, hallucinations, emotional flatness, lack of motivation, and disorganized speech. Psychotic disorders are a loss of contact with reality.

Axis II is employed for personality and mental retardation diagnoses. When a patient or client has an Axis I and Axis II diagnosis, and the principal diagnosis is on Axis II, it is common to qualify that Axis II has the principal diagnosis by employing the phase principal diagnosis. Axis II disorders include mental retardation and the following personality disorders:

Paranoid – traits clients have that are associated with distrust of others. Clients tend to have eccentric paranoia.
Schizoid – a personality disorder characterized by a disinterest in others and an aloofness within interpersonal relations that is not the result of fear.
Antisocial – a personality disorder with pervasive patterns of disregard for the rights of others.
Borderline – a personality disorder that is characterized by instability in moods, relationships, and the self-image.
Histrionic – a personality disorder associated with overly emotional and attention-seeking behaviors.
Narcissistic – is characterized by grandiosity, self-centeredness, and a lack of empathy toward others.
Avoidant – is associated with fear in social situations, but unlike the schizoid personality, these clients want to enjoy interactions with others.
Dependent – is marked by traits of dependent and submissive behaviors, and these clients require enormous amounts of reassurance from others.
Obsessive-compulsive – is characterized by a preoccupation with perfectionism, orderliness, and the rigid control of self and others, but unlike obsessive-compulsive disorder, there are not repetitive actions related to persistent thoughts.

Axis III is used for general medical conditions, diagnosed by a medical practitioner or physician, that are pertinent to the patient's mental disorder. Examples of some of these disorders are the following:

Diseases of the digestive system
Diseases of the circulatory system
Diseases of the nervous system and sense organs
Diseases of the skin and subcutaneous tissue
Endocrinal, nutritional, and metabolic diseases and immunity disorders
Diseases of the respiratory system

Axis IV is employed for psychosocial and environmental concerns that may influence the diagnosis and prognosis of Axis I and Axis II diagnoses. These are negative life events that produce interpersonal stress. Some of these categories are the following:

Problems with primary support group: divorce, death of family member, sexual abuse, physical abuse.
Problems related to the social environment, such as death of a friend, living alone, adjustment to retirement.
Educational problems, such as academic difficulties and negative school experiences.
Occupational difficulties, such as unemployment or the threat of losing one's job.

Axis V is employed to report the client's overall level of functioning, and it is referred to as the global assessment of functioning scale (GAF). The scale has values that range from 0, inadequate information; to 10, persistent danger to self and others; to 50, moderate symptoms; to 100, superior functioning in a variety of areas.

The following section outlines such multicultural applications of psychoanalysis, and it provides a multiaxial diagnosis of an African American male client and a transcription of a therapeutic session.

Psychoanalysis and the Use of Semantics: Understanding the Internal Dialogue of an Adult African Male Client

Introduction[2]

From a literary point of view, psychoanalysis and its derivations,

[2] This paper was part of the proceedings of the 14th International Conference on Literature and Psychoanalysis: 53-56 that was held in Las Navas, Avila, Spain, 1997.

such as psychodynamic and other analytic therapies, are based on psychic energy and unconscious conflicts; therefore, at a literary level, language has manifest meanings and latent meanings. Specifically, Freud stated that psychic energy existed within the psyche, a compartment that contained psychic energy. In addition, psychic energy can move throughout the entire body, such as the mouth, anus, genitals, and so on. This movement of energy refers to Freud's famous psychosexual stages of development. Also within a person's psyche are the psychic structures called the id, ego, and superego. Each has its own linguistic style. For example, the id's communication is amoral, and it uses symbols that are pleasure oriented. For example, the id expresses itself by childishly requesting to have its desires fulfilled, and it is illogical and largely unconscious.

The language of the ego is logic, order, reality testing, and it moderates the other personality structures by interacting between the linguistic communications of the id and superego. To appease the id, the ego realistically figures out methods of satisfying its desires. The communication style of the superego is largely judgmental; it involves the moral language that one uses to represent abstractly the ideal.

The superego strives for perfection, and it often expresses itself as parental and societal standards. Some of the specific language of the superego are "shoulds," "ought tos," "don'ts," and "musts." The superego is capable of using damaging language against the person's self, against others, and against the world.

For example, language such as, "If I cannot be perfect at everything I do, and if I cannot win the approval of everyone, I am a total failure" would illustrate damnation of the self. Hence, language is used to damn the self, others, and the world. Others can be damned with the following language: "I have to be treated fairly by everyone. When they don't, it is outrageous. I must be treated fairly." Damnations of the world would be as follows: "The world must operate the way I demand. I want all of my desires granted instantly. If I do not get what I want, when I want it, life is awful." The interpretation of language is important from a psychoanalytic and psychodynamic standpoint. The way a client uses language correlates with the degree of his/her psychological state of mind. For example, once a client becomes aware of how language intensifies feelings and how language can exaggerate the significance of events, often he/she can learn to change his/her internal dialogue and hence change the degree of his/her psychological disturbance.

Psychoanalysis has many applications for the majority culture; however, little is known about the intrapsychic communication styles of African American adult males. Specifically, a modern language computer search conducted on April 26, 1997, did not find a single article that discussed psychoanalysis, African American males, and literature. The conclusions one can draw from this search is that there is little known about the communication styles of African American males using a psychoanalytic literary communications analysis. The purpose of this paper is to present a brief transcript of a free association session during psychoanalysis and to provide an analysis in terms of the methods this African American male used to communicate. The following transcription highlights the critical differences and yet the importance of language within the African American culture.

The transcription is from an 18-year-old African American male who was experiencing intrapsychic conflict within himself. He had the following multiaxial Diagnostic and Statistical Manual of Mental Disorders, fourth education (DSM-IV): Axis I, 300.02, Generalized Anxiety Disorder; Axis II, 301.81, Narcissistic Personality Disorder; 301.7, Antisocial Personality Disorder; Axis III, None; Axis IV, Problems with Primary Support Group; Axis V, GAF 60 (current). His internal dialogue shows how, even using Black English, intrapsychic conflict manifests itself through the communication of his id, ego, and superego.

> Ma peeps are really gettin on ma nerves. Ah hear voices in ma head telling me ah can't make it, can't be cool, can't be mella. Yo, ah just wont, and wont, and wont. But ah don't know wa ah wont so much. Most of wha ah wont, ah don't need. Ma famla, ma peeps, and ma homies voices tell wha ah should wont. Ah in a fight with good and bad, and ah don't know if ah is good or bad. Ma mama told ma, be good and hona the Lold. Ah just wish everythang waz perfect and ah could be happa. Ah know nothin will change. Life be just holdin ma down. Ah just a brotha tryin to git ova, tryin to understand ma self and the sistas. Ah realla got a jones fo this one sista. She be bad, a brick house. Ah thank of bonin ha and bustin ma nuts. Sometimes ah jackoff thankin about that bad sista. Ma mama say this is wrong and ah should be married and shouldn't bon and thank of bustin out. Ah thank ah can make it. Ah must be strong and use ma head.

The standard English interpretation of the transcription is as follows:

> My friends are really getting on my nerves. I hear voices in my head telling me I can't make it, can't be cool, can't be mellow. You know, I just want, and want, and want. But I don't know why I want so much. Most of what I want, I don't need. My family, my friends, and my neighbors' voices tell what I should want. I am in a fight with good and bad, and I don't know if I am good or bad. My mother told me to be good and honor the Lord. I just wish everything was perfect and I could be happy. I know nothing will change. Life is just holding me down. I am just a brother [African American male] trying to get over, trying to understand myself and the sisters. I really have a strong sexual desire for this one sister [African American female]. She is bad [attractive], a brick house [very attractive]. I think of having sex with her and reaching an orgasm. Sometimes I masturbate when I am thinking about that bad [attractive] sister. My mother says this is wrong, and I should be married or should not have sex or think of having it. I think I can make it. I must be strong and use my head.

Within the client's unconscious are many repressed childhood issues, especially issues regarding the Oedipus complex. Because this client did not have an African American male figure to identify with during childhood, he is using the current client-therapist relationship as a means to develop an identity of an adult African American male. The client's covert language shows that he has unconscious sexual desires for his mother that are symbolically represented by mentally and physically engaging in sexual relations with several African American women. In addition, sexual release is used to allow the client to displace feelings of anger and aggression that have origins in the lack of mature bonding with both parents. In terms of psychosexual development, this client is clearly at the genital stage.

From an object-relations viewpoint, this client fits the diagnosis of a personality disorder that has narcissistic and antisocial features. Object-relations describes the process this client must undergo to become a mature adult. Specifically, the objects are significant persons from the client's past, and in this case they are his mother and father. To be more precise, this client had difficulty during the differentiation and separation/individuation process of object relations. His narcissism is his inability to differentiate himself and to idealize others. This suggests that he also has borderline feature, and he has failed to separate and become a mature adult; hence, his object borders are blurred.

The client's collective unconscious or nonpersonal unconscious is the most perplexing aspect of how he manipulates language. Carl Jung argued that the collective unconscious contains archetypes, mental representations of universal experiences expressed as images. I argue that Black English is an archetype within African American culture, and it is used to connect African Americans to a common history. What is critical about analyzing the collective unconscious is that it is not accessible to conscious experiences; however, the images that underlie language processes are clues to the collective unconscious.

Another aspect of the client's collective unconscious is his reference to God. Here, God is an archetype with contextual experiences that are related to the evolutionary history of African Americans. God and other religious symbols are associated with African Americans' collective unconscious.

Because the client's shadow is unconscious, it is projected onto his mother, African American women, and African American males. Just as the shadow is a combination of evil and creative parts, this client has exaggerated feelings of self-love and strong feelings of hate for other African American males. This is consistent with the high homicide rate for African American males between the ages of 18 and 24. The shadow produces psychic energy by the principle of opposites – conflicts between opposing forces. The love relationship the client has with himself and the hatred he has for other African American males illustrates this concept of opposites. To summarize, this client's shadow can be evil and good, weak and strong, monotonous and creative, have the desire to kill and the desire to create life; these are all illustrations of the concept of opposites. The most important aspect of this shadow is that it cannot be totally suppressed by the ego without the client losing creativity, spontaneity, and dying spiritually.

Summary and Conclusions

The foregoing transcription clearly showed how intrapsychic conflicts occur within a Black English context. Specifically, even within an African American context, language has superficial (manifest) and latent (deep) or unconscious meanings. Moreover, the preceding transcription clearly showed how the client experienced conflict that was expressed in the following quote: "I am in a fight with good and bad, and I don't know if I am good or bad." Moreover, the client expressed sexual conflict, and he realized that the sexual values of his mother were at odds with his own. Furthermore, he has several irrational beliefs, such as confusing wants with biological needs (food, clothing, shelter, etc.). Likewise, the client believed irrationally that life can be perfect and that if his life were perfect, he would be happy. In addition, this client assumed that life should be orderly, fair, painless, and perfect. In contrast to assuming personal responsibility for things that can be changed, this client assumed irrationally that "Life is holding me down."

The goal of therapy is to show the client how his language affects his thoughts (internal dialogue), feelings, and actions. In addition, another goal of therapy is to get the client to see how he uses language to damn himself, others, and the world. Moreover, careful analysis of the client's language shows how unconscious meanings (latent content) that are embedded within Black English can lead to self-defeating thoughts, feelings, and actions. In conclusion, the careful analysis of the internal dialogue of this adult African American male client can lead to psychoanalytic treatment options. In conclusion, this article showed how psychoanalysis and the interpretation of language can lead to an understanding of the internal dialogue of an adult African American male client. Finally, this paper showed how sex and aggression are integral aspects of the life of an African American adult.

Short-Term Dynamically Oriented Psychotherapy

During the 1960s, the first generation of short-term dynamically oriented psychotherapists began modifying psychodynamic therapies, and they included Davanloo (1979) in Montreal, Malan (1963, 1976), Mann in Boston (Mann, 1973; Mann & Goldman, 1982), Sifneos (1972, 1979), and the Tavistock group in England (Balint, Ornstein & Balint, 1972).

David Malan investigated modifying psychodynamic therapy in Britain and used many analytic techniques except passivity in role of the analyst. Malan found that a modified form of dynamically oriented therapy could be used with certain clients who met a selection criteria.

While Malan worked at the Tavistock Clinic in Britain, Sifneos started his work at Massachusetts General Hospital in Boson. Sifneos reached conclusions similar to those of Malan: with the appropriate selection of clients, traditional psychoanalysis could be modified into a short-term dynamically oriented psychotherapy.

Davanloo began his work in short-term dynamically oriented psychotherapy at Montreal General Hospital in Canada during the 1960s, and he noticed that long-term psychotherapy was inefficient in the hospital's outpatient psychiatric unit (Bauer & Kobos, 1993).

The dynamic hypothesis and transference are the two fundamental principles of all psychodynamic therapies (Anderson & Lambert, 1995). The influence of unconscious primary process mentation on secondary process mentation is called the dynamic hypothesis. Primary process mentations are nonlogical or id-associated mentations, and they are associated with the pleasure principle. Actually, primary process mentation can be found in dreams, poetry, myths, and magic, and the ultimate form of primary process mentation is psychosis. In contrast to primary process mentation, secondary process mentation is governed by laws of logic and is associated with the ego and the reality principle.

The selection criteria of clients for short-term therapy is stringent (Crits-Christoph & Barber, 1991; Malan, 1976; Davanloo, 1979; Sifneos, 1979), and there are five features (Binder, 2004). First, clients must have conscious awareness of the areas of conflict. Second, clients must be able to recall early childhood memories connected with the areas of conflict. Third, clients must have the ego strength to tolerate high emotional tension. Fourth, clients need strong motivations to explore internal conflicts. Fifth, clients must be able to engage and disengage from the therapeutic relationship within a relatively short period of time.

Traditional psychoanalysis can take three to eight years and may require four to five sessions per week. Short-term dynamically oriented psychotherapy is usually between 12 and 40 sessions; however, there are several time-limited approaches that range from 12 to 16 sessions. Because short-term dynamic therapy is time limited, free association is seldom part of the process.

In summary, the goal of short-term dynamically oriented psychotherapy is insight into events that contribute to present conflict. Even though short-term dynamic therapy uses some of the basic principles of traditional psychoanalysis, the therapist takes a more active and directive role. For example, defenses are identified early within the therapeutic process and interpretation is used to get clients to understand the dynamics of their symptoms and how psychotherapy will proceed. Moreover, thoughts and feelings that represent repressed material are quickly exposed by the therapist. Like the Levels I and II skills discussed earlier, these same skills are needed to help clients develop trust. In addition, abreactions are encouraged within the therapeutic process. Interestingly, depression is viewed as unexpressed affect, and clients are encouraged to reexperience painful events as a means to resolve them. Unlike traditional psychoanalysis, transference is more global and includes links from the past as well as current links, including the relationship with the therapist. Finally, short-term can be completed within 10 sessions, but 20 sessions are not unusual.

Relational Psychoanalysis

Relational psychoanalysis differs from drive theories, object relations, and self psychology in that the therapeutic relationship is stressed. Traditional psychoanalysis stresses a therapeutically neutral role of the therapist, but relational psychoanalysis stresses the influence that a therapist can have on a client due to the personality of the analyst. In fact, relational psychoanalysis stresses the analyst–patient dyad as a unique feature of psychotherapy (Greenberg & Mitchell, 1983; Sharf, 2008). Readers interested in relational psychoanalysis can consult Mitchell's (1998) book entitled *Relational Concepts in Psychoanalysis.*

The terminology that follows gives one a feel for terms connected with psychoanalysis.

Glossary of Key Terms

Abreaction: Reexperiencing of painful emotions in psychotherapy. Usually involves the conscious awareness of previously repressed or unconscious material.

Borderline personality: A personality disorder characterized by patterns of instability in self-image, mood, interpersonal relationships, sexual orientation, and career choices. Individuals diagnosed with this disorder will make suicidal threats or gestures as a means of manipulating friends and family members. Moreover, individuals with borderline personality disorders will self-mutilate by cutting their wrists and so on. In sum, these individuals commonly report chronic boredom and emptiness.

Determinism: The assumption that all present functioning is causally linked to the past.

Catharsis: The expression of strong emotions that are normally repressed. A synonymous term is abreaction.

Cathexes: Driving forces or the movement of psychic energy.

Complexes: A core of emotions that are organized around a common theme.

Countertransference: The tendency of a therapist to project unconscious wishes and fantasies onto the client.

Electra complex: The erotic attraction that a girl shows toward her father while displaying hostility toward her mother.

Free association: Reporting without censure whatever comes to the mind. A basic tool used in psychoanalysis, it is designed to access the unconscious.

Libido: The basic driving energy or force in psychoanalysis. This includes sexual and aggressive energy and so on.

Narcissism: Excessive self-love by investing psychic energy within the self. Specifically, narcissism is believed to be the result of the inability to differentiate from the self and to idealize others. Persons with the borderline personality disorder fail to separate and become distinct individuals; hence, object borders are blurred.

Object-relations theory: A theory developed by ego psychologists Margaret Mahler (1879–1985) and Heinz Kohut (1913–1981). During the 1950s and 1960s, object-relations theorists dominated psychoanalysis. The object-relations theory describes the process a client undergoes to become an individual. In this sense, the object used is a significant person from the past. These theorists believe that narcissistic and borderline personality disorders are caused by a person's having difficulty during the differentiation and separation/individuation process.

Oedipus complex: The erotic attraction of a male toward his mother and display of hostility toward the father. This is the male's version of the Electra complex. According to theory, if this complex is successfully resolved, one's sexual identity emerges.

Intrapsychic: Within the psyche (mind). This is the compartment Freud conceptualized as containing psychic energy and personality structures.

Sublimation: Is not viewed as a defense mechanism by some theorists, but it involves the redirection of psychic energy throughout the life span. According to theory, psychic energy is redirected using socially accepted norms, such as relationships, friendship, sports, art, and other forms of social expression.

Multicultural Applications and Limitations

If psychoanalytic and psychodynamic theories are modified, they can be applied to culturally diverse groups. The major limitation for minority clients is the amount of time and money needed for these therapies. Also, many minority clients are dealing with practical problems such as survival and environmental security; therefore, intrapsychic personality reconstruction is not practical. Nevertheless, if ethnic minority groups have their survival and security needs met, they could benefit from modified versions of psychoanalysis and psychodynamic therapies. Finally, time-limited or brief psychodynamic therapies have application for minority clients.

Critique

Comprehensiveness. Psychoanalysis is probably the most comprehensive theory of psychotherapy. It can explain almost every facet of human behavior, from human development to psychopathology. Nevertheless, the psychodynamic theories are not as comprehensive as psychoanalysis, especially time limited or brief dynamic.

Parsimony. Based primarily on sex and aggression, psychoanalysis presents a bleak view of human nature. It consists of many concepts such as defense mechanisms, psychosexual development, character types, Electra and Oedipus complexes, free association, transference, and countertransference. In summary, psychoanalysis and many of the psychodynamic theories do not meet the criteria for parsimony, but short-term dynamic therapy is parsimonious.

Empirical Validity. Thousands of studies have investigated psychoanalysis. There is empirical support for the defense mechanisms of psychoanalysis and for the psychosexual stage of development. Meta-analytic studies have shown that psychoanalysis is effective as a psychotherapy. Readers may remember that psychodynamic therapy had a 95% confidence interval of .2523, .4374, whereas short-term dynamic therapy had a 95% confidence interval of –.0451, .7483. In essence, there is empirical support for these therapies.

Precision and Testability. Many of the concepts of psychoanalysis and psychodynamic therapies are vague, such as id, ego, superego, life and death instincts, and unconscious. Moreover, many constructs of these theories are presented as metaphors; therefore, these theories fail in the area of precision and testability.
Heuristic Value. One of the major legacies of psychoanalysis is its influence on other forms of psychotherapy such as Gestalt therapy, transactional analysis, psychodrama, and so forth. In addition, psychoanalysis has had an influence on literature, history, sociology, anthropology, and philosophy. Moreover, psychoanalysis has had a stronger influence on the field than psychodynamic approaches have had. The psychodynamic approaches have not had an impact on the field as strongly as psychoanalysis has.
Applied Value. Psychoanalysis has had strong applied value. For example, research on posttraumatic stress disorder, repressed memory syndromes, and so on has led to the development of treatment partly through an understanding of psychoanalysis. Finally, applications of the psychodynamic approaches are not as strong as those of psychoanalysis, but brief dynamic therapy is becoming more popular.

Summary

Psychoanalysis and psychodynamic approaches are past oriented, and they stress helping clients resolve unconscious conflict. Jung's theory, followed by Freud's, is probably the most abstract. Actually, Jung presented a theory that was not only ethereal but also mystical. These approaches appear to have confidence intervals as large as other therapies. Finally, in 2006, the first *Psychodynamic Diagnostic Manual* (*PDM*) was published as an alternative to the *DSM-IV-TR*.

Review Questions

1. Culturally, why does psychoanalysis remain popular within the twenty-first century?
2. Use a Google search to find information about some of the personality theories mentioned in this chapter, and use Google to find information about some of the defense mechanisms.
3. Use a Google search to compare and contrast drive-oriented,

object-relations, and time-limited psychotherapies.

4. Compare and contrast transference within a traditional psychodynamic perspective and a short-term dynamic perspective.
5. Perform a case conceptualization of the African American male who was presented within this chapter.
6. Use a Google search to compare and contrast the approaches to psychoanalysis of Carl Jung, Karen Horney, Erich Fromm, Harry Stack Sullivan, and Wilhelm Reich.
7. Use a Google search to determine the training required for psychoanalysis.

Psychoanalytic Associations and Journals

- **American Psychoanalytic Association**
  309 East 49th Street, New York, NY 10017
  Telephone: (212) 752-0450
  Fax: (212) 593-0571
  Web site: http://www.apsa.org
  Journal: *Journal of the American Psychoanalytic Association* (quarterly)
- **American Psychological Association Division**
  39 – Psychoanalysis
  Membership Information: www.division39.org/membership_application.php
  Journal: *Psychoanalytic Psychology* (quarterly)
  Editor: Joseph Reppen, PhD, New York, NY
  Journal: *Psychoanalytic Abstracts* (quarterly)

Chapter 4

BEHAVIOR THERAPY

Chapter Overview

Behavior therapy became a challenge to the dominant form of psychotherapy of the 1950s and 1960s: psychoanalysis (Siegel, 1983, 1984). For example, within the United States, Joseph Wolpe developed systematic desensitization; Arnold Lazarus (in South Africa) and Hans Eysenck (in the United Kingdom) were beginning to employ results from animal psychology to treat anxiety disorders with humans. During the 1970s, it was clear that behavior therapy was the dominant paradigm in both psychology and education. For example, new procedures called self-control procedures were being developed. Likewise, there was an explosion of cognitive-behavioral therapies and techniques. To the regret of some therapists and theories, during the 1980s, behavior therapy became more diverse and moved beyond its earlier roots of learning theories (Day, 1983).

For example, more emphasis was being given to client–therapist relationship issues and working with clients' feelings. During the 1990s, theories started emphasizing the common elements that are found in both behavior therapy and humanistic therapies. Moreover, also during the 1990s and into the twenty-first century, two new techniques have been incorporated into behavior therapies to treat anxiety disorders: Francine Shapiro's EMDR, and a more general procedure called the eye movement technique (EMT). In addition, these eye movement procedures have been also combined with psychological hypnosis (Sapp, 2004a).

Note: Part of the material in this chapter was adapted from Sapp (2004a).

Finally, during the twenty-first century, Barber (1999, 2000) presented evidence that may end a major debate within the area of psychological hypnosis. Traditionally, psychologists have debated whether hypnosis was an altered state of consciousness or was due to cognitive abilities and social cues. Barber found that there were three types of hypnotizable clients: one type that fit the altered state of consciousness notion, but with three subtypes, and another type that fit the nonstate hypnosis camp. Interestingly, Barber also found a third type that did not fit the state or nonstate position. In closing, during the twenty-first century, researchers have found that there are brain correlates of hypnotizability and behavior (Ray & Oathes, 2003: Raz & Shapiro, 2002).

The Evolution of Behavior Therapy

Frew and Spiegler (2008) divided behavior therapy into traditional behavior therapy that consists of stimulus control procedures, reinforcement, punishment, exposure therapies, and modeling. The early origins of behavior therapy started with the Russian physiologist Ivan Pavlov, who discovered classical conditioning during the 1920s. Also during the 1920s, John Watson, an experimental psychologist at Johns Hopkins University, founded behaviorism as a reaction to Wundt's structuralism. Watson extended the learning theory of Pavlov-classical conditioning. In addition, during the 1920s, Mary Cover Jones, one of Watson's students, used modeling therapy and in vivo exposure to therapy to treat a phobia in a three-year-old male child called Peter.

During the 1930s, Edward Thorndike at Columbia University developed instrumental or operant conditioning by finding that behavior could be changed by modifying consequences. Following Thorndike, B. F. Skinner wrote a book on operant conditioning and extended the work of Thorndike.

During the 1950s, Joseph Wolpe, a psychiatrist in South Africa, developed systematic desensitization that was designed to treat anxiety disorders. Wolpe trained Arnold Lazarus and Stanley Rachman. Lazarus immigrated to the United States; Rachman immigrated to the United Kingdom.

At Stanford University in the 1960s, Albert Bandura developed a social learning theory, and during the 1960s cognitive therapies were developed by Albert Ellis in private practice in New York City and by psychiatrist Aaron Beck at the University of Pennsylvania. In the 1970s, at the University of Waterloo in Ontario, Canada, Meichenbaum developed self-instructional training and stress inoculation.

The Association for Advancement of Behavior Therapy (AABT) was founded in the United States in 1966. AABT became a major organization advocating behavior therapy, but in 2004, AABT became the Association for Behavioral and Cognitive Therapies (ABCT).

Approaches to Behavior Therapy

Becker (1987) stated that there are at least five forms of behavior therapy, and they are the following: applied behavior analysis, neobehaviorism, cognitive-behavioral therapy, social learning theory, and multimodal behavior therapy.

Applied Behavior Analysis

A popular American experimental psychologist, Skinner is associated with applied behavior analysis. Simply stated, applied behavior analysis studies the relationship between behavior and the environment. For example, how does behavior change as a result of environmental events. "Applied" suggests that events have social importance (Gambrill, 1994), while behaviors are the things that we do (Skinner, 1974, 1987, 1988a, b).

Unlike some other behaviorists, Skinner endorsed a philosophy of science called **radical behaviorism**, which is an attempt to account for behavior using only natural contingencies having survival, reinforcement, and social evolutionary links. Moreover, radical behaviorism is a radical departure for **Watsonian behaviorism** and **methodological behaviorism**.

According to Skinner, feelings are the products of one's experiences and they are the by-products of reinforcement, and Skinner emphasized this point by stating we do not cry because we are sad, but because something has happened. Moreover, unlike Watson, Skinner did not embrace associationism, operationalism, positivism, or **environmental determinism**, the notion that the environment totally determines behavior. Finally, radical behaviorism is an attempt to account for behaviorism entirely in terms of natural contingencies – such as survival, reinforcement, and social evolution.

Skinner's form of behavior therapy modifies antecedents, consequences, or both (Spiegler & Guevremont, 2003), and Skinner described an **ABC model** that described a time sequence of antecedents, behavior, and consequences. Not all antecedents and consequences are maintaining conditions, and only a small number of antecedents and consequences influence behavior. An interesting area of Skinner's approach, called **operant conditioning**, is stimulus control. First, operant conditioning means that an organism operates on the environment. Stimulus control is where cues set the stage for behaviors that will occur. Prompts are used to guide behavior. For example, when one says "sit" to a dog and the dog sits, the dog is responding to cues that guide behavior. Moreover, when one is interested in studying, the **setting events** are important. For example, a quiet room, free from distraction, is conducive to studying. Simply stated, setting events are environmental conditions that bring about a behavior. A Skinnerian behavior therapist would look for antecedents and consequences that cause a problem behavior, and it is these possible maintaining conditions that are modified (Spiegler & Guevremont, 2003). In summary, Skinner emphasized that behaviors are influenced by environmental events and consequences.

Neobehaviorism

During the 1930s, neobehaviorism was a school of psychology that challenged Wundt's structuralism. Even though Watson was the most famous neobehaviorist, Tolman, Guthrie, Hull, and others contributed to a sophisticated and elaborate form of behaviorism. The major goal of neobehaviorism was to make psychology scientific and to free it from the introspection methods of structuralism.

Watson endorsed the philosophy called **methodological behaviorism**, which is based on truth by agreement, logical positivism. Things are true only if a group of people can agree on them. During the 1900s, Watson (1879–1958) criticized Wundt's introspective psychology and stressed an objective form of psychology. Therefore, he did not emphasize environmental events, and he did not accept covert internal events; in essence, all behavior could be explained by stimulus and response learning or classical conditioning. Methodological behaviorism is based on public or consensual validation, and it is a **nomothetic approach**, traditional group experimentation and statistical inference approach. Watson (1930) shocked the world when he stated; "Give me a dozen healthy infants, well-formed, and my specified world to bring them up in and I will guarantee to take any one random and train him or her to become any type of specialist I might choose – doctor, lawyer, artist, merchant-chief and yes, even beggarman and thief, regardless of his or her talents, penchants, tendencies, abilities, vocations, and race of his or her ancestors. **I am going beyond my facts and I admit it, but so as have the advocates of the contrary, and they have been doing it for many thousands of years**" (p. 104; emphasis added). The section that is bold within the quote is often omitted from books. This quote suggests that Watson knew he was going beyond his facts and wanted to popularize psychology.

In 1920, Watson was forced to leave the academic world because he had engaged in inappropriate sexual intercourse with his female research assistant. After this incident, Watson's wife sued him and divorced him and destroyed his data on sexuality. This scandal forced Watson to resign from Johns Hopkins University, and in 1921, after marrying his former research assistant, he entered advertising and worked until his retirement in 1945. In 1957, Watson received an award for influencing modern psychology. Because Watson was still angry about being forced out of academic psychology, he burned all of his writing so that nothing could be left to science. Unlike Skinner, Watson viewed feelings, thoughts, and other internal states of mind as nonexistent. In contrast, Skinner's radical behaviorism is based on the **idiographic approach**, and it does not insist on truth by agreement. It can consider private events, but without a causal inference. In addition, what is radical about Skinner's position is that he viewed feelings, thoughts, and private events as behaviors like other behaviors that have environmental, evolutionary, and biological origins.

The **mediational notion of neobehaviorism** states that within the stimulus-response model there are intervening variables, or internal processes, that occur within the individual. In actuality, neobehaviorism is a stimulus, organism, response model (S-O-R), in which an organism is an intervening variable and the internal processes that occur within the individual (Hull, 1952).

To summarize, Sapp (1997a) presented the following table to summarize the difference between Skinner's radical behaviorism and Watson's neobehaviorism, a form of behaviorism based on classical conditioning.

Table 4-1

Skinner's radical behaviorism	***Watson's behaviorism***
1. Idiographic: single subject's research or case study methodology	1. Nomothetic: experimental group research
2. Nonassociationism, nonoperationism, and nonpositivism	2. Association, operationalism, and positivism
3. Relationship between environmental events and behavior	3. Stimulus-response psychology
4. Operant conditioning	4. Classical conditioning
5. Nonmediational theory	5. Mediational theory
6. No insistence on truth by agreement	6. Insistence on truth by agreement
7. Inductive	7. Deductive
8. Atheoretical	8. Theoretical

Cognitive-Behavioral Therapy

Cognitive-behavioral therapy is an eclectic range of techniques that combines strategies or techniques from cognitive and behavioral psychology. Dr. Albert Ellis, the grandfather of cognitive-behavioral therapy, the president of the Albert Ellis institute, and the pioneer of cognitive-behavioral therapy within the area of clinical psychology, founded cognitive-behavioral therapy. Dr. Aaron T. Beck, a psychiatrist, is a prominent figure who followed Ellis with his emphasis on what he called "cognitive therapy" (Beck & Freeman, 1990; Ellis & Dryden, 1987). Dr. Donald Meichenbaum (1994), another clinical psychologist, gained a great deal of attention in terms of stress inoculation training, a cognitive-behavioral method for reducing stress. Within the area of adolescence, Dr. Philip C. Kendall (1992) has used cognitive-behavioral strategies with youths.

There is a relatively new form of cognitive-behavioral therapy called **dialectical behavior therapy (DBT)**. Dialectics is defined as the synthesis of opposing opposites. It was developed by Dr. Marsha Linehan at the University of Washington (Linehan, 1993; Linehan, Dimeff & Reynolds, 2002) and she and her colleagues have developed techniques for dealing with riskier behaviors, such as suicide, self-mutilation, substance abuse, borderline personality disorder (BPD), and other disorders. Leahy (2003) pointed out that DBT places more of an emphasis on the behavioral dimension of cognitive-behavioral theory. For example, a greater emphasis is placed on teaching clients behavioral skills for regulating negative cognitions, behaviors, and emotions.

Another relatively new form of cognitive-behavioral therapy is **mindfulness-based cognitive therapy (MBCT)**. **MBCT** teaches clients to process cognitions and affect without judging their origins. For example, clients are taught meditation and other mindfulness strategies such as yoga. Instead of trying to control thoughts and feelings, clients are taught to let them rise without judgment during meditative exercises (Germer, 2005).

There are at least four aspects of cognitive-behavioral therapy: schemata theory, continuity assumption, Socratic method, and cognitive-behavioral attributions. **Schemata theory** was originally described by two noted theorists, Piaget (1926) and Barlett (1932). Freeman (1990) stated that schemata are formed during childhood and constantly change, even though they remained relatively stable. Schemata are conceptual frameworks that describe how thought processes develop within children. For example, society and socialization help determine how schemata are formed. In addition, as schemata develop they are both conscious and unconscious, or below the level of awareness (Garner, Rockett, Davis, Garner, Olmstead & Eagle 1993).

In terms of structures, schemata are composed of four interrelated concepts or structure: cognitive structure, cognitive propositions, cognitive operations, and cognitive products (Granvold, 1994). **Cognitive structure** is the way information is stored, represented, and processed within the mind. **Cognitive propositions** are information processing mechanisms that are selected, stored, encoded, and retrieved. **Cognitive products** are the results of information processing, and they exist within the mind as opinions, self-cognitions, beliefs, attitudes, conclusion, judgments, and so on. *Cognitive operations* are the active mechanisms of processing information such as attention, encoding, storage, and retrieval. **Cognitive products** are the results of cognitive operations and are attributions, cognitions, beliefs, self-verbalizations, opinions, values, judgments, and images. In summary, information processing consists of several structures, such as short-term memory, long-term memory, iconic sensory memory, cognitive networks, and memory modes. Schema involve cognitive structures and cognitive propositions such as episodic knowledge, semantic knowledge, and internally generated beliefs. In addition, schema consists of cognitive propositions and cognitive operations (Clark, 1989; Granvold, 1994).

Schemata on an abstract level are philosophies that guide a client's life, and synonyms for this term are irrational beliefs (Ellis and Dryden, 1987), personal constructs (Kelly, 1955), deep structures (Guidano, 1987), and dysfunctional cognitions (Beck, 1976). In closing, schemata can be rigid, broad, and irrational and rational beliefs (Blackburn, Eunsun & Bishop, 1986).

The **continuity assumption** simply states that the same rules that govern overt learning such as operant conditioning and classical conditioning also govern thoughts or cognitions. In essence, covert learning (cognitive learning) occurs through the same rules that govern observable behavior. Finally, the continuity assumption is assumed with all the cognitive-behavioral therapies.

Individuals familiar with **Socratic method**, which is taken from philosophy, realize that it is a method of skillful questioning. The goal is to permit clients to discover solutions for themselves. Sapp (1997a) provided the following examples: "What makes this assumption so or true?" "Provide evidence to support your belief." "What is the proof that your belief is true?" "Is this notion totally true?"

Cognitive-behavioral attributions, also called **cognitive distortions** by Beck (1976), which are taken from the area of social psychology, state that clients make inferential causal explanations about their behaviors and the behaviors of others (Epstein, 1982). Actually, clients tend to make **major attributional errors**, and they tend to blame others for situational events. This is more likely to occur for others and not oneself. In reality, clients tend to underestimate situational explanations of behavior when the situations involve others. This leads to blame and, as the reader will see, with therapies like REBT, blame is one of the core emotional disturbances – blaming others, blaming oneself, and blaming the world. Moreover, blame can be viewed as a broad schema. There are a variety of cognitive-behavioral attributions or cognitive distortions such as negative attributions; misattribution; personalization; dichotomous or polarized thinking; selective abstraction; arbitrary inference, which includes mind reading and negative predictions; and overgeneralization, which includes magnification and minimization.

Negative attribution is the attribution of blame toward others as the core schema. For example, "I could not help myself." "You made me do this." "You made me mad." "I cannot stand you." "You make my life hell."

In addition to the words cognitive distortion, Beck refers to personalization, dichotomous thinking, selective abstraction, arbitrary inference, and overgeneralizations as **misattributions**.

Personalization is where a client assumes responsibility for things that are outside of his or her control. Often the client is apologizing for things that are out of his or her control. For example, once when I was seeing a client during a thunderstorm and the lights went out, the client stated "I am sorry." I indicated to the client that the thunderstorm had made the lights go off. On a cognitive level, the client had assumed that she was the cause of object of the lights going out. This assumption was made through an implication that I, the subject, caused the lights to go out, and that I am the object of the negative events.

Dichotomous or **polarized thinking** is extreme or absolutistic or polarized thinking. Things are viewed in black or white terms, right or wrong, good or evil. Some cognitive-behavioral therapies refer to this thinking as all-or-nothing thinking because the client does not leave any room for in-between or gray areas of seeing things. This form of thinking is a distortion, and it tends to simplify life events. Sapp (1997a; 2004a) provided the following examples: "I am a total fool." "I am always wrong." "I am the worst bitch." These statements suggest that the subject is nothing other than a fool, wrong, worst bitch, and so on. Usually as the result of such thinking, the clients experience negative effects such as depression, anger, misery, and so on.

Selective abstraction focuses only on the negative aspects of a situation, and this form of thinking ignores other salient features of a situation. Actually, a situation is viewed as totally bad or negative. For example, suppose you asked your boss for a 15% raise and your boss agrees to a 10% raise. As a result of this interaction, you could feel worthless and underpaid but only after focusing on the exact outcome as opposed to the fact that you received a raise. If you focused on the process of obtaining a raise it would be difficult to have extreme negative emotions connected with the encounter.

Often clients reach a negative conclusion, and this is called an arbitrary inference. If a client cannot provide data to support his or her inference, chances are it is an arbitrary one. **Mind reading** and **negative predictions** are two examples of this form of misattribution of cognitive distortion. **Mind reading** is when clients attempt to predict what someone is thinking based on random nonverbal cues or clues. For example, "I knew that our relationship would end, because I had bad feelings toward my husband, and I assumed that my feelings represented what he was thinking." It has to be pointed out to a client that it is not possible to determine another's thoughts based on arbitrary circumstantial evidence. When clients report that they have a feeling that something bad is going to happen without evidence or data to support the prediction, through a self-fulfilling prophesy, the client can unconsciously bring about the desired negative prediction or outcome.

Overgeneralization is drawing conclusions from one or a few isolated pieces of data and applying the conclusion in a broad way. Clients can magnify or exaggerate the negative aspects of a situation or they can minimize the positive aspects of a situation. In summary, when clients tend to magnify negative aspects of a situation and minimize the positive aspects of the situation, the clients are overgeneralizing.

Finally, **cognitive-behavioral attributions** or **cognitive distortions** are the results of processing information improperly, and cognitive distortions are partly the result of individual differences and partly the results of socialization (Wilson, 1989; Blaine et al., 1989; Guidano & Liotti, 1983). The following scale was designed to measure irrational beliefs and was based on Ellis' theory of irrational beliefs. (Ellis & Dryden 1982).

Ellis' Thirteen Irrational Beliefs

Directions: For each question, please circle the response which most accurately reflects your beliefs. There are no right or wrong answers so please answer honestly.

1. It is necessary to be loved and approved by significant others.

1	2	3	4	5	6
Strongly Disagree	*Moderately Disagree*	*Mildly Disagree*	*Mildly Agree*	*Moderately Agree*	*Strongly Agree*

2. It is necessary to be competent, adequate, and achieving 100% of the time in order to be worthwhile.

1	2	3	4	5	6
Strongly Disagree	*Moderately Disagree*	*Mildly Disagree*	*Mildly Agree*	*Moderately Agree*	*Strongly Agree*

3. When individuals act obnoxiously (bad, wicked, and villainous), we should blame them for their wrongdoing.

1	2	3	4	5	6
Strongly Disagree	*Moderately Disagree*	*Mildly Disagree*	*Mildly Agree*	*Moderately Agree*	*Strongly Agree*

4. It is catastrophic and awful when things do not go the way I would like.

1	2	3	4	5	6
Strongly Disagree	*Moderately Disagree*	*Mildly Disagree*	*Mildly Agree*	*Moderately Agree*	*Strongly Agree*

5. Unhappiness is the result of external events that are beyond my control.

1	2	3	4	5	6
Strongly Disagree	*Moderately Disagree*	*Mildly Disagree*	*Mildly Agree*	*Moderately Agree*	*Strongly Agree*

6. If certain things are dangerous and fearsome, the individual should constantly be preoccupied with them.

1	2	3	4	5	6
Strongly Disagree	*Moderately Disagree*	*Mildly Disagree*	*Mildly Agree*	*Moderately Agree*	*Strongly Agree*

7. It is easier to avoid facing difficult life situations than to face them.

1	2	3	4	5	6
Strongly Disagree	*Moderately Disagree*	*Mildly Disagree*	*Mildly Agree*	*Moderately Agree*	*Strongly Agree*

8. Individuals should be dependent on others, and individuals should need others – especially someone who is stronger to rely on.

1	2	3	4	5	6
Strongly Disagree	*Moderately Disagree*	*Mildly Disagree*	*Mildly Agree*	*Moderately Agree*	*Strongly Agree*

9. The past is the sole determinant of present behavior.

1	2	3	4	5	6
Strongly Disagree	*Moderately Disagree*	*Mildly Disagree*	*Mildly Agree*	*Moderately Agree*	*Strongly Agree*

10. Individuals should worry, be upset, and be concerned about other people's concerns.

1	2	3	4	5	6
Strongly Disagree	*Moderately Disagree*	*Mildly Disagree*	*Mildly Agree*	*Moderately Agree*	*Strongly Agree*

11. A correct or perfect solution exists for every problem, and it is terrible if such a solution is not found.

1	2	3	4	5	6
Strongly Disagree	*Moderately Disagree*	*Mildly Disagree*	*Mildly Agree*	*Moderately Agree*	*Strongly Agree*

12. The notion that human happiness can be achieved by not actively engaging in creative pursuits.

1	2	3	4	5	6
Strongly Disagree	*Moderately Disagree*	*Mildly Disagree*	*Mildly Agree*	*Moderately Agree*	*Strongly Agree*

13. One can have no control over emotions.

1	2	3	4	5	6
Strongly Disagree	*Moderately Disagree*	*Mildly Disagree*	*Mildly Agree*	*Moderately Agree*	*Strongly Agree*

This final scale was developed by Dr. Amanda J. Gregas and my research team, and it was designed to measure the cognitive distortions of Aaron Beck.

1. **I tend to discount the positive and dwell on the negative aspects of a situation or issue.** For example, a student receives many positive comments about a class presentation but receives one piece of mildly critical feedback. Afterwards, the student obsesses about the negative comment and ignores all of the positive feedback.

1	2	3	4	5	6
Almost Never	Rarely	Seldom	Occasionally	Frequently	Almost Always

2. **I tend to think in terms of all-or-nothing, such that if a situation falls short of perfect, I see it as total failure.** For example, a woman who eats one cookie thinks she has blown her diet and as a result, gives up and eats the entire bag of cookies.

1	2	3	4	5	6
Almost Never	Rarely	Seldom	Occasionally	Frequently	Almost Always

3. **I tend to believe that my feelings about a situation are an accurate reflection of the way things really are, even if there is evidence to the contrary.** For example, a man is afraid of flying so he reasons that air travel must be very dangerous.

1	2	3	4	5	6
Almost Never	Rarely	Seldom	Occasionally	Frequently	Almost Always

4. **I tend to anticipate that things will turn out badly.** For example, before going on a job interview, a student predicts that he will not get the job.

1	2	3	4	5	6
Almost Never	Rarely	Seldom	Occasionally	Frequently	Almost Always

5. **I tend to assume I know what other people are thinking based on their behaviors.** For example, a young man assumes his girlfriend is thinking about breaking up with him because she has been quiet lately.

1	2	3	4	5	6
Almost Never	Rarely	Seldom	Occasionally	Frequently	Almost Always

6. **I tend to overgeneralize by taking one event to be the proof of a series or pattern of events.** For example, a student becomes terribly upset when she finds a parking ticket on her car. She tells herself, "This kind of a thing always happens to me. I never catch any breaks."

1	2	3	4	5	6
Almost Never	Rarely	Seldom	Occasionally	Frequently	Almost Always

7. **I tend to hold myself personally responsible for events that are not necessarily under my control.** For example, when a student learns

that her mother is having some health problems she tells herself, "This shows what a neglectful daughter that I have been – if I spent more time at home or called more often this probably wouldn't have happened."

1	2	3	4	5	6
Almost Never	Rarely	Seldom	Occasionally	Frequently	Almost Always

8. **I tend to catastrophize by assuming the worst is going to happen.** For example, after receiving a speeding ticket, a student begins to think about not being able to afford the ticket, or higher car insurance, his car payment, rent, tuition, and eventually the student assumes he will have to drop out of school.

1	2	3	4	5	6
Almost Never	Rarely	Seldom	Occasionally	Frequently	Almost Always

9. **I tend to focus on the negative aspects of situations.** For example, a student receives an honorary scholarship yet when her friends congratulate her, she says "But now my financial aid will get messed up and I won't be offered any work-study or loans!"

1	2	3	4	5	6
Almost Never	Rarely	Seldom	Occasionally	Frequently	Almost Always

10. **I tend to say harsh things to myself when I make a mistake.** For example, a student discovers he forgot to bring his calculator with him on the day of his statistics exam, and he thinks to himself, "You're such an idiot. I can't believe you could be such a fool!"

1	2	3	4	5	6
Almost Never	Rarely	Seldom	Occasionally	Frequently	Almost Always

Social Learning Theories

There is a **family of social learning theories**, and, Bandura (1985) has contributed a great deal to this area. Unlike radical behaviorism, social theory, also a cognitive-behavioral or sociocognitive theory, gives explanatory roles to cognitions. As the reader may remember, radical behaviorism was a radical rejection of Watsonian behaviorism and it did not view cognitions or thoughts as an explanation of behavior. Simply stated cognitions are by-products of behaviors, and they do not initiate behaviors.

Bandura endorsed **reciprocal determinism** or the notion that environmental, cognitive, and behavioral factors interacted simultaneously to determine behavior. In essence, social learning theory is a blend of cognitive-behavioral therapies and social-psychological theories. In contrast to cognitive-behavioral therapies, which place most of their emphasis on cognitions as determinants of behaviors, social learning theories are more comprehensive in that they place emphasis on the client, his or her environment, and cognitions as mutually interactive factors in determining behaviors.

The notion of **expectancies theory** was discussed earlier (*see* Chapter 1), and the notion of expectancy is derived from social learning theories. Rotter (1966), another social learning theorist, defined expectancy as a client's subjective perceptions about an event, situation, or person. It is a client's covert perception about reality. Readers may have heard about a common expectancy called **internal locus of control**, or the belief that one has the ability to produce certain outcomes. In addition, there is another expectancy called **self-efficacy**, or the belief or conviction that one can produce a certain outcome. Moreover, Seligman (1975) defined another common expectancy within psychology that he referred to as **learned helpless**, and this concept is the opposite of self-efficacy. This expectancy, learned helplessness, also corresponds to Rotter's notion of external locus of control expectancy or the belief that things are totally out of one's control. Therefore, outcomes are the results of outside events or pure luck. The concept of learned helplessness describes clients' expectations of being depressed, helpless, paralyzed, and ineffective.

Multimodal Behavioral Therapy

Lazarus (1980) refers to this as eclectic behaviorism, and he was the first theorist or therapist to coin the term behavior therapy. He uses the term **technical eclecticism** to refer to using procedures and techniques from various theories without subscribing to the individual theories. In addition, he noted that **theoretical eclecticism**, drawing from diverse theories and trying to integrate them, leads to confusion in that certain theories are epistemologically incompatible and cannot be logically integrated. Lazarus recommended analyzing and treating clients in terms of their behavior from seven interacting modalities: behavior, affect, sensation, imagery, cognition, interpersonal relationships, and drugs and physiology. Lazarus refers to his form of assessing and analyzing clients as the BASIC-ID, an acronym for a client's behavior, affect, sensations, imagery, cognitions, interpersonal relationships, and drugs and/or biology or physiology. An assessment is made in terms of a client's strengths and weaknesses with these seven modalities. Clearly, multimodal behavior therapy is the most comprehensive intraindividually based behavior theory, and social learning theories are the comprehensive nonintraindividually based theories (Burnett & Pulvino, 1990; Lazarus, 1976, 1986, 1989c, 1992, 1995).

Common Characteristics of Behavior Therapies

Even though there are not any unifying sets of assumptions about behavior therapies that can incorporate all existing procedures and theories within the behavioral field, there are three shared common characteristics (Becker, 1987). All therapies view the client's concerns within behavioral terms – the changing of behavior. Second, all behavior therapies use principles of learning, such as respondent (classical) and instrumental (operant) conditioning (Day, 1980). Third, all behavior therapies, implicitly or explicitly, employ the scientific method. The scientific method involves testing hypotheses and making adjustments to hypotheses based on data that are collected. In essence, the scientific method is an investigative or experimental approach. The next section discusses anxiety disorders that have been more thoroughly investigated and treated by behavioral therapies than any other group of therapies (Guidano, 1987).

Anxiety Disorders

Anxiety disorders are affective or mood disorders in which a client experiences debilitating anxiety. Most of the research about anxiety disorder came from the area of test anxiety. Sapp (2006a, b), Scholze and Sapp (2006), and Sapp (1999) defined test anxiety as a special case of a general anxiety disorder consisting of phenomenological, physiological, and behavioral responses related to the fear of failure. These feelings are the harsh feelings that have physiological and behavioral concomitants that clients experience in evaluative situations. Spielberger and Vagg (1995) theorized that test anxiety is composed of at least two factors or constructs – worry and emotionality – and this theory is a state trait, one where worry is analogous to trait anxiety and emotionality corresponds to state anxiety. This theory of anxiety states that the interaction of high worry and high emotionality produce test anxiety. In essence, worry is the cognitive concern about performance, whereas emotionality is the physiological arousal response to anxiety.

Recently, Spielberger and Vagg (1995) introduced a transactional process model of test anxiety. This comprehensive model of test anxiety specifies that interpersonal perceptions, cognitions, informational processing, and retrieval mechanisms mediate the effects of worry and emotionality on performance. Moreover, they identified other important correlates of test anxiety such as study skills or habits, test-taking skills, test-wiseness, and task-irrelevant cognitions. This, too, is an essentially trait-state theory of test anxiety that states that test anxiety is a trait evoked by state during evaluative situations.

Sarason (1984) extended Spielberger's model of test anxiety into four factors; first, worry and emotionality, but he conceptualized worry as existing of two distinct dimensions he called bodily arousal and tension. Finally, his fourth dimension was test-irrelevant cognitions. Sapp (1999) also found that test anxiety was composed of two constructs that correspond to Sarason's model. Sapp (1994a, 1996a, c) conceptualized test anxiety within a cognitive-behavioral theory, and he viewed worry as the cognitive component of test anxiety and emotionality as the behavioral response. He viewed the cognitions and affects that result from test anxiety as behaviors and logically cognitive-behavioral treatments would be the treatments of choice.

The *DSM-IV-TR* describes nine anxiety disorders: panic disorder with agoraphobia, panic disorder without agoraphobia, agoraphobia with history of panic disorder, specific phobia, obsessive-compulsive disorder, posttraumatic stress disorder, acute stress disorder, generalized anxiety disorder, anxiety disorder due to [indicate the general medical condition]. Specify if diagnosis is With Generalized Anxiety/With Panic Attacks/With Obsessive-Compulsive Symptoms, and anxiety disorder not otherwise specified. The reader can review the *DSM-IV-TR* (pp. 429–484) for a detailed discussion of each disorder; however, there are some general features of anxiety disorder that are important from a clinical standpoint. Panic attacks are common characteristics of anxiety, and these are sudden feelings that something horrible will happen. Often, clients will have feelings of shortness of breath, heart palpitations, choking sensations, chest pains, a sense of going crazy, and losing control. Actually, panic disorder parallels test anxiety in that there are somatic complaints and excessive worry.

Kendall and Hammen (1998) defined the following anxiety disorders: generalized anxiety disorder, specific phobia, agoraphobia, obsessive-compulsive disorder, posttraumatic stress disorder (PTSD), and acute stress disorder.

Generalized anxiety disorder (GAD) is excessive worry anxiety and emotionality anxiety that lasts for six months. **Specific phobias** are simple phobias, or the unrealistic fear of a certain situation or object. **Social phobia** is worry anxiety about social or performance situations. **Agoraphobia** is worry anxiety and emotionality anxiety in which escape from a situation is difficult, and this disorder can occur with or without panic attacks. **Obsessive-compulsive disorder (OCD)** can be diagnosed if a client presents obsessions – recurrent cognitions or images, and compulsions – rituals or repetitive behaviors that a client is driven to perform. **PTSD** is an anxiety disorder that is the result of extreme psychological trauma. PTSD can include symptoms such as an exaggerated startle response, reliving the traumatic event, sleep difficulties, and cognitive distortions. When a client presents symptoms of PTSD that have occurred less than a year, the appropriate diagnosis is acute **stress disorder**.

Anxiety disorders can be treated by psychological or medical means. Cognitive-behavioral approaches view anxiety disorders as the results of error in information processing and irrationality philosophies about life. Medical therapies such as benzodiazepines or anxiolytics are antianxiety medications; these include such brand name drugs as Xanax, Valium, Ativan, and Dalmine. These medications reduce central nervous activity by lessening anxiety and by producing calming effects. Kendall and Hammen (1998) reported that antianxiety medications or minor tranquilizers work by increasing the activity of a neurotransmitter gamma-aminobutyric acid (**GABA**), which is an inhibitory neurotransmitter. In summary, the theory states that benzodiazepines increase the effects of GABA. OCD is believed to be the result of high levels of the neurotransmitter serotonin, and antidepressant medications such as clomipramine or anafranil have been shown to be effective within dosage ranges of 75 to 300 milligrams. Clearly, some anxiety disorders run within families, and there are biological aspects of these disorders.

As previously stated, there are many cognitive-behavioral techniques that can be used to treat anxiety disorders such as relaxation therapies, systematic desensitization, hypnosis, EMT, exposure procedures, and so on.

Therapies Based on Principles of Classical Conditioning

Van Den Hout and Merckelbach (1991) have challenged the notion that classical conditioning is just the temporal pairing of conditioned and unconditioned stimuli, and they have stated that clients' expectations lead to the reaction of one stimulus to another. Furthermore, they presented a **neo-Pavlovian model** of classical conditioning: conditioned stimulus → cognitive representation of unconditioned stimulus → evaluation of unconditioned stimulus → conditioned stimulus. This model asserts that we are genetically prepared to respond to certain conditioned stimuli (Rescorla, 1988).

Systematic desensitization is a therapy based on the reciprocal inhibitions theory of counterconditioning. Wolpe (1958, 1973, 1997) stated that if an antagonistic response is made during the presence of an anxiety-producing stimulus, the feared response can be decreased. Wolpe labeled this process whereby two antagonistic responses could not occur simultaneously as **reciprocal inhibition**. For example, Wolpe theorized one could not experience bodily tension and relaxation at the same time. In essence, bodily relaxation cancels out bodily tension.

Systematic desensitization (SD) can be used not only to reduce stress, anxiety, and anger but also sexual disorders and so on. Unlike the claims of Wolpe's theory of reciprocal inhibition, it appears that SD works because of imaginal exposure and in vivo exposure. The reader who is interested in treatment scripts for SD can consult Sapp (1993, 1999); however, there are several steps to this treatment. The first step is **muscular relaxation**. The client is taught to tense and relax muscle groups throughout the body, and eventually through the process of conditioning, the client is able to mentally relax the body without muscular tension.

The second step of SD is an anxiety or **stress hierarchy**, or the arrangement of feared or stressed items or situations from least to most stressful or anxiety evoking. The third step of SD is teaching clients the **Subjective Units of Distress Scale** or **(SUDS)**, which is a method of teaching clients to rate the amount of stress or anxiety evoked during the stress or anxiety scenes. There are a variety of ways of presenting SUDS to clients, and some psychologists use a scale from 0 to 100; others use a scale from 0 to 10. The smaller the value, the smaller the degree of stress or anxiety.

The fourth stage of SD is **interposition**, or the pairing of relaxation with the anxiety or stress scenes using the clients' imaginations. The final phase of SD is **in vivo desensitization** or real-life exposure to the things that produce stress or anxiety. Sapp (1997a) reported that clients with agoraphobia or the fear of social situations respond better to in vivo desensitization than to SD without in vivo exposure. In addition, Sapp reported that the entire process of SD is more effective than exposure or relaxation is alone. The mechanisms that underlie SD are exposure and response expectancies. Clients have a belief in SD, and it meets their expectations; coupled with exposure it is a powerful treatment. Finally, expectations are factors that probably influence all psychological and medical treatments.

Suinn and Richardson (1971; Suinn, 2001) developed **anxiety management training (AMT)** due to the length of time needed for the development of hierarchies and the length of treatment with SD. Unlike SD, this process can take less than three hours, and it employs a variety of visual and fantasy techniques to elicit anxiety within clients. Suinn theorized that anxiety was a drive state, and he stated that we can learn behaviors to eliminate that drive. In summary, clients are taught first to identify the internal signal of anxiety and then later to learn to react to these signals with responses that are designed to remove them, such as relaxation, self-monitoring, and so on. Finally, Suinn described how AMT can be conducted within five structured sessions (Heimberg, 1990).

Aversive counterconditioning is another technique or therapy based on classical conditioning principles. An **aversive stimulus** is an unpleasant or undesirable stimulus. For example, Antabuse® (Disulfiram) a drug used to treat alcoholism, is an aversive drug because it produces nausea. Antabuse is given to a client each time he or she consumes alcohol. The drug works by being repeatedly paired with alcohol and eventually, through conditioning, produces nausea. In addition, apomorphine is another drug that produces nausea and has been used with smoking cessation. When the drug is repeatedly paired with smoking, the result is **counterconditioning**, and eventually smoking produces nausea. Moreover, stale cigarettes and electric shock have been used as part of aversive conditioning with smoking cessation. Finally, aversive conditioning has been used to treat childhood enuresis. Special ethical considerations are needed with aversive techniques, but as the reader will see, covert sensitization is an alternative.

Joseph Cautela (1967) developed **covert sensitization** as an alternative to aversive conditioning. This technique uses imaginal aversive stimuli as opposed to actual aversive stimuli. For covert sensitization to be effective, a client must be capable of elaborate mental imagery and committed to mentally exposing himself or herself to mentally aversive stimuli.

Behavior therapy is also popular in the treatment of sexual disorders. For example, **sensate focus**, a technique based on classical conditioning, involves in vivo desensitization. This technique is common for couples with sexual disorders. First, couples are requested to abstain from sexual intercourse and to explore a series of graduated exercises such as touching, caressing, and holding. Once a couple is able to touch each other without feeling extreme anxiety, which is a relaxing response, they are instructed to gradually engage in sexual activity. Sensate focus is used to reduce sexual performance anxiety by having couples learn to associate pleasurable sensations (relaxation) with what were once anxiety producing situations.

Assertion training like all the techniques discussed within this section, is based on classical conditioning. Wolpe (1973) viewed assertion training as the correct response for emotional expression in contrast to anxiety toward others. In essence, assertion training is used to reduce anxiety, and it differs from aggression in that the goal is expression without harming others. Clients are taught to express their feelings without interfering with the expression of feelings of others. Often, relaxation, behavioral rehearsal, in vivo, and modeling are combined with assertion training.

Therapies Based on Extinction

Many therapies based on classical conditioning are based on gradual exposure to anxiety-eliciting stimuli; extinction is based on the immediate and intense exposure to anxiety-eliciting stimuli (Sapp, 1997a). Because these techniques are based on immediate exposure, clients are at an added risk of psychological harm and should be carefully assessed to determine if they can tolerate immediate exposure. The techniques that are discussed within this section are flooding, implosive therapy, paradoxical intention, aversive conditioning, and covert sensitization.

Flooding is usually conducted in vivo, and it prevents a client from making an avoidance response. Similarly, flooding can be conducted through a client's imagery, but it is probably more effective when used in vivo. If a psychologist combines flooding with modeling, the client can learn effective coping and decrease the anxiety response.

T. F. Stampfl, a distinguished professor emeritus of the department of psychology at the University of Wisconsin–Milwaukee, developed implosive therapy, and it was popular mainly during the 1960s (Stampfl & Levis, 1967). Like flooding, implosive therapy is designed to implode or extinguish anxiety by repeatedly having a client expose herself or himself to the conditioned anxiety-eliciting stimulus via imagery. In contrast to flooding, implosive therapy is an imaginally based therapy only. Another difference between flooding and implosive therapy is that implosive therapy uses psychoanalytically oriented concepts during the imagery process. In addition, one goal of implosive therapy is to elicit unconscious conflicts.

It was the existential psychotherapist Viktor Frankl (1959) who developed the technique of paradoxical intention or prescribing the client's symptoms. With paradoxical intentions, clients are instructed to increase their symptoms; the goal is to show clients that they have voluntary control of their symptoms. Even though paradoxical techniques have been used to treat a variety of disorders, such as anxiety disorders, insomnia and so on, it is contraindicated in the treatment of suicide, violence, and substance abuse (Dattilio, 1994; Huddleston & Engles, 1986).

Aversive techniques were described in the previous section under therapies based on classical conditioning; however, aversive conditioning results in behavioral responses that prevent the occurrence of aversive stimuli (Sapp, 1997a). Moreover, aversive conditioning uses aversive stimuli such as physical punishment and electrical shocks that can be useful in extinguishing maladaptive behaviors (Iverson, 1994).

Aversive techniques, like covert sensitization, were also described in the section about therapies based on classical conditioning. In contrast to the use of actual aversive techniques, convert sensitization asks clients to imagine aversive stimuli, and it is an alternative to aversive conditioning and in vivo aversive counterconditioning.

Therapies Based on Instrumental or Operant Conditioning

Even though Skinner considered himself atheoretical, he developed the theory of instrumental conditioning, following the work of experimental animal psychologist Edward Lee Thorndike (1874–1949). Skinner did not see the value in giving causal emphasis to cognitions, emotions, or neuropsychology. He emphasized the primacy of behavior, or the connection between the environment and behavior, and he believed cognitions, emotions, and so on were the by-products of behavior or responses to things that happened within the environment. In addition, Skinner accepted evolutionary theory and believed that many behaviors were part of the evolutionary process.

In order to apply instrumental conditioning, Cormier and colleagues (2009) recommended applying an ABC model for the relationship between behavior and environmental events. This model suggests that behavior (B) is influenced by things that precede it (A, antecedents) and by things that follow it (C, consequences). Clearly, consequences can strengthen or weaken behavior.

Next, the following instrumental conditioning techniques will be discussed: positive reinforcement, negative reinforcement, schedules of reinforcement, successive approximation, Premack principle, token economy, contracts, punishment, time out, overcorrection, response cost, reinforcing incompatible behaviors, and operant extinction.

Both **positive reinforcers** and **negative reinforcers** increase behavior. Positive reinforcement is the application of rewards or some pleasurable event following a certain behavior or set of behaviors that leads to an increase in responding. Now, the notion of pleasurable is a matter of interpretation or judgment. Some examples of positive reinforcement are praise for a child following the completion of homework, encouragement, hugs, stars for good behavior and so on. The goal of reinforcements is to increase the desired behavior.

Negative reinforcement is reinforcement that is connected with the **termination of an aversive stimulus**. In other words, it is the **removal of negative consequence** following a performance of a certain behavior. For example, taking cold medication to remove or lessen the symptoms of a cold is an example of a negative reinforcer.

In addition, in some cars, a buzzer sounds to alert the driver to put on the seat belt. The sounding buzzer serves as a negative reinforcer, because each time the driver hears the sounding buzzer he or she puts on his or her seat belt in order to stop the negative consequence – the sounding buzzer. If parents prevent their children from watching television until they complete their homework, preventing children from watching television is a negative consequence that is removed once homework is completed.

Reinforcers must be contingent on target behaviors, and they are the most effective when immediately following certain performances. Continuous or excessive reinforcement leads to satiation, and this is why primary reinforcers like food and water are more susceptible to satiation than are secondary reinforcers like money, stocks, bonds, and so on.

The **schedules of reinforcement** also determine the rate of satiation. By definition, continuous reinforcement is providing reinforcement after each response. When continuous reinforcement is reduced to a partial reinforcement schedule, the process is called **thinning**. In addition, variable reinforcement, providing reinforcement on a variable rate, results in the highest rate of responding and is extremely resistant to extinction. For example, gambling casinos and lotteries operate on a variable ratio schedule of reinforcement in that they provide intermittent or irregular reinforcement. Since a person who is gambling never knows when he or she will win, the persons continues gambling even though he or she loses money because the expectation is that he or she will win eventually. In many casinos, initially people are permitted to win early on, but, once hooked, people continue playing hoping to win or receive reinforcement.

Successive approximation is a method of teaching complex tasks, especially to children. For example, it has been used to teach speech to autistic and schizophrenic children and those with other complex behaviors. Differential reinforcement of successive approximations is reinforcing behaviors that are similar to the approximated ones. Differential reinforcement is not providing continuous reinforcement, and it is used to shape behavior. Finally, this process involves the gradual withdrawal of reinforcement until the desired behavior is performed.

The Premack principle can be useful when it is difficult to come up with reinforcers for a client, and it is the reinforcement of low-frequency behaviors with high-frequency behaviors. This is the performance of low-frequency behaviors before high-frequency behaviors. For example, if you are required to exercise and usually you enjoy watching television, you could make yourself exercise before watching television. Here, you would be linking exercise, a low frequency behavior, with watching television, a high frequency behavior (Premack, 1959).

Token economy is very useful for structured environments like schools and institutional settings, and it is the establishment of environment in which tokens are given for desired behaviors. After clients collect tokens, they can trade them in for pleasurable items or activities. Within institutions, token economy requires that everyone work together, and this includes therapists, institutional workers, and others. Even though token economy loses its reinforcing power once clients leave structured settings, parents, family members, and friends can keep the process going.

Contracts or behavioral contracting is a self-management strategy in which a client enters into an agreement with one or more persons to perform specific predetermined behaviors or responses (James & Gilliland, 2003). Usually, the contract specifies consequences for not following the contracted behaviors. Clearly, for contracts to be effective, they must be explicit, and monitoring and record keeping is important for feedback. The following is a general contract.

General Contract ____

I agree to agree to follow the terms of this contract, and if I do not meet the terms of this contract forfeit the right to the following activity or rewards.

Signature ______________

The next contract is one to prevent suicide.

Suicide Prevention Contract ______________________________

I agree to not harm myself, and if I get to the point of not being able to comply with this contract, I will call 911 and seek immediate help.

Signature ______________

In summary, contracts can be elaborate or simple, but the notion is that it allows the client and psychologist to agree on terms that can strengthen the therapeutic relationship, and often when clients do not believe in or are unwilling to comply with a contract, they will not sign.

In contrast to reinforcers, punishment is an operant or instrumental procedure designed to decrease behavior; however, very similar to negative reinforcement, it uses aversive stimuli but the goal is to decrease behavior and not to increase it. What is often missed with punishment is the fact that it has to be intense and immediate to be effective. When punishment is intense, it can suppress behavior. Moreover, punishment must be consistent to be effective, and when desirable behaviors are reinforced, it is even more effective. Finally, there are ethical concerns in using punishment, but with injurious behavior, sometimes it becomes the last resort.

Time out has been a common instrumental or operant procedure used by parents and teachers, and it is the removal of positive reinforcers. For example, children who fight or misbehave are often removed from the classroom or other reinforcing environments. In essence, time outs are given when children perform undesirable behaviors. In order for time out to work, it is necessary to see if the environment is reinforcing to the client.

Overcorrection uses corrective procedures following disruptive episodes. For example, when a child has a temper tantrum, it can be useful to have the child straighten out a destroyed room, put away chairs, and place items back in order. Overcorrection uses a penalty after undesirable behavioral episodes, where is it hoped that overcorrection will reduce disruptive behaviors. Response cost is the removal of positive reinforcers following inappropriate behaviors. For example, if a child misbehaves, his or her allowance can be lowered. Often, response cost is combined with token economy, especially if alternative behaviors can be positively reinforced.

Reinforcing incompatible behaviors is the reinforcing of all appropriate behaviors but not inappropriate behaviors, and it is another operant or instrumental procedure.

Operant extinction is the process of removing reinforcement, and extinction is more likely to occur if continuous versus partial reinforcement has been applied. Moreover, often before behavior is extinguished, it can increase before gradually decreasing. Finally, with extinction, there can be spontaneous recovery, or the temporary reoccurrence of a response or behavior without reinforcement.

EMDR was developed by Dr. Francine Shapiro (1989, 1991, 1994; Beere, 1992; Fish, 1992) as a treatment for PTSD. Shapiro discovered EMDR while noticing, within herself, that disturbing memories disappeared as she became relaxed from performing back and forth eye movements (Sapp, 1997a). James and Gilliland (2003) noted that the R was added to indicate the reprocessing of information that changed from negative cognitions to positive cognitions and the desensitization of the traumatic memory. Even through Shapiro claims that EMDR has roots in both psychodynamic and behavior theories, James and Gilliland and the current writer believe it more closely fits within the cognitive-behavioral umbrella. According to Sapp (1997a) and James Gilliland (2003), EMDR treats negative memories by working on one or more of the following concepts that the client hold within conscious awareness:

1. The image of the memory
2. Negative self-statements
3. Assessment of the trauma
4. Anxiety response.

Shapiro believes that it is best when all four concepts are held by the client at the same time, but she believes that any one can be used for desensitization.

The process of EMDR is similar to many other desensitization procedures. First, the client is taught to assess anxiety using Wolpe's (1982) SUDS. Next, an assessment of the cognitive view of the traumatic event is done using Shapiro's validity of cognition (VOC) scale, in which the value of 1 means the cognition is completely untrue, and 7 means the cognition is completely true. Now, the client is asked to focus on the traumatic event and to think about the most traumatic aspect of the memory. This process is similar to other mental imagery exposure procedures described within this chapter. Essentially, the client is exposed repeatedly to the traumatic event and asked to rate SUDS levels and VOC levels. During this juncture of therapy, the client is asked to report exactly what is happening cognitively. Specifically, the client is asked to report when mental pictures or images change and when they do not change. Moreover, clients are asked to let happen whatever happens and just report it. At this point of therapy, the client is instructed to continue visualizing the traumatic image or picture and to rehearse negative statements, to concentrate on emotional sensations, and to visually track the therapist's finger. The therapist moves his or her index finger rhythmically back and forth, from left to right, across the client's visual field. Between twelve and twenty-four movements are called a set or saccade.

During this process, the client is asked to think about the traumatic event and to let emotions surface and to assess them with SUDS levels. After about two sets, the client is asked if the image has changed or if anything new has happened. After each set, the client is asked to blank out the image and take a deep breath and relax. Throughout this process, the therapist is looking for insights in terms of how to proceed during therapy and which images to explore again. Shapiro noted that when the client experiences a mismatch among the images, cognitions, and emotions, the SUDS levels may not decrease; therefore, it is important for all three to be congruent for therapy to be successful. Eventually the client will report a positive cognition, and he or she is asked to focus on that image. Finally the client is asked to return to the earlier traumatic image only when constructive insights no longer surface. Shapiro reported that after three to fifteen sets, clients usually report SUDS of 0 to 1. If the VOC increases or the client reports new images or memories, the desensitization process is repeated.

Even though EMDR appears to be a single technique, Shapiro has pointed out that it is an eight-phase process. The EMDR website (http://www.seinstitute.com/EMDR.html) claims that his approach brings together many elements of a variety of psychological approaches, including psychodynamic, cognitive-behavioral, person-centered, gestalt, and bioenergetic. In addition to being a treatment for trauma, it is claimed that EMDR can treat anxiety, depression, guilt, and anger. The theory of EMDR is that stress, anxiety, and trauma are processed differently by the brain than nonstressful emotions are. It is believed that during acute stress the amygdala, the part of the brain that regulates emotions, shuts down the hippocampus, a part of the brain that processes memory. Hence, stressful events are trapped outside of the normal brain processing centers, and EMDR helps a client access the experiences and transform them into declarative memory using the hippocampus. It is believed that with EMDR, the hippocampus is not shut down by evoked stressful emotions and that clients can tolerate the processing by distracting their attention by bilateral stimulation. How bilateral stimulation works, however, is not understood.

There are **eight phases** of EMDR (Shapiro, 2001). During **phase one**, a client's history is gathered, and over several sessions a treatment plan is developed. With **phase two**, the therapist works at establishing a relationship with the client, and if the two decide to use

EMDR, the steps in the process of the therapy are described. In addition, clients are taught soothing techniques such as mentally going to a safe place and relaxation and breathing techniques that tend to be soothing. The reader should remember that these techniques are mindfulness-based cognitive therapy strategies. Finally, the therapist and client decide which type of bilateral stimulation is preferred by the client. **Phase three** is the assessment phase, and the client is asked which target incident produced the trauma. Moreover, the client is asked which picture captures the worst part of the traumatic incident, and the client connects words that best describe the negative cognitions, or negative beliefs. Next, the client determines what he or she would like to believe instead of the negative thoughts, or what are referred to as positive cognitions. The validity of the positive cognitions are assessed on a seven-point scale, and the client describes the bodily feelings.

During **phase four**, desensitization starts with the client holding a focused picture of the negative self-perceptions and bodily feelings associated with the traumatic event. The therapist employs the bilateral stimulation procedure that was agreed on during phase two, and usually this is the eye-movement desensitization procedure. In addition, the bilateral stimulation could consist of moving lights in the client's visual field, alternating tones to the ears, or alternating taps on the hands. The bilateral stimulus can last for a few moments to several minutes, depending on the client's responses. Next, the client is asked to clear his or her mind and to allow whichever thoughts surface to rise within his or her mind. Once the client describes what has surfaced to conscious awareness, he or she is given another set of bilateral stimulation. After each set of bilateral stimulations, the client is guided through the process of letting whatever surfaces to conscious awareness to rise.

Phase five is the installation of positive cognitions. Once the processing of traumatic memory is complete, positive cognitions are revisited along with additional bilateral stimulations until the positive cognitions are expressed as being totally valid as compared to the original traumatic event.

Phase six is the body scan, and the client is asked to mentally scan his or her total body and if negative sensations or a lack of sensations are reported, additional bilateral stimulations are applied until positive sensations are reported.

Phase seven is called the closure phase, and the client continues to process the mental material obtained through the therapeutic process, which may take weeks. At this juncture of therapy, the client can become retraumatized and needs to be monitored closely by the therapist for potential relapses (Puk, 1994; Rosen, 1992; Sweet, 1995).

Phase eight is the reevaluation. The client reviews the week and discusses any new experiences or sensations from his or her log. Essentially, the disturbances of previous sessions are assessed to determine the course of treatment.

In summary, Shapiro provided a number of precautions when using EMDR therapy. For example, she stated that unresolved memories can surface through EMDR, and some clients experience high levels of emotional and physical sensations. In addition, she claimed that memories of past events may be altered. Finally, she recommended that therapists be formally trained in EMDR so that the risk to clients is minimized. Readers interested in a dialogue with Dr. Francine Shapiro can read about her explanations of the process at the following website: http://www.behavior.net/cgi-bin/nph-display.cgi?MessageID=4&Top=-1&config=emdr

For an interesting debate about EMDR, *Behavior Therapist* (October, 2001; volume 24[9]) provides a detailed critique of EMDR. In addition, Davidson and Parker (2001) stressed that EMDR is not any more effective than other exposure techniques are, and the most important technique from the process is imaginal exposure. The *American Journal of Clinical Hypnosis* (2001, volume 43[3–4]) described many applications of combining EMDR with hypnosis. Dr. Shapiro has a website at http://www.emdr, and she has an institute located at Pacific Grove, California, 93950-6010; telephone number (831) 382-3900; fax: (831) 647-9881.

Recent meta-analyses have shown that EMDR is a first-line treatment for traumas and has had more randomized trials conducted on it than any other treatment for traumas (Silver, Rogers, & Russell, 2008). (*See* the *Journal of Clinical Psychology*, August, 2008, 64(8): 947–957 for a through description of this research.) In term of effect sizes, Davidson and Parker (2001) found an effect size $r = .64$ for pretest and posttest changes for EMDR and a 95% confidence interval of .55 to .72 for EMDR. Moreover, they did not find any significant effect for EMDR when compared to other exposure treatments. Finally, they suggest that the eye movements are unnecessary for successful treatment.

Eye-Movement Technique

Dr. Larry Smyth has developed another protocol for the treatment of PTSD and trauma (Smyth, 1999). Unlike Shapiro, Smyth's protocol is based on traditional cognitive-behavioral strategies for PTSD. He starts by showing clients the eye technique that is similar to the strategy discussed in the EMDR portion of this chapter, but unlike Shapiro, he gradually turns the eye-movement technique into a self-control procedure in which the client learns to do it without the direction of the therapist. In addition, Smyth points that there is nothing spectacular about the eye-movement technique except its novelty and placebo effects. He emphasizes, like many cognitive-behavioral therapists, that imagery exposure and in vivo exposure is the best treatment for PTSD and traumas. In summary, Smyth has a protocol that will appeal to cognitive-behavioral therapists that uses the eye-movement technique, relaxation response, cognitive-restructuring, and imaginal exposure to treat PTSD. Dr. Smyth has a website at http://qualityfilmvideo.com/smyth/seven.html, and Dr. Fred Friedberg has a do-it-yourself eye-movement technique book that teaches the reader how to self-administer a variety of eye-movement techniques.

Applications of Progressive Relaxation Techniques

Within this section, there are two treatment transcripts, one employing traditional muscle tension relaxation exercises and the other employing guided imagery. A therapist needs to assess which transcript is appropriate for a client and, if a client has good imagery capacity, the possibility of combining both transcripts. Finally, each transcript can be read to a client in a slow soft voice in about 30 minutes. It is important to instruct the client that he or she should tense muscles for about 5 to 10 seconds to allow tension to build up and not to tense muscle to the point of building up pain. For additional transcripts and similar procedures the reader can consult Sapp (1997a; 1999; *see also* Jacobson 1938).

Transcript

Can you get into a relaxed position? Please close your eyes. I want you to first take a few deep breaths. I want you to inhale

– hold it and relax. Once again – inhale and exhale and just focus on your breathing. Notice as you inhale and exhale that you become more and more relaxed. Focus on your breathing. Inhale. One...two...three...now you can exhale. Let us do this again. Inhale...one...two...three...now exhale and slowly relax. I want you to bring attention to your arms. That is it. I want you to tense both arms. This includes the biceps, hands and so on. Bring tension into your arms. Now, let the tension go, and I want you to notice the difference between tension and relaxation. Let us do this again. Bring tension into both arms. Allow the tension to slowly build, and let it go. Let both arms feel very relaxed.

Now we will move to the muscles in both legs. This includes the feet, calves, and so on. Tense both legs by allowing the tension to slowly build up. Now, let the tension go. Let us repeat this process. Allow tension to build up in both legs. Slowly allow the tension to increase. Now, slowly let the tension go. Yes, feel the difference in your legs and arms. Notice how different they feel in comparison to other parts of your body.

Now, let us move to the stomach muscles. I want you to draw in your stomach as though someone punched at your stomach. Tightly draw in your stomach muscles. Hold the tension for a few seconds. Let it go and relax and focus on the rhythm of your breathing. Notice as you inhale and exhale that you become more and more relaxed. Notice how relaxed your stomach, legs and arms are. Allow the relaxation to spread throughout your body.

Let us tense the neck muscles. Make your neck really tight. Allow the tension to build. Now, relax these muscles. Let us do it again. Tense the neck muscles, and now you can relax. Notice the relaxation spreading throughout the relaxed parts of your body.

I want you to now make your shoulders very tense. Tense your shoulder muscles. Try to bring your shoulder muscles up to your ears. Notice the tension and relax. Let us do this again. Try to bring your shoulders up to your ears. Steady the tension and relax. Notice the difference in the relaxed parts of your body.

Let us relax the facial muscles. Tense the muscles of your forehead by raising the eyebrows of your forehead. Steady the tension and relax and let it go. Now, I want you to wrinkle your face. Make a very wrinkled face by holding the tension and now slowly relax and let the tension go. Now, let us move to the lips. I want you to pucker your lips as though you were kissing someone. Really pucker your lips. Hold the tension and now you can relax. Let us move to the eyes. Tightly close your eyes. That is it. And now relax and let the tension go.

I want you to notice your breathing and by noticing it you can become even more and more relaxed, and if there is tension in any part of your body, just relax and let it go. Now, we have relaxed the muscles of your arms, legs, stomach, neck and face. Again, if there is any tension in your body, just relax and let it go by breathing or retensing muscles and relaxing.

It is now time to start ending this exercise, and I will count from one to three as a way to terminate this process. One...two...three. Whenever you sleep, you will find that you will get a restful and wonderful sleep. Now, it is up to you at your own rate and pace.

Debriefing

It is important to process this experience with the client. You can do this by asking, "How was the exercise?" Allow the client to express any concerns or areas of the body that were difficult to relax, and use this information to adapt the transcript to the client. Finally, it is important to stress to clients that relaxation is a conditioning process that involves practice.

Guided Imagery

Transcript

Close your eyes and I will describe a very relaxing beach scene. I want you to picture this scene as clearly as possible. Let us begin. I want you to think about the time that you saw a beach. This could be an actual beach or in a movie or from television, but it does not matter because your imagination can create a scene just from an image. We can start with creating the image of the sun in your mind. If you want, there is the sun within your mind's eye. It is in the sky, and you can notice that its imaginary warmth relaxes your hands, arms, face, neck, chest, stomach, back, and legs. Use your imagination to create relaxation moving throughout your entire body.

I want you to now imagine walking near a lake and beach on a warm sunny day. As you are walking, be aware of your surroundings. Notice what is around you, and if you want, you can give your attention to things within your environment. It could be the sound of the waves or the birds. Maybe it is the sounds of people playing volleyball or the sounds of people relaxing and enjoying the lake and the beach. What you choose is completely up to you. If you want, you can include some friends within your scene. Think about this scene and relax very deeply. Notice how free you feel being at the beach and near the lake. You are getting energy and you feel very free. If you need some additional energy or added amounts of self-esteem, imagine yourself taking it from the sun. Take in as much energy as you need to feel strong, alert and relaxed. Allow yourself to experience this scene as though it were real. Let your mind expand throughout the entire beach scene by being aware and relaxing and letting go. Let your mind and body experience infinite relaxation, peace and wisdom. Take in as much energy and relaxation as you need. And if there are any parts of your body that need more relaxation, just let the imaginary sun relax those parts. If you want, you can take off your shoes and walk on this imaginary beach. Let your mind feel the sand that is beneath your feet, and if you want, just stretch out and relax by erasing any tension, worries, or discomfort from your mind. Take a few moments to enjoy this scene and knowing that whenever you want, you can return to this place and relax and enjoy yourself again.

It is now time to start ending this experience. I will count from one to three as a means of ending this experience. When I am counting, you will feel yourself becoming more relaxed. Once this experience is over, it will seem as though you have had a wonderful nap, and when you go to sleep you will get a very pleasant rest. Now, one...two...three. It is up to you at your own rate and pace.

Debriefing

Like the progressive muscle relaxation exercise, it is important to process this experience with the client. For example, ask the client, "How were the imagery scenes?" If the client mentions scenes that were unpleasant or difficult to imagine, you can modify the scene during the next session. Finally, like the muscle-tension exercises, mental imagery relaxation requires practice.

Psychological Hypnosis

Sapp (2000) defines hypnosis as a situation or set of procedures when one person (therapist) offers suggestions to another person (client) that can produce psychophysiological changes and responses (Golden, Dowd, & Friedberg, 1987). This is one approach that clearly emphasizes the connection between the mind and the body, and the applications for hypnosis tend to be underutilized by the medical community (Libet, 1985). For example, hypnosis is useful for pain control, burn patients, the control of bleeding, the control of hypertension, cardiovascular disease, and many other medically related problems (Wester 1987). Kihslinger and Sapp (2006) described the applications of hypnosis to the treatment of diabetes, and what the medical community tends to forget is the fact that almost any medical condition has psychological aspects and that it makes sense to treat a client medically as well as psychologically (Hensel, Sapp, Farrell & Hitchcock, 2001; Kroger, 1977; Kroger & Fezler, 1976; Sapp, 1995; Sapp, Ioannidis & Farrell, 1995). In addition, hypnosis is useful for a wide range of psychological disorders such as dissociative disorders, anxiety disorders, eating disorders, sexual disorders, and others (Bowers, 1992; Sapp, 2002b). In addition, hypnosis is one of the techniques that has multicultural applications; for example, after more than 40 years Sapp and Hitchcock (2001, 2003a, b) have provided data about hypnosis and African Americans (Hensel et al., 2001). In addition, hypnosis data exist for several populations, such as Canadians, Australians, the British, European Americans, Germans, Finnish, Italians, and Spaniards. In reality, it is possible to look at hypnosis across several cultures and the multicultural applications appear to be infinite (Crasilneck & Hall, 1985).

Sapp (2002b) reported that current thinking within hypnosis research is that hypnosis is a multidimensional construct (Wagstaff, 1981, 1991). For example, recently, Dr. Theodore X. Barber (1999; 2000) proposed a multidimensional paradigm or theory of hypnosis. However, during the 1950s, Dr. Theodore Sarbin was one of the first theorists to reject the altered state of consciousness notion of hypnosis, and he viewed hypnosis as a social psychological construct. Sarbin theoretically viewed hypnosis as a dramaturgical metaphor, and he used role theory to explain hypnosis. From Sarbin's point of view, clients enact the role of how a hypnotized client is supposed to behave (Sarbin & Coe, 1972). Clearly, Sarbin did not suggest that hypnosis was a sham, but he did not view it as a conscious-altering state, because he found that many psychological variables affected hypnotic responsiveness, such as increasing clients' expectations and motivations. Sarbin and Barber explained hypnosis without proposing an altered state of consciousness paradigm, and they viewed contextual variables like defining a situation as hypnotic and goal-directed behavior as the theoretical basis for hypnosis. Theodore X. Barber (1969) was the second major theorist to reject the altered-state notion of hypnosis. He found that hypnosis could be elicited without hypnotic inductions and that motivation and expectations influenced hypnotizability.

Currently, Barber argued that the reason that researchers disagree about whether hypnosis is an altered state of consciousness is due to the fact that they tend to see one or two of the three hypnotic types that he has referred to as fantasy prone (with three subgroups: sex fantasizers, escape fantasizers, and encouraged fantasizers), amnesic prone, and positively set. Barber referred to the fantasy prone as very good hypnotic subjects with excellent fantasy capacity and the amnesic prone as also good hypnotic subjects but with amnesia for hypnosis and general proneness to forgetting (Wilson & Barber, 1981, 1983). Recently, Barber (2000) has further broken down the fantasy prone into the following three subtypes: the sex fantasizers, who engage in romantic and sexual fantasies; escape fantasizers, who use fantasies to escape from isolation, loneliness, and unstable living conditions; and encouraged fantasizers, who were encouraged to fantasize as children. Finally, about 75% of the fantasy-prone individuals are sex fantasizers. The positively set are not hypnotic virtuosos like the fantasy prone and amnesic prone, but they have a positive attitude toward hypnosis and tend to respond to the social psychological aspects of hypnosis. Several researchers have described this type of subject (Coe & Sarbin, 1991; Kirsch, 1991, 1997; Lynn & Rhue, 1991; Sarbin, 1998, 1999; Spanos, 1991; Wagstaff, 1991). Interestingly, the positively set clients tend not to report that hypnosis is an altered state of consciousness like the amnesic prone clients (Connery, 1982).

Kirsch and Lynn (1999) have proposed a response set theory of hypnosis that has become popular within the area of the nonstate view of hypnosis. As this writer alluded to in Chapter 1, Kirsch and Lynn have a new sociocognitive therapy of hypnotic automaticity. Response set theory states that at the moment of activation all behavior is automatic and that automaticity is the result of a client's response expectancies. One assumption of this theory is that clients prevent hypnosis from occurring as a voluntary act; as a result, clients experience hypnosis as automatic (Kirsch, Burgess & Braffman, 1999; Kirsch & Council, 1992; Kirsch & Lynn, 1995a, b; Kirsch, Montgomery & Sapirstein, 1995).

However, hypnosis is far more complex than Kirsch and Lynn's position (Sheehan & McConkey, 1982). In fact, one would not expect clients with inattention disorders to be very responsive to hypnosis; nevertheless, Barabasz and Barabasz (1996) and Kirsch and Sapp (2000) found that clients with attention deficit hyperactivity disorder were extremely hypnotizable. Apparently, attentional resources may be needed for some hypnotically suggested effects but not for others. Bartis and Zamansky (1990) found that clients could respond to hypnotic suggestions when they visualized conflicting scenes (Pekala, Kumar & Marcano, 1995). This would indicate that Kirsch and Lynn are incorrect with their theory that clients always use imagery or visualizations to produce hypnosis. Moreover, the evidence suggests that clients can experience hypnosis with and without mental imagery. Apparently, there are aspects of hypnosis that do not depend on just cognitive abilities and expectations (Shor, 1959). In addition, Barber (1999, 2000) provided evidence that supports the state or trance view of hypnosis for the amnesic prone. The nonstate or sociocognitive theories he believes describe hypnosis for the positively set clients. In conclusion, Barber believes that the tension that exists between the state and nonstate theories is due to the fact that neither group has seen the amnesic prone clients and positively set clients simultaneously, and neither group has seen the fantasy prone clients (Hammond, 1992; Hilgard, 1973, 1994; King & Council, 1998; Rhue, Lynn & Kirsch, 1993).

What is absent from Barber's new paradigm is the connection between hypnosis and the brain. Barabasz and coworkers (1999) found that participants with high hypnotic abilities showed greater cortical hallucinations – suggestions to experience competing stimuli instead of the presented one. Nevertheless, low hypnotizable individuals did not show amplitudes in cortical event-related potential when experiencing negative hallucinations. These researchers concluded that now it is possible to distinguish hypnotic conditions from normal waking states of consciousness using physiological markers (Ray & Oathes, 2003). Other researchers have presented an explicit relationship between hypnosis and the brain (Balthazard & Woody, 1989; Woody & Bowers, 1994). In addition, Woody and Bowers found that routine hypnotic responding is correlated with response expectancies, but difficult hypnotic responding has little to do with response expectancies. Clearly, there is an overlap in brain functioning and hypnosis, and many new brain imaging techniques will show more specific connection between the brain and hypnosis (Barabasz et al., 1999; Laurence & Perry, 1983; Raz & Shapiro, 2002).

Finally, hypnosis has features that include, but are not limited to, automaticity, dissociation, absorption, suggestibility, fantasy proneness, amnesic proneness, response expectancies, and alterations in consciousness (Tellegen & Atkinson, 1974). In conclusion, hypnosis is a complex phenomenon that will take the complex synthesis of several areas to continue to shed more light on this elusive construct (Crasilneck & Hall, 1985; Woody & Farvolden, 1998).

Hypnosis as Adaptive Regression

Edwards and Sapp (2002), and Nash (1987) presented evidence that hypnosis can be viewed as a form of adaptive regression. The notion of adaptive regression stems from the psychoanalytic theory that held that hypnosis elicits a regressive shift from secondary to primary process thinking. This process is produced by relaxation of ego control and a shift toward unconscious thinking. This theory of viewing hypnosis, which is called topographical regression, is based on a reversal or change in thinking from reality based to non reality based. Adaptive regression is using hypnotic regression as a healing process for psychological disorders (Shor 1959). Edwards and Sapp used a nonrandomized two-group pretest posttest design to see if a regression hypnotic transcript would produce greater reduction in conflict responses than a relaxation transcript, and they found that hypnotic regression produced greater changes in conflict responses than hypnotic relaxation (Edmonston, 1981).

These researchers believed that this was the first study to show that hypnosis can produce adaptive regression (Orne, 1959, 1979). This study showed that one form of hypnosis is psychological regression; however, this notion is similar to dissociation theories of hypnosis in that participants produce changes in conscious experiences. In addition, relaxation is another process that can produce hypnosis and a change and shift from conscious to unconscious experiencing. In essence, there are many forms of hypnosis, and this study suggests that there are many features of hypnosis such as regression, relaxation, dissociation, and so on (Zeig, 1980). Moreover, this study offers support for Barber's new multidimensional theory in that it found that there are a variety of forms of hypnosis. Finally, this study suggested that hypnosis is a multivariate construct that has many features (Crawford, Kendel & Vendemia, 1998; Erickson, 1944, 1958, 1967, 1980; Erickson & Rossi, 1979).

Cognitive-Behavioral Hypnosis (CBH)

Cognitive-behavioral hypnosis (CBH) is a term for combining hypnosis with cognitive-behavioral strategies. One assumption of this approach is that psychological problems are the result of negative self-hypnosis (Arazoz, 1981; Spanos, 1986; Spanos & Chaves, 1989). This is similar to the principles emphasized by Ellis (1993), who stated that emotional disturbances are the result of irrational thinking. The CBH approach is a nonstate theoretical approach (Coe & Sarbin, 1991; Sapp, Farrell, Johnson, Kirby & Pumphrey, 1997). The transcript that follows is a CBH one.

Transcript

> Get into a relaxed position, close your eyes, and I will show you how to elicit cognitive-behavioral hypnosis within yourself. First, I would just like you to relax. You can relax by just thinking about relaxation. Use your thoughts to relax your mind, which in turn will relax your body. Learning to use cognitive-

behavioral hypnosis involves controlling your thinking and attention. Thoughts are the things we say to ourselves. Thinking or using your mind is the first step toward change.

We can talk more about thinking. Many of our thoughts are based on the way we think about social situations. Often, social situations such as public speaking and so on do not produce anxiety, but it is the way we look or think about social situations that produce anxiety and fear. For example, some students who have difficulty in school will tell themselves that negative things are going to happen, that they are not good, and the result is negative emotions. If you can get rid of self-defeating thoughts, all the musts, and other derivatives, you will be better off. You will be even better off if you can replace self-defeating thoughts with realistic ones.

Now let's proceed with cognitive-behavioral hypnosis. If the phone rings or if someone comes to the door, I will take care of it. The important thing for you is just relaxing. If you think about relaxation, your body will feel relaxed. And to help you, I will count from ten to one. As the numbers are going down, your level of relaxation will increase. 10...9...8...7...6...5...4...3...2...1.

Cognitive-behavioral hypnosis involves cognitively imagining a scene. In your mind's eye, imagine a very relaxing scene. You can choose a scene that is indoors or outdoors. Take your time and visualize every aspect of that scene. See it as clearly as possible. Notice the time of day or night. Yes, cognitive-behavioral hypnosis uses your imagination to produce changes in your inner experiences. Really let your imagination get into this scene. When I say the word "now," you will count to yourself from one to ten. When you say the number ten, you will come out of cognitive-behavioral hypnosis feeling relaxed, refreshed, and confident in your ability to use cognitive-behavioral hypnosis.

Debriefing

Have the client describe his or her experience and make adjustments in the script based on the client's comments.

Therapeutic Process

Therapeutic Goals

One goal of behavioral therapy is for the client to learn new ways of behaving. Interpersonal concerns are conceptualized behaviorally, such as with antecedents, contingencies, consequences, reinforcement, and so on. Essentially, the therapeutic process parallels the scientific method. Once a client's concerns are put into behavioral terms and a case history has been obtained, the client and therapist select treatments and determine ways of monitoring progress. Throughout the therapeutic process, modifications are made due to individual differences within a client, and finally, the therapist discusses with the client ways of continuing to implement treatment using self-control procedures.

Role of Therapist

Even though behavior therapists use Levels I and II counseling skills to establish a counseling relationship, after a relationship is established, mainly Level III counseling skills are used. In addition, the therapist uses himself or herself as a model, and he or she models adaptive responses for the client. One important point that is sometimes misunderstood by professionals with a superficial understanding of behavior therapy is that the client determines which behavior to change, and the therapist shows the client how to change the behavior. The relationship between client and therapist is collaborative. Finally, even though there is structure within behavior therapy, it does not have to be employed in a robotic fashion and the therapist–client relationship is important.

Therapeutic Relationship

Most behavioral therapists admit that the therapeutic relationship is important – except for Ellis. Unlike the theorization of psychodynamic theorists, clients tend not to develop symptom substitution (Kazdin & Wilson, 1978; Sloane, Staples, Cristol, Yorkston, & Whippler, 1975). Moreover, as opposed to seeing behavioral therapy as treating symptoms, behavioral therapists see themselves as changing maladaptive behavioral, and, as mentioned earlier, concepts are used to negotiate behavioral changes and to strengthen the therapeutic relationship.

Multicultural Applications and Limitations

Unlike psychoanalysis, which requires insight, behavioral therapies focus on behavioral changes and have applications to many cultural groups who may want changes in maladaptive behavior and not deep insight. For cultural groups wanting deep emotional and psychological understanding, they may find behavioral therapies limiting in that they can be viewed as simple because they deal with overt behavior and do not address the historical roots of maladaptive behavior. In addition, due to the fact that behavior therapies have large effect sizes, the potential for harm increases with the large effect sizes. Understanding the potential for early therapy termination, multiculturally skillful therapists can make adjustment to minimize the potential of harm. Sapp, Torres, and McNelly (1998) and Sapp, Torres, and McNelly (2007) described applying REBT to the death and dying process of aged African Americans and Latinos. In addition, Sapp, McNeely , and Torres (2007) described applying hypnosis to African American and Latino clients within the area of health psychology.

Critique

Comprehensiveness: In comparison to psychoanalysis and psychodynamic therapies, behavior therapies are not comprehensive. Moreover, paradigms of behavior therapy do not address unconscious factors that underlie behavior. Possibly, only social learning theories approximate comprehensive theories of behaviorism. Finally, behavior therapies are not comprehensive systems of psychotherapy.

Parsimony: Modern behavior theories are not parsimonious because there are hundreds of techniques. Moreover, some of the modern behavioral theories are far more complex than the early stimulus and response theories of the 1950s and 1960s. For example, the automaticity theories are quite complex, and they offer some links of behavior with the brain.

Empirical Validity: In terms of the treatment of anxiety, depression, weight reduction, sexual dysfunction, and many other disorders, behavior therapy has very high empirical validity. Unlike some psy-

choanalytic, Adlerian, and humanistic therapists, behavioral therapists encourage research and the testing of hypotheses.
Precision and Testability: Since empirical validity is extremely good with behavior therapy, precision and testability are also good. In addition, with EMDR and EMT, behavior therapy has two new techniques for the treatment of PTSD and traumas, and this research has strengthened the forces of behavior therapy within psychology (Parrot & Howes, 1991). In addition, cognitive-behavioral therapies are the strongest paradigms within counseling and clinical psychology.
Applied Value: Behavior therapy has applications that have not actually been realized. For example, it has applications within medicine for pain reduction, the control of bleeding, the treatment of burns, and the prevention of cardiovascular disease, and they are relatively unexplored areas. Moreover, in terms of general public health, behavior therapy is a good approach to use for educating the public about mental and physical health. Finally, behavior therapy has been used to treat groups, families, and couples (Abram, 1983; Bauer, Sapp & Johnson, 2000; Farrell, Sapp, Johnson & Pollard, 1994; Sapp & Hitchcock, 2003a).

Summary

Unlike the naive notion of some therapists and theorists, behavioral therapies are collections of techniques and are not a unitary approach. In addition, techniques like relaxation therapy, guided imagery, hypnosis, reinforcement, covert sensitization, EMDR, and EMT are all behavioral techniques. Behavioral therapy is the strongest paradigm within psychology. During the 1950s, behavioral therapy developed into a systematic assessment and treatment for psychological disorders. The ABCT, the largest behavioral therapy organization, continues to spearhead changes within behavior theory and practice. As previously stated, behavior therapy has large effect sizes, and ABCT tends to encourage research. Finally, this writer believes that behavioral therapy will continue to be the leader for empirical treatment strategies (Fairburn, Jones, Peveler, Hope & Doll, 1991; Farrell et al., 1994; Munuchin, 1974; Piccone, Hilgard & Zimbardo, 1989; Sapp, 1990, 1991, 1992a, b, 1993, 1994a, 1995, 1997a–d, 2000, 2002a, b; Sapp, Durand & Farrell, 1995; Sapp, Farrell & Durand, 1995a, b; Sapp & Evanow, 1998; Sapp, Farrell, Hitchcock & Johnson, 1999; Sapp,

Ioannidis & Farrell, 1995; Sapp, Farrell, Johnson & Ioannidis, 1997; Smith, Sapp, Farrell & Johnson, 1998), Kihslinger & Sapp, 2006).

Glossary of Key Terms

Adaptive regression: A theory of hypnosis that states hypnosis is the result of adaptive regression. This is a psychoanalytic theory of regression.
Applied behavioral analysis: An instrumental conditioning theory that emphasizes the relationship between behavior and the environment and that states that behavior can be controlled by the environment.
Assertion training: A set of procedures that teaches clients appropriate social skills that involve behavioral rehearsal and coping skills.
Automaticity: A theory that states at the point of initiation all behavior is automatic.
BASIC-ID: Arnold Lazarus' theory of multimodal therapy that assesses personality through seven interacting modalities: behavior, affect, sensations, images, cognitions, interpersonal relationships, and drugs/physiological bases of behavior.
Behavioral rehearsal: A technique in which clients role play new behavior during therapy. It is hoped that this will help with generalizing the new behaviors in actual situations.
Biofeedback: The use of technology and other means to provide clients with feedback of physiological processes.
Classical conditioning: A learning theory based on how reflexes are an integral part of learning and popularized by the work of Pavlov.
Cognitive-behavioral therapy: A theory that blends cognitive psychology and behavioral psychology. The goal is to show clients how thoughts affect behavior.
Counterconditioning: The opposite of learning in which a learned stimulus loses its capacity to bring about a learned response.
Covert desensitization: An imagery-based theory that uses aversive stimuli.
Extinction: The presentation of a stimulus without a response that can be viewed as a form of satiation.
Eye movement desensitization-reprocessing (EMDR): A desensitization technique created by psychologist Francine Shapiro to treat traumas. Part of this therapy involves clients visually tracking the fingers of therapists.

Eye movement technique (EMT): An alternative to EMDR that was developed by psychologist Larry Smyth based on traditional cognitive-behavioral strategies and self-control.
Fading: The slow withdrawal of behavioral prompts during the learning process.
Flooding: An imagery-based technique that is used to extinguish undesirable behavior.
Guided imagery: The process of presenting imagery scenes to clients during therapy.
Hypnosis: A process by which suggestions are given to a client and the results are psychophysiological changes.
Implosive therapy: An imagination technique that is similar to flooding but uses psychodynamic-based imagery.
Modeling: A process of demonstrating new behaviors to clients so they learn parts of the behaviors through observing.
Negative reinforcement: The removal of a negative consequence after performing a certain behavior. Like all forms of reinforcement, behavior increases and does not decrease in contrast to punishment that suppresses behavior.
Operant conditioning: Instrument learning or learning through operating on the environment.
Positive reinforcement: The applications of positive stimuli followed by a behavioral response such as money, candy, tokens, and so on.
Premack principle: Connecting low-frequency behaviors with high-frequency behaviors to increase low-frequency behaviors.
Progressive relaxation: Edmund Jacobson developed this muscle tension process that is often used with systematic desensitization. In addition, imagery-based techniques can also produce relaxation.
Prompting: The use of prompts or cues to modify behavior.
Punishment: The application of aversive stimuli following behavior. The goal is to decrease or suppress behavior.
Radical behaviorism: A radical departure from neobehaviorism and popularized by Skinner, who believed that behaviorism was just simply the relationship between behavior and environmental events and evolution. Skinner did not believe in giving primacy to cognitions, affect, brain science, or social psychological factors.
Reciprocal inhibitions: This is Wolpe's theory of why systematic desensitization works, and it states that two incompatible responses, such as relaxation and tension, cannot happen at the same time.

Response cost: A form of punishment in which there are penalties following undesirable behaviors.
Self-control: These are techniques that a client can implement himself or herself.
Self-monitoring: A form of self-control in which the client charts or monitors his or her behavior.
Sensate focus: A strategy for reducing the anxiety connected with sexual intimacy.
Shaping: The use of prompts or cues to teach new behavior. Eventually the prompts are slowly faded through the method of successive approximation.
Social learning theory: A group of social-cognitive-behavioral theories that state that the client, situation, and social context all interact to influence behavior.
Stress inoculation training: Donald Meichenbaum developed this cognitive-behavioral technique to reduce stress through a process of cognitive inoculation.
Subjective Units of Distress Scale (SUDS): A scale used by clients to rate their levels of anxiety; it is used in other therapies such as EMDR, EMT, and systematic desensitization.
Systematic desensitization: Joseph Wolpe developed this technique to treat anxiety-related and other disorders. Essentially, it is the pairing of relaxation with anxiety-evoking imagery.
Thinning: The movement from continuous reinforcements to variable or intermittent reinforcement.
Token economy: A structured environment in which tokens are used as positive reinforcers, and the tokens are traded for secondary reinforcers such as toys, food, and so on.

Review Questions

1. Describe five forms of behavior therapy.
2. Describe Barber's multidimensional theory of hypnosis.
3. Compare and contrast Watson's and Skinner's theories of behaviorism.
4. What is the mediational notion of neobehaviorism?
5. What is dialectical behavior therapy?
6. What is the importance of viewing hypnosis as adaptive regression?

Behavior Organizations and Journals

Professional Organizations:

- **Association for Behavioral Analysis (ABA)**
  1219 South Park Street, Kalamazoo, MI 49001
  Telephone: 269-492-9310
  Fax: 269-492-9316
  Email: mail@abainternational.org
  Website: http://www.abainternational.org/
- **Association for Behavioral and Cognitive Therapies (ABCT)**
  305 7th Avenue, 16th Floor
  New York, NY 10001
  Telephone: 800-685-2228
  Website: http://www.aabt.org/
- **National Association of Cognitive-Behavioral Therapists (NACBT)**
  P.O. Box 2195
  Weirton, WV 26062
  Telephone: 800-853-1135
  Website: http://www/nacbt.org/
- **Academy of Cognitive Therapy (ACT)**
  One Belmont Avenue, Suite 700
  Bala Cynwyd, PA 19004-1610
  Telephone: 610-664-1273
  Website: http://www.academyofct.org/
- **International Association for Cognitive Psychotherapy (IACP)**
  Website: http://www.cognitivetherapyassociation.org/

Professional Journals:

- ***Behavior Modification***
  Website: http://bmo.sagepub.com/
- ***Behavior Therapy***
  Website: http://www.elsevier.com/locate/bt

- ***Behavior Research and Therapy***
  Website: http://www.elsevier.com/locate/bt
- ***Behavioural and Cognitive Psychotherapy***
  Website: http://www.cambridge.org/journals/journal_catalogue.asp?mnemonic=BCP
- ***Child and Family Behavior Therapy***
  Website: http://www.haworthpress.com/store/find.asp
- ***Cognitive and Behavioral Practice***
  Website: http://www.elsevier.com/locate/bt
- ***Cognitive Behaviour Therapy***
  Website: http://journalsonline.tandf.co.uk/(501ld42nw0rsh045mhh2obml)/app/home/journal.asp?referrer=parent&backto=linkingpublicationresults;1:300302,1&linkin=
- ***Cognitive Therapy and Research***
  Website: http://www.springer.com/west/home/generic/search/results?SGWID=4-40109-70-35753187-0
- ***Journal of Applied Behavior Analysis***
  Website: http://www.seab.envmed.rochester.edu/jaba/
- ***Journal of Behavior Therapy and Experimental Psychiatry***
  Website: http://www.elsevier.com/locate/bt
- ***Journal of Behavioral Education***
  Website: http://www.ovid.com/site/catalog/Journal/1521.jsp?top=2&mid=3&bottom=7&subsection=12
- ***Journal of Cognitive Psychotherapy: An International Journal***
  Website: http://www.cognitivetherapyassociation.org/jorunal/default1.aspx?pagename=jcp.aspx
- **Journal of Psychopathology and Behavioral Assessment**
  Website: http://www.springer.com/west/home/generic/search/results?SGWID=4-40109-70-35608747-0
- ***Journal of Rational-Emotive and Cognitive-Behavioral Therapy***
  Website: http://www.rebt.org/journal.htm
- ***The Behavior Therapist***
  Website: http://www.abct.org/mentalhealth/journals/?fa=tBT

Other Organizations:

- **B. F. Skinner Foundation**
  12 Arrow Street, Suite 303
  Cambridge, MA 02138
  Telephone: 617-661-9209
  Website: www.bfskinner.org

- **Joseph Wolpe Archive**
  University of Southern California (USC)
  Doheny Memorial Library
  3550 Trousdale Parkway
  University Park Campus
  Los Angeles, CA 90089-0185
  Telephone: 213-740-2924

Chapter 5

EXISTENTIAL PSYCHOTHERAPY

Chapter Overview

Existential psychotherapy is called the **third force** within psychology. Readers may remember that psychoanalysis was the **first force** and behavior therapy was the **second force**. Many of the theories presented in this text have existential roots. For example, Person-centered therapy, Gestalt therapy, REBT, reality therapy, transactional analysis (TA), and Fromm's psychodynamic theory all have roots in existential therapy. Philosophy guides the practice of existential therapy, and it is not a neatly defined therapy with techniques; however, it uses Levels I, II, and III counseling skills and can be classified as an affective and experiential approach to psychotherapy (Corey, 2004; Sapp, 1997a; Sharf, 2008).

Philosophies

Morris (1999) described ten philosophers who influenced existentialism. First, Socrates was a philosopher who lived in ancient Athens, but he did not write books. He just liked to ask probing questions, which gave rise to the terms Socratic method of teaching and Socratic questioning. Socrates was executed for allegedly corrupting the youth. Second, Plato, whose real name was Aristocles, was a student of Socrates and lived in Greece during the mid-fourth to mid-fifth century. Plato believed in the preexistence and immortality of the soul, and he viewed humans as souls trapped within bodies. Plato stressed themes such as justice and equality.

Third, Aristotle was a student of Plato, and he and Plato lived in Greece during the fourth century before the birth of Christ. Aristotle was a peripatetic (*peripateo* means to walk around) philosopher, since he walked while lecturing to his students. A group of philosophers who influenced REBT and other existential therapies called Stoics sat around porches (stoa). Aristotle brought the concepts of happiness as the goal of life and logical theory to philosophy.

Fourth, Thomas Aquinas, the eighteenth-century Italian philosopher, provided philosophy with complex arguments for the existence of God.

Fifth, William of Ockham (often spelled "Occam)" contributed the parsimony principle to science. He was known for his logical skills, and he viewed simplicity as preferable to complexity.

Sixth, René Descartes was a seventeenth-century French philosopher and is regarded as the father of modern philosophy. Descartes was the philosopher who split humans into minds and bodies: **dualism** is the philosophical belief that the body is physical and the mind, spirit, or soul is immaterial. In contrast, the philosophical belief called **monism** views the world as consisting of matter and energy, and the mind or brain is the by-product of the nervous system.

Seventh, Immanuel Kant, born in Koningsberg, Prussia, was a famous eighteenth-century German philosopher, who contributed to conceptions of morality and ethics. He viewed morality as absolute.

Eighth, Georg Wilhelm Friedrich (G.W.F.) Hegel was a nineteenth-century German philosopher who described a three-phase process of dialectical reasoning on which Karl Marx based his theory called dialectical materialism. The notion of dialectics means as one thing happens, the opposite or antithesis happens. Finally, Hegel viewed art, religion, and beauty as forms of thought, and the higher form of thought was philosophy.

Ninth, Sören Kierkegaard was a famous nineteenth-century Danish philosopher and was the father of existentialism. He focused on what it means to be human and what it means to be in the world.

Tenth, Bertrand Russell was a twentieth-century British philosopher whose work in logic and love influenced the existential movement.

Existential philosophy took its form after World War II, and philosophers such as Sören Kierkegaard (1813–1855), Martin Heidegger (1889–1976), Martin Buber (1878–1965), Jean Paul Sartre (1905–1980), Albert Camus (1913–1960), and Karl Jaspers

(1883–1969) gave existentialism its voice.

Ludwig Binswanger (1881–1966) and Victor Frankl (1905–1997) were the first psychotherapists to apply existential philosophy to psychotherapy; however, it was Frankl and Rollo May (1909–1994) who influenced existential philosophy within psychology.

Frankl published 32 psychospiritual books, and his most famous book, *Man's Search for Meaning*, was a worldwide best seller. This book was based on Frankl's experience as a Holocaust survivor in Nazi Germany. Once Frankl's family was killed in Nazi concentration camps, he was still able to find meaning in his life (Frankl, 1963, 1969). As the result of an extreme traumatic experience, Frankl realized that he had the freedom of choice despite his tragic circumstances. Finally, Frankl developed logotherapy, an existential form of therapy that means "healing through meaning."

Rollo May was one of the first prominent psychologists to combine existential humanistic approaches to psychotherapy, and he was concerned with "being or existence," not problem solving. May dealt with topics such as life, death, love, freedom, anxiety, intimacy, and existence. Like May, James Bugenthal (1967) systematically combined strands of existential-humanism to psychotherapy.

View of Human Nature

Existential psychotherapy focuses on the meaning of being human, and some issues of existential psychotherapy are the following (Vontress, 2008):

1. Ability to experience awareness
2. Freedom and responsibility
3. Ability to make a commitment
4. Choices in life
5. Uncertainty of life
6. Discovering one's uniqueness
7. Being intimate with others in a meaningful way
8. Accepting aloneness
9. Human search for meaning, values, purpose, and goals
10. Anxiety as a natural part of life
11. Death as a natural process of life
12. Nonbeing

May and Yalom (2005) distinguish existential psychotherapy from interpersonal psychotherapy. Specifically, interpersonal psychotherapy does not have a theoretical basis for dealing directly with **Mitwelt**, or the social environment. Nevertheless, **Eigenwelt**, or the world of the self, is often omitted in interpersonal psychotherapy (May & Yalom, 2005). **Uberwelt**, or the spiritual world, is not addressed during interpersonal psychotherapy. In summary, existential psychotherapy addresses three worlds: **Umwelt**, the physical world, **Mitwelt**, the social world, and **Eigenwelt**, the world of the self.

As alluded to previously, existential psychotherapy is not a single method but a divergent group of methods that help clients gain understanding about what it means to be human. Unlike some forms of psychodynamic theories, existential psychotherapy is grounded on the assumption that humans are free.

Humanistic psychologists Abraham Maslow (1968, 1971) and Carl Rogers (1942, 1951, 1957) were influenced by existential philosophy. In contrast to psychodynamic approaches, Maslow focused on how humans could actualize or become all they were capable of becoming. He emphasized topics such as love, joy, creativity, and peak experiences – experiences that can propel one toward self-actualization. Maslow's conceptualization of self-actualization leads to the following:

1. High tolerance for uncertainty
2. Acceptance of oneself and others
3. General caring for others
4. Creativity
5. Spontaneity
6. Desire for privacy, solitude, and autonomy
7. Ability to form profound interpersonal relationships
8. Risibility, or the ability to laugh readily
9. Novel attitude toward life
10. Internal locus of evaluation and inner directedness

Rogers built upon existential philosophy by emphasizing that humans are trustworthy and have a tendency to become actualized. Even though existential psychotherapy and humanistic psychology are related, they also differ. As previously stated, existential psychotherapy is the by-product of existential philosophy, whereas humanistic psychology is a form of psychology that reacted against psychoanalysis and behaviorism.

Both existential psychotherapy and existential philosophy address conscious experiences, in contrast to unconscious processes. Moreover, both approaches stress clients' phenomenological experiences and clients' immediate here and now experiences.

Existential psychotherapy stresses wholeness and integrity, and this is similar to Adler's concept of unity. Both existential psychotherapy and humanistic psychology view clients in a process of becoming, not as a product. Existential psychotherapy differs from humanistic psychology in that it does not directly address psychotherapeutic issues, rather it is an attitudinal way of viewing life. Finally, both existential psychotherapy and humanistic psychology stress that human choices and responsibilities are experiential and affective.

Therapeutic Process and Goals

The basic goal of existential psychotherapy is to help clients develop an existential attitude toward life and to accept freedom and personal responsibility for their actions. Existential psychotherapy stresses that clients cannot avoid freedom and responsibility, and clients with limited awareness of themselves and their existential existences are excellent candidates for existential psychotherapy.

Role of Therapist

The role of the existential therapist is similar to the person-centered therapist, but in contrast to person-centered therapists, existential therapists use not only Levels I and II counseling skills but also Level III counseling skills. Finally, unlike person-centered therapists, existential therapists confront their clients in terms of existential dilemmas.

Therapeutic Relationship

For existential psychotherapy to be successful, there must be a I–thou encounter between the client and therapist, and unlike some other psychotherapists, existential psychotherapists are eclectic and can use techniques from various theoretical approaches. Finally, existential psychotherapy does not concentrate on specific techniques, but rather the therapeutic process.

As previously mentioned, existential psychotherapy addresses forms of the world. First, there is **Umwelt**, the environment or external world; second, **Mitwelt**, the world of others; and third, **Eigenwelt**, one's own world. Existential psychotherapists attempt to understand clients from all three forms or worlds.

As humans mature, they have a natural inclination to explain the meanings of their lives. Within my practice, I find clients searching for their individual identities, and they tend to struggle with several questions, such as: "Who am I?" "What am I here to do?" "What is the purpose of my life?" "Who or what created me?" These questions lead to six existential propositions described by Corey (2004):

1. Capacity for self-awareness
2. Freedom and responsibility
3. Striving for identity and relationships with others
4. Searching for meaning
5. Anxiety as a condition of living
6. Awareness of death and nonbeing

Once a client understands that he or she has options, the greater the client's awareness and the greater the client's capacity for freedom.

Existential psychotherapy allows clients to explore their identities and relationships with others, and when clients cannot relate with others, often they experience isolation and loneliness.

Existential psychotherapists view anxiety not as an ego defense but as a natural and normal part of life. Actually, anxiety is viewed as part of the growth process. In contrast to trying to uncover unconscious reasons for anxiety, existential psychotherapists explore the process of anxiety and not the underlying cause.

Existential psychotherapists view death as part of the life cycle, and it has meaning to clients. In fact, one can be alive physiologically and yet be existentially dead. Life has meaning because of the limitations of death. After one becomes aware of death, life becomes more valuable. Finally, existential psychotherapists focus on or deal with the meaning that death has for a client within the present moment.

Multicultural Applications and Limitations

African Americans who, as a group, were not always free in the

United States, could benefit from the existential concept of freedom. For example, some African Americans avoid freedom and responsibility, and they can become empowered when they accept freedom and responsibility. Moreover, existential psychotherapy can be used to help minority, gay, and female clients to confront existential dilemmas. The themes of choice and responsibility are important attitudes to explore with various cultural groups. One limitation of existential psychotherapy is that it does not focus on oppression, racism, sexism, and social class discrimination. Finally, it does not adequately address sociocultural factors and environmental factors that affect the lives of various cultural groups.

Critique

Comprehensiveness: Since existential psychotherapy does not focus on developmental, historical, and unconscious processes, it is not comprehensive. In fact, this approach only partially, using existential and phenomenological perspectives, addresses the affective domain. In conclusion, cognitive and behavioral dimensions are not adequately addressed.

Parsimony: Existential psychotherapy is parsimonious, but it fails to define operationally terms such as self-actualization, nonbeing, and authenticity. Essentially, this approach lacks systematic and concise definitions and many existential psychotherapists use vague and abstract terms that have not been operationally defined.

Empirical Validity: Since this approach has not been subjected extensively to scientific investigation, empirical validity is not very good. For group psychotherapy, Opalic (1989) and Yalom and Lieberman (1991) found some support. Finally, additional empirical validity is needed for existential psychotherapy (Elliot, Greenberg & Lieter, 2004; Keshen, 2006).

Precision and Testability: Because of the dearth of empirical validity, precision, and testability are poor with existential psychotherapy, it is not easy to test operationally the constructs of existential psychotherapy.

Heuristic Value: Even though heuristic value is satisfactory with existential psychotherapy, it has not stimulated much empirical research; however, therapists with backgrounds in cognitive-behavioral therapy, Gestalt therapy, and Jungian psychotherapy have began integrating existential constructs within their approaches.

Applied Value: Existential psychotherapy has satisfactory applied value, and it has been used to treat unipolar reactive depression, borderline personality disorder, anxiety disorders, and alcoholism (Van Deurzen-Smith, 1988). In closing, existential psychotherapy has been applied to couples, families, and groups.

Summary

Existential psychotherapy cannot be defined by techniques, but rather it is a philosophical approach to the human condition. Even though Frankl developed paradoxical intention and had a strong influence on existential psychotherapy, the goal of existential psychotherapy is to help clients to determine the meanings of their lives and to reduce existential dilemmas. Although existential psychotherapy is affective and experiential, it differs from other affective approaches in that it uses Level I through Level III counseling strategies. If a client wants to explore personal growth, existential psychotherapy maybe an adequate approach.

Glossary of Key Terms

Existential psychotherapy: An affective and experiential approach to psychotherapy that was influenced by philosophy.
Humanistic psychology: This is an affective approach to psychology that is closely related to existential psychotherapy.
Logotherapy: A form of psychotherapy developed by Frankl that addresses healing through meaning.
Phenomenology: The exploration of clients' subjective worlds.

Review Questions

1. Why is existential psychotherapy the third force within psychology?
2. Describe the 10 philosophers who influenced existentialism.
3. What are some multicultural applications and limitations of existential psychotherapy?
4. Which roles did Rollo May and Carl Rogers serve in the development of existential psychotherapy?

5. What is the existential view of anxiety?
6. Describe some similarities and differences between existential psychotherapy and Fromm's theory?

Existential Societies, Journals, and Websites

- **Society for Existential Analysis**
  BM Existential
  London, WCIN 3XX, England
  E-mail: exist@cwcom.net
  Website: www.existential.mcmail.com
- **Existential Humanistic Institute**
  870 Market Street, Suite 463
  San Francisco, CA 94102
  Telephone: 415-421-3355
- **International Society for Existential Psychology and Psychotherapy** and ***International Journal of Existential Psychology and Psychotherapy***
  c/o Trinity Western University
  Graduate Counseling Psychology Department
  7600 Glover Road
  Langley, BC V2Y Y1, Canada
  Telephone: 604-513-2034
- ***Journal of Existentialism***
  11 Main Street
  Germantown, NY 12526
  Telephone: 518-537-4700
- ***Review of Existential Psychology and Psychiatry***
  11 Main Street
  Germantown, NY 12526
  Telephone: 518-537-4700
- **Existential Links, Organizations, and Listservs**
  Website: www.existentialk-therapy.com/Links.htm
- **Existential Psychotherapy**
  Website: www.Existential.dsl.pipex.com/Existential/home.htm

Chapter 6

PERSON-CENTERED PSYCHOTHERAPY: LEVELS I AND II COUNSELING APPROACH

Chapter Overview

Person-centered psychotherapy is somewhere between a Level I and a Level II form of counseling, and similarly to existential psychotherapy and Gestalt psychotherapy it is humanistic-existential. Carl R. Rogers founded person-centered psychotherapy during the 1940s, when psychoanalysis was the dominant paradigm within the area of psychotherapy. However, Rogers rejected psychoanalysis and postulated that only three conditions were necessary and sufficient for therapeutic changes to occur: congruence, unconditional positive regard, and empathy. Even though Rogers stated that his theory was a set of tentative principles, not dogma, his approach has changed little in over 60 years.

Biographical Sketch

Carl Ranson Rogers was born in Oak Park, Illinois, in 1902, and fundamentalist religions shaped his development (McMillan, 2004). Rogers received his bachelor's degree in 1924 from the University of Wisconsin–Madison and married Helen Elliot. In 1931, Rogers earned his Ph.D. from Teachers College at Columbia University. Rogers held academic positions at Ohio State University, the University of Chicago, and the University of Wisconsin–Madison. In 1964, he left the University of Wisconsin–Madison and moved to La Jolla, California, where he worked as a private practice psychologist, writer, and teacher of the person-centered approach until 1987, when he died from heart failure following hip surgery.

Nineteen Propositions

Rogers, in 1951, stated that his theory was based on the following nineteen propositions:

1. Everyone exists in a changing phenomenal field in which he or she is the center.
2. Everyone reacts to his or her phenomenal field as reality.
3. Clients react as an organized whole to their phenomenal fields.
4. The self is a portion of the total perceptual field.
5. The self is the result of interactions with others and the environment.
6. Humans have a tendency to become actualized.
7. The key to understanding a client is through the internal vantage point of the client.
8. Behavior is goal directed to satisfy needs within a perceptual field.
9. Goal-directed behaviors are accompanied by emotions.
10. Humans introject the values of others and often distort these as though they were experienced directly.
11. Experiences are either symbolized, ignored, or distorted.
12. Behaviors that are consistent with the concept of self are assimilated.
13. Some behaviors may be inconsistent with the self and not accepted by the client.
14. Psychological adjustment is the assimilation of the concept of self.
15. Psychological maladjustment is the lack of assimilation of the concept of self.
16. Anxiety is the inconsistency in the organization of the structure of self.
17. The lack of anxiety is the complete absence of threat to the self.
18. When an individual integrates all of his or her experiences, he or she is more accepting of others.
19. An integrated person accepts his or her self structure and has an evolving organismic valuing process.

In summary, person-centered therapy is humanistic and phenomenological and is based on a phenomenological field theory of personality.

Key Concepts

Raskin and Rogers (2005) listed 10 characteristics of the person-centered approach, and they are the following:

Distinctive Features of the Person-Centered Approach

1. The attitudes of the therapists are necessary and sufficient to bring about therapeutic effectiveness.
2. The immediacy or moment-to-moment experiences of the therapeutic relationship and the availability of the therapist in the present facilitates the therapeutic relationship.
3. Person-centered therapy is an intensive focus on the phenomenological world.
4. A person-centered relationship results in a client's living more fully in the present.
5. Person-centered therapy is concerned with the process of therapy and personality change.
6. Person-centered therapy emphasizes the need to continue doing research on the process of psychotherapy.
7. Person-centered therapy is based on the hypothesis that the sesame principles of therapy apply to **all** clients.
8. Person-centered therapy is a specialized example of a constructive interpersonal relationship.
9. Person-centered therapy is based on the experiences of the client. Because all theoretical formulations are the results of clients' experiences, clients are not manipulated to fit a theory.
10. Person-centered therapy is concerned with humanistic-existential issues of therapy.

Person-centered therapy is similar and different from REBT. Readers may remember that REBT has an emotive component, and Raskin and Rogers (2005) listed five ways that person-centered therapy is similar to REBT and other cognitive-behavioral therapies.

Five Similarities Person-Centered Therapy Has with REBT and Other Cognitive-Behavioral Therapies

1. Clients can change, even if they are deeply disturbed.
2. Clients can turn negative self-attitudes into positive ones.
3. The willingness to work hard in helping clients, particularly through professional therapy and nontechnical writing.
4. The willingness to demonstrate psychotherapy in public.
5. Encouraging the scientific study and research of psychotherapy.

Five Ways Person-Centered Therapy Differs from REBT and Other Cognitive-Behavioral Therapies

1. The person-centered approach values the therapeutic relationship; Ellis said it is neither necessary nor sufficient in promoting therapeutic change.
2. Person-centered therapy allows the client to determine the direction of therapy, whereas REBT and cognitive-behavioral approaches provide direction.
3. Person-centered therapy accepts clients' thinking and perceiving; REBT and other cognitive-behavioral approaches challenge clients' thinking processes.
4. Person-centered therapy allows the clients to determine action; in contrast, REBT and other cognitive-behavioral approaches assign homework for clients.
5. REBT and other cognitive behavioral approaches are inclined to interrupt a client's affective process to indicate irrational and automatic cognitions that affect feelings. Person-centered therapists relate to clients on an affective level, and they respect and accept clients' affect.

Historical Background

The person-centered approach is the humanistic extension of existential philosophy, and this approach has a great deal in common with existential psychotherapy; however, Rogers assumed that clients were basically trustworthy and have vast human potential.

Earlier, Rogers postulated that the therapist's attitude, the client–therapist relationship, and a trusting environment were the key ingredients of therapeutic outcome. Additionally, Rogers viewed the expertness of a psychotherapist, theory, and techniques as secondary determinants when considering therapeutic outcomes.

Raskin and Rogers (2005) traced four periods in the development of person-centered therapy. First, during the 1940s, Rogers developed nondirective therapy as a reaction to the directive and interpretive approaches of psychodynamic approaches. Nondirective therapy emphasized creating a flexible, permissive, and nondirective environment for the client. Because Rogers saw diagnostic procedures as nonhumanistic, he omitted them from his theory, but insurance companies require a *DSM-IV-TR* diagnosis before they will reimburse for psychotherapy services.

Second, during the 1950s, Rogers published *Client-Centered Therapy* (1951). Here, Rogers changed the name of his therapy from nondirective to client-centered and then reflected the emphasis on the client. In addition, he theorized that the actualizing tendency was the motivational force that leads to the client choosing to change.

Third, Rogers published *On Becoming a Person* (Rogers, 1961). It was during this phase that Rogers developed his self theory, or the process of the self that a client is capable of becoming. Moreover, this process included an emphasis on the client's developing an internal locus of evaluation, being open to experiences, and being willing to participate in a therapeutic process. In addition, Rogers conducted process and outcome research during this phase, and he applied his approach to groups, education, and the teaching of psychotherapy. During the 1960s, psychotherapy changed, and many psychotherapists became interested in the "third force" or humanistic approaches as alternatives to psychodynamic and behavioral approaches. Specifically, Gestalt therapy, existential therapy, person-centered therapy, and other humanistic approaches became popular during this phase.

Fourth, during the 1970s and 1980s, Rogers expanded his theory to industry, conflict resolution, and the search for world peace (Rogers, 1980, 1983, 1986). It was during this fourth phase that Rogers' theory became known as *person-centered therapy*. Finally, Rogers' emphasis on world peace characterized this fourth phase.

Rogers along with psychologist Abraham Maslow (1970) were instrumental in integrating humanism into psychology and the area of psychotherapy. For example, Maslow's scholarship was on *self-actualization*, or the tendency for clients to grow and develop their potentialities. From Maslow's perspective, clients undergo *peak experiences*;

that is, they experience strong feelings of ecstasy and awe with the belief that something significant has occurred. Essentially, self-actualizing clients are in a constant state of growth.

One major contribution of Rogers' theory is his notion of **self** or **self-concept**. For example, the self develops during early childhood, and it is the child's subjective distinction of himself or herself from others. Theoretically, the self is the phenomenological view of "me," and it is a subjective view that one has about oneself. In summary, the characteristics a client attributes to himself or herself is the self-concept.

Rogers claimed that clients employ their actualizing tendency when they interact with their environments, and he theorized that humans were born with an **organismic valuing process or system** that determines which experiences determine self-actualization and which ones do not. In terms of promoting self-actualization, experiences that promote self-actualization are valued positively, whereas experiences that obstruct self-actualization are valued negatively. Rogers believed, however, that all clients have a need for **positive regard**, or the tendency to seek the approval of others. This need for positive regard leads to **conditions of worth**, and these are behaviors that are viewed as acceptable only if they meet the approval of significant others.

Q-Sort Technique

Rogers argued that clients' self-concepts would change as the result of psychotherapy, and he designed the **Q-sort technique** to measure clients' self-concepts. Rogers thought that, as a result of psychotherapy, the variance is reduced between the way a client views himself or herself and the way a client would like to view himself or herself. The Q-sort technique involves a client sorting self-referent states on a 7-point Likert scale, ranging from "not like me" (1) to "like me" (7). Some examples of self-referent statements could be "I am weak," "I am stupid." "I am a loser," "I am immature," and "I am intelligent." After a client sorts the self-referents according to the way he or she actually sees himself or herself, the client is asked to resort the statements to reflect the ideal self, or the way he or she would like to see himself or herself. In order to measure the reliability of these items, a correlation is obtained between the two sorts. Rogers theorized that as therapy progresses, it is expected that a strong positive correlation should occur for scores between the actual and the ideal self.

Therapeutic Process

Person-centered therapy is based on the following 19 propositions (Raskin & Rogers, 2005; Raskin, Rogers & Witty, 2008):

1. A client exists in an ever-changing world of experiences in which he or she is the center.
2. A client's perceptual field is reality.
3. Clients react as a Gestalt to their phenomenal field.
4. Clients have a basic tendency for self-actualization.
5. Clients' behaviors are goal-directed attempts to meet needs.
6. Affect facilitates goal-directed behavior.
7. The best frame of reference is from the client's vantage point.
8. The self is a portion of a client's perceptual field.
9. The self forms as a result of interactions with the environment and others, and it is characterized by "I" or "me," along with self-referent values.
10. Introjected values can be perceived in distorted fashions. When a client is in a state of incongruence – external experiences of the client do not correspond to internal ones – distortion of experiences can occur.
11. As clients experience life, they can do the following: (a) symbolize the experience – organize it into a significant relationship to the self; (b) ignore the experience and assume no relationship to the self-structure; or (c) deny symbolization or distort symbolization because the experience is incompatible with the self.
12. Many of a client's behaviors are the result of his or her self-concept.
13. Organic experiences can bring about behaviors inconsistent with the self; however, the client does not "own" these organic experiences, and they are not symbolized.
14. Psychological tension is the result of a client's denying awareness and other sensory experiences.
15. Psychological adjustment occurs when a client assimilates sensory and visceral experiences into self-concept.
16. When a client feels threatened, he or she has experiences that are inconsistent with the organizational structure of self.
17. Clients can become aware of nonconscious experiences that are inconsistent with the self, and the client can revise the self

to include the assimilation of previously unconscious experiences.

18. When clients accept Gestalt, sensory and visceral experiences, they are more understanding of others and more accepting of others as independent beings.
19. A client's organismic valuing process allows him or her to replace introjected values with present actualizing ones.

Therapeutic Goals

The goal of person-centered therapy is for the client to become actualized and for the client's true self to emerge. If this occurs, the client is more open to experiences, is more trusting of himself or herself, operates from an internal locus of evaluation, and is opened to continued growth. Finally, a person-centered therapist allow clients to choose their own goals.

Role of Therapist

Person-centered therapy allows the client to explore aspects of the self without judgment or evaluation, and, unlike behavior therapists, person-centered therapists do not use techniques. They use themselves as instrument of change.

Therapeutic Relationship

Raskin and associates (2008) and Cain (2008) stated that there are three conditions that are *necessary* and *sufficient* for therapeutic change to occur:

1. The client and therapist are in psychological contact.
2. The client experiences incongruence, anxiety, or vulnerability.
3. The client experiences the condition provided by the therapist, such as congruence, unconditional positive regard, and empathy.

To restate, Raskin and colleagues (2008) said that three characteristics, that is congruence, unconditional positive regard, and empathy, of the therapist are necessary and sufficient to help the client to change. The most significant factor, however, is congruence or genuineness, and this implies that the therapist is authentic during therapy. Moreover, it suggests that the therapist is not presenting a facade, and the therapist uses self-disclosure when it is appropriate. Interestingly, Rogers pointed out that therapists do not have to be fully functioning to be effective, but if a therapist is congruent during a therapeutic relationship, the probability that changes will occur within a client increases. In addition, Rogers noted that change is on a continuum, and the therapeutic characteristics of therapists exist on a continuum, too. The second characteristic a therapist needs to communicate to a client is unconditional positive regard or acceptance. **Unconditional positive** regard connotes caring for clients without evaluating clients' feelings, thoughts, and behaviors. This is the philosophical acceptance of a client as a human being, and the therapist helps the client express feelings without fear of judgment. Like congruence, unconditional positive regard is also on a continuum. **Empathy** involves the therapist's phenomenologically entering a client's world and reflecting the client's feelings so the client can feel understood. In essence, empathy is feeling with the client without losing one's own separateness or identity.

Applications: Reflecting Content and Feelings – Level I Counseling Skills

Directions: Reflect the content and feelings for the following scenarios, and write down your responses.

1. A 13-year-old girl says to you:
   "I love hooking up, and no one can control my body! I am mature, and I do as I please, and I hate bastards who attempt to control me!"
   Note: Use the Internet to research the laws that govern sexual activity of minors within your state. What are some ethical issues to consider with this scenario? For example, are there any issues around duty to warn or protect or confidentiality?
   a. What are the ethical issues surrounding this case?

   ____
   ____
   ____
   ____

   b. What is the content that this adolescent is communicating?

c. What are the feeling this adolescent is communicating?

Use this list of affect words to guide your responses.

List of Affect Words

anger	lonely	betrayed	exhausted
threatened	defeated	misunderstood	restricted
sad	crushed	closed	jealous
worried	helped	frustrated	energized
shame	calm	powerless	competent
confused	depressed	lost	incompetent
listless	stymied	cowardly	weak
stuck	powerful	courageous	inadequate
rejected	weird	disturbed	courageous
frightened	strange	uncertain	actualized
hurt	irritated	embarrassed	nervous
pessimistic	assertive	scared	happy
optimistic	confident	odd	ashamed

2. A 26-year old man says the following to you:
"I have the hots for you, and you really turn me on. You are a giving person, and you have not rejected me, and for that, I love you."
   a. List the ethical issue that may relate to this scenario. Could countertransference be an issue?

   ____

   ____

   ____

   b. What is the content that this young man is communicating?
   c. What are the feelings this young man is communicating?

   ____

   ____

   ____

Critique: Multicultural Applications and Limitations

Person-centered therapy has made major contributions to the area of multicultural counseling. For example, therapists in Europe, Australia, New Zealand, Japan, Mexico, and South America have adapted the practice of person-centered therapy to fit their cultures (McMillan, 2004). From a multicultural perspective, one limitation of this approach is the tendency for therapists to use only Level I and/or II counseling skills and to never confront the client. Moreover, some African American clients may want more from a therapist than paraphrasing of feelings and content, and they want may specific strategies (Sapp, 1997a).

Comprehensiveness: Person-centered therapy has evolved into an approach that is more comprehensive than it was originally. For example, Rogers broadened this approach to include areas such as group therapy, marriage, family, race relations, and world peace. However, this approach does not describe how or why clients develop emotional issues. In addition, this approach does not address unconscious behavior in great detail; therefore, this approach is not as comprehensive as psychodynamic or social learning theories. Moreover, this approach focuses mainly on the client's affective domain, whereas cognitive-behavioral approaches focus on cognitions and behaviors and possibly affect. Clearly, REBT is more comprehensive than person-centered therapy is, and Adlerian therapy, which places more emphasis on social interests and the family, is more comprehensive than person-centered therapy is.

Parsimony: Person-centered therapy is very parsimonious in that Rogers believed that three core conditions were necessary and sufficient to bring about therapeutic change. Specifically, person-centered therapy is more parsimonious than are Adlerian therapy, cognitive-behavioral therapies, and psychodynamic therapies.

Empirical Validity: Person-centered therapy has a d effect size of .63 and a 95% confidence interval for d of .2111, .4185. Levels I and II counseling skills, which were derived from this approach, are the micro or foundational counseling skills that are used by training programs throughout the country. In addition, qualitative studies support the efficacy of person-centered therapy (Braaten, 1986; Cain, 1986, 1987, 1990, 1993; Thorne, 1992).

Precision and Testability: Although there are many studies supporting the empirical validity of person-centered therapy, it is lacking in precision and testability because concepts such the self, empathy, unconditional positive regard, conditions of worth, and congruence have not been operationally defined.

Heuristic Value: Person-centered therapy has strong heuristic value, and it has stimulated a great deal of research by challenging the notion that therapists know best. This approach has been controversial and still provokes debate within counseling psychology and education. Clearly, person-centered therapy has strong heuristic values.

Applied Value: Person-centered approach has strong applied value, and as previously stated it is used to teach Levels I and II counseling skills. In addition, person-centered therapy is the preferred mode of therapy for crisis-intervention counseling. Finally, this approach has been used within education, applied to groups, politics, human relations, and community mental health counseling.

Summary

Person-centered therapy is a humanistic-existential form of psychotherapy, and it is an affective form of psychotherapy. Carl Rogers founded this approach as a reaction to psychoanalysis and behavior therapy, and he believed that three core conditions were necessary and sufficient to move clients toward growth and change. They are congruence, unconditional positive regard, and empathy. Finally, Rogers believed that the therapeutic relationship was the most important determinant of therapeutic outcome.

Associations and Institutes

- **World Association for Person-Centered and Experiential Psychotherapy and Counseling (WAPCEPC)**
  P.O. Box 142
  Ross-on-Wye, HR9 9AG, United Kingdom
  Website: www.pce-world-org/idxjournal.htm
- **Rogerian Training Institute**
  Center for Studies of the Person
  1150 Silverado Street Suite 112
  La Jolla, CA 92037
  Telephone: 858-459-3861
  Website: www.centerfortheperson.org
- **Associate for Humanistic Psychology (AHP)**
  1516 Oak Street, #320A
  Alameda, CA 94501-2947
  Telephone: 510-769-6495
  Website: www.ahpweb.org

- **Person Centered Expressive Therapy Institute (PCETI)**
  726 Mendocino Avenue
  Santa Rosa, CA 95401
  Website: www.pceti.org
  This organization is run by Dr. Carl Rogers' daughter, Dr. Natalie Rogers.

Chapter 7

GESTALT THERAPY: AFFECTIVE-EXPERIENTIAL LEVEL III COUNSELING THEORY

Chapter Overview

During the 1940s, Frederick Salomon (Fritz) Perls and his wife, Laura Posner Perls, developed Gestalt therapy. The Perlses were influenced by psychoanalysis, Wilhelm Reich, Karen Horney, Gestalt psychology, psychodrama (a form of group psychotherapy), existentialism, and phenomenology. Gestalt therapy is viewed as an integrative approach in that the therapist encourages the client to integrate thoughts, feelings, and behavior. Specifically, the therapist uses experiments to increase the client's self-awareness. In addition, Gestalt therapy is an affective-experiential noninterpretive approach because clients must find their own way. In contrast to psychoanalysis and dynamic approaches, Gestalt therapy is a here and now, present-oriented form of psychotherapy.

Very similar to existential therapy and humanistic psychology, Gestalt therapy is a reaction to behaviorism and psychoanalysis. The German Gestalt psychologists Kohler, Koffka, and Wertheimer influenced Fritz Perls' development of Gestalt therapy. Like the cognitive-behavioral approaches to psychotherapy, Gestalt therapy is an action-oriented Level III theory of psychotherapy. In contrast to psychoanalysis, Gestalt therapy is experiential and affectively oriented. In addition, it is a short-term form of therapy in which awareness is seen as curative in and of itself. Furthermore, Gestalt therapy is an existential form of therapy based on the premise that clients must find their own way in life and learn to accept personal responsibility as a means to achieve maturity (Yontef & Simkin, 1989).

The term Gestalt originated from German psychologists working in the area of perception. They found that humans do not perceive objects as unrelated parts but rather as meaningful wholes. These German psychologists stated that the whole was greater than the sum of the parts (Maples, 1995). Even though a relationship exists between Gestalt psychology and Gestalt therapy, Gestalt psychology investigates perception and cognition, whereas Gestalt therapy is concerned with field theory, phenomenology, dialogue, and psychotherapeutic issues (Corey, 2009; Frew & Spiegler, 2008).

One basic assumption of Gestalt therapy is that clients must deal effectively with their concerns. The therapist merely assists clients to fully experience the here and now and to determine how they prevent themselves from experiencing the present, and clients experience the cycle of awareness and contact. Again, unlike psychodynamic approaches, Gestalt therapy is noninterpretive in that clients interpret the meanings of their own experiences, and they must find closure in their cycles of awareness and contact.

Biographical Sketches

Born in Berlin in 1893 to a middle-class Jewish family, Fritz Perls received his medical degree in 1920 and served in the medical corps during World War I. After the war, the famed neurologist Kurt Goldstein supervised Perls. Perls had difficulty with his training in psychoanalysis, and he rejected behaviorism and structuralism. Perls was influenced by Wilhelm Reich and Karen Horney. Specifically, Reich analyzed him, and Horney supervised his training.

Perls immigrated to the United States in 1946, and he published *Gestalt Therapy: Excitement and Growth in Human Personality* in 1951. In 1969, Perls published two more books: *In and Out of the Garbage Pail* and *Gestalt Therapy Verbatim* (Perls, 1948, 1969a, b).

Maples (1995) pointed out that Wertheimer, Koffka, and Kohler influenced Perls. Max Wertheimer (1880–1943), a Berlin psychologist who studied motivation and perception, was credited as the founder of Gestalt psychology. In addition, his students, Kurt Koffka and Wolfgang Kohler, continued experimentation within the area.

Koffka (1886–1941) described Gestalt psychology as the study of "shape or pattern." Perls used the term Gestalt to mean the configuration of parts into a whole. This notion of whole is used in Gestalt psychology and the general area of psychotherapy. Kohler (1887–1967) resisted structuralism and behaviorism, the favored psychological theories of the 1920s and 1930s, and brought a sense of humanism to Gestalt psychology. Later, this emphasis influenced Perls and helped serve as a precursor to the phenomenological nature of Gestalt therapy.

During the 1960s, Perls was already in his 70s, and this was the second phase of Gestalt therapy (1947–1969). The first phase, 1912 to 1960, was established by Wertheimer, Koffka, and Kohler. Perls extended the work of phase one into the affective aspects. The final phase of Gestalt therapy stressed the importance of the therapist in the psychotherapy process. Moreover, Perls focused on the how and where in the process of psychotherapy – not on the why. He stressed noticing the obvious during psychotherapy, and he thought this was a good way to affect the entire Gestalt of a client (Perls, 1970, 1973; Perls, Hefferline & Goodman, 1951).

Perls' wife, Laura Posner Perls, was a cofounder of Gestalt therapy. She wrote several chapters in *Ego, Hunger, and Aggression.* She received her Ph.D. in Gestalt psychology from the University of Frankfurt in 1932. Yontef and Simkin (1989) pointed out that she incorporated most of the phenomenological and existential influences into Gestalt therapy. Specifically, Laura Perls was influenced by the existential theologians Martin Buber and Paul Tillich.

Laura worked with the New York Institute for Gestalt therapy, and she influenced the Cleveland school, where Erving Polster, Miriam Poster, and Joseph Zinker were faculty members during the 1960s. In contrast to Perls, who left his family to pursue popularizing Gestalt therapy with a confrontation style, Laura stressed support, empathy, dialogue, and challenging with clients.

Key Concepts

Gestalt therapy is based on a **phenomenological perspective**, and the goals of Gestalt therapy are the phenomenological exploration of awareness and insight. Insight is the perceptual focusing of patterns in such a way that significant realities are seen in the perceptual field.

The theory that underlies Gestalt's phenomenological perspective is **field theory**. In contrast to analyzing events as individual classes, **field theory** is a descriptive method of describing the entire field in which events are parts. The observer defines the phenomenological field, which only has meaning from the observer's point of reference. The unfolding nature of Gestalt therapy stresses the existential perspective of this therapy. Moreover, the here and now orientation of Gestalt is also part of existentialism (Maples, 1995).

The relationship between the therapist and client is called **dialogue**. The Gestalt relationship grows through **contact**, which is when the client experiences the boundary of "me and not me." Contact is the existential equivalent of the I–thou relationship. In contrast to behavioral therapy, Adlerian therapy, transactional analysis, and reality therapy, which are goal oriented, Gestalt therapy is content, process, and dialogue oriented. In fact, the therapist works through engaging the client in dialogue during therapy and the client must learn inner dialogue to maintain self-awareness (Yontef & Simkin, 1989).

A critical concept of Gestalt therapy that is related to the organismic valuing concept of person-centered therapy is **organismic self-regulation**, or the view that clients have the ability to understand their needs and to relate to their environment to satisfy their needs. Because Gestalt therapy is a process-based existential approach, change occurs automatically.

Dialogue has **four characteristics**: **inclusion**, **presence**, **commitment to dialogue**, and **dialogue is lived**. **Inclusion** is putting oneself into the experience of another without evaluating the experience but still maintaining individual self-awareness. Inclusion provides a safe environment for phenomenological work and client self-awareness. In contrast to psychoanalytic approaches, the Gestalt therapists express themselves to clients. This underscores the notion of **presence**. The therapist uses phenomenological reporting to help guide the client to develop trust and awareness with the existential process. Contact is the interaction that happens between two people (the client and the therapist). Clearly, contact is not manipulated; it is allowed to happen. This is what is meant by **commitment to dialogue**. Dialogue occurs rather than being discussed; however, it is limited by appropriateness and ethical considerations. This is what is meant by the expression **dialogue is lived**.

Although Gestalt therapy is phenomenological, it deals with the unconscious in the form of **unfinished business**. Any form of unawareness can be viewed as unfinished business (unconsciousness). Earlier it was stated that Perls viewed awareness as curative and that awareness represents itself through *contact.*

According to Perls, Hefferline, and Goodman (1951), contact is **figure-ground bound**. Contact can only be understood by considering the structures of the ground or **phenomenological field**. Gestalt psychotherapy is the reorganization of structures of ground over time. However, unfinished business is often part of the figure-ground relationship (Yontef, 1987, 1988). Figure is something that is within awareness, and ground is something that is not within awareness.

Defense Mechanisms: Disturbances in Contact Boundary

If the boundary between the self and others becomes blurred, the result is defense mechanisms that attempt to maintain the disturbance (lack of clarity) between the self and others, and this is similar to the process called dissociation, in which two or more mental processes are not integrated. For example, dissociation can occur when clients detach from their environment by day dreaming or seeing themselves performing actions outside of their body. The **contact boundary** can be lost by two polar-opposite defense mechanisms – **confluence** and **isolation**. Through fusion, **confluence** is lost in the boundary between the self, environment, and others. **Confluence** occurs when individuals blend into relationships and become so fused with others that there is a blending of feelings, thoughts, and behavior and a lack of constructive conflict (Maples, 1990; Zinker, 1991). **Isolation** is the result of an impermeable boundary that does not have connections with others. When the importance of others is lost from awareness, the result is the defense mechanism called **isolation**.

Retroflection, **introjection**, **projection**, and **deflection** are other defense mechanisms used to avoid contact. **Retroflection** occurs when clients turn emotions back onto themselves, and like dissociation it is the splitting of the self when clients turn their emotions back onto themselves. Similarly, when clients do to themselves what they would like others to do to themselves, it also represents retroflection.

Introjection has the same meaning that it has within the psychodynamic context. It is the indiscriminant absorption of beliefs and standards of others without assimilation. **Assimilation** allows a client to accommodate and to make ideas congruent with himself or herself. For example, a child may introject or "swallow whole" parental values of morality without fully understanding them but at adolescence realizes that his or her values differ from his or her parents.

Projection is the blurring of the boundaries of self and others; it is the opposite of introjection. It involves attributing things to the outside that are actually being generated by the self. Personality attributes that are inconsistent with one's self-image are disowned and attributed to others. **Deflection** is avoiding awareness or contact by being indirect. For example, person to person contact, being vague, or talking about someone instead of to someone are examples of deflection. The reader should be aware that these five processes can be healthy because they allow clients to interact with their environments, and interpreting them as defense mechanisms would depend on the context in which they are used.

Gestalt therapy stresses integrating polarities. For example, the Gestalt phenomenological field is differentiated into **polarities** – opposite parts that are complementary contributions to a whole. In contrast, dichotomies are splits in the phenomenological field that are competing unrelated parts. Unlike polarities, dichotomies do not explicate each other. Gestalt therapy employs integrative techniques to assimilate various aspects of a client's personality. Finally, Gestalt techniques, hypnotic integrative techniques, and other procedures can be used to integrate parts of a client's personality.

The Now

Due to an existential stance, Gestalt therapists believe that only the **now** exists. They argue that the past is gone and the future has not arrived; therefore, the only significant point in time is the now. For example, anxiety is the gap between the now and later. If clients are distracted by the past or future, they experience anxiety. Clients create anxiety by attempting to bridge the gap between the now and later with plans, activities, rituals, and resolutions. Gestalt therapists use **what** and **how** questions to promote the client's experience of the now awareness.

Action Strategy: Gestalt Questioning

Gestalt therapists believe that **"why"** questions lead to rationalizations, self-deceptions, and ruminations into the past and future. Some examples of Gestalt inquiries are as follows:

"Tell me what's happening now."
"What is occurring now?"
"What is going on now?"
"What are you experiencing now?"
"What are you experiencing as you try to talk?"
"How you have attempted to withdraw at this moment."

Other Action Strategies

Corey (2008) described the following ten Gestalt action strategies: dialogue exercise, empty-chair or two-chair technique, making the rounds, unfinished business, I take responsibility for, playing the projection, reversals, rehearsal, exaggeration, and staying with feelings.

Dialogue Exercises. Involves role-playing polarities that exist within the self. One of Gestalt therapy's common polarities is the struggle between the "top dog" and the "underdog." The top dog is the critical parental part (superego) of the personality that cajoles with shoulds, oughts, and other moralistic manipulations. In contrast, the underdog is the helpless or powerless side of the personality. Often, the therapist uses empty chairs to get the client to externalize the introjected top dog and underdog. Usually, the therapist asks the client to sit in one chair and become the top dog and then to move to another chair and become the underdog. In addition, a client can stay in one chair but switch on and off aspects of the top dog and underdog. Some other applicable dialogues include commitment versus noncommitment, responsibility versus impulsivity, good person versus bad person, and adult versus child. Gestalt therapy, especially techniques such as the dialogue exercise, can be conducted in both individual and group therapy

Empty-Chair or Two-Chair Technique. This technique is a popular strategy that has been incorporated into other theories (Clarke & Greenberg, 1986; Greenberg, 1989). This strategy is a form of confrontation and enactment in which the therapist asks a client to play one or more roles by moving back and forth from chair to chair. For example, the top dog–underdog dialogue can be enacted by having a client speak from the perspective of the top dog in one chair and then respond, in the other chair, as the underdog. Greenberg (1980) has shown that the empty-chair or two-chair technique can be used to resolve decisional conflicts. This research appears to support Perls' contention that this technique helps integrate disparate parts of the client and leads to conflict resolution. Greenberg and Webster (1982) showed that their research demonstrates that the two-chair technique is more effective than are cognitive-behavioral or traditional problem-solving strategies used in psychotherapy. Also, this strategy, like hypnosis, has potential for integrating personalities for clients experiencing dissociative identity disorder (formerly called multiple personality disorder).

Making the Rounds. A group technique that involves asking group members to approach each other and either say or do something to each other. The purpose of the exercise is for members to reveal aspects of the self.

Unfinished Business. The nonconscious aspect of Gestalt therapy, and it is similar to the psychodynamic notion of unconscious, but it is not based on primaty process mentation. In addition, it is unexpressed feelings such as rage, hatred, pain, anxiety, resentment, and so on that are not fully experienced within awareness. They have an impact on intrapersonal and interpersonal interactions. When a person does not express unfinished business, it can result in self-defeating responses. Perls stated that resentment, which can turn to guilt; was the most frequent and devastating form of unfinished business. Perls suggested that when a person feels guilty, he or she should find out what is being resented (Paivio & Greenberg, 1995). Finally, unfinished business is the Gestalt method of accessing the nonconscious.

I Take Responsibility for... During **I take responsibility for**, the therapist asks the client to make a statement and add "I take responsibility for it." This exercise allows clients to accept responsibility for their feelings. Often, feelings of isolation, rejection, alienation, depression, and so on surface from this exercise.

Playing the Projections. With **playing the projections,** the therapist requests the client to play the role of projections, dynamics the client does not want to admit exist within himself or herself. For example, if a client expresses difficulty in feeling independent, the therapist can ask the client to play the role of a weak, dependent individual. Finally, projections have a meaning similar to what it had with psychodynamic approaches.

Reversals. The therapist can use **reversal** techniques to allow clients to get into contact with parts of themselves that are denied. The theory underlying this technique is that by exposing clients to the parts of themselves that they fear it will lead to a reduction in anxiety and increased self-acceptance. When the therapist has the client play the opposite of the symptoms he or she is presenting, it may awaken underlying impulses. For example, a client who presents herself as a "nice woman" may be covering angry or negative feelings toward others. When it is therapeutically indicated, reversal techniques – that is, playing a "tough woman" – could lend to the assimilation of both aspects of the personality.

Rehearsals. Perls believed that much of our thinking is **rehearsal**. In fantasy, we commonly rehearse roles we are expected to play. Perls used this exercise during group therapy and had clients rehearse aloud pros and cons of various roles (Perls, 1970, 1973).

Exaggerations. Perls concentrated on having clients exaggerate nonverbal behavior as a means to complete a Gestalt experience. He helped clients exaggerate nonverbal behavior by paying attention to their trembling hands, legs, and so on, and he would notice facial expressions such as smiles and eye movements. The purpose of this technique was to intensify clients' feelings and to make the meanings of their nonverbal behavior more apparent.

Staying with the Feelings. When clients expressed feelings with which they were uncomfortable, Perls would often have them stay with and retain the feelings. For example, if a client was experiencing emotional pain, Perls might ask the client to go deeper into the pain. It is hoped that going deeper into feelings will unblock energy and lead to further growth.

Dream Work

In contrast to a psychoanalyst's interpretative and unconscious approach to dreams, Gestalt therapists do not interpret or analyze dreams into parts, but they have clients relive dreams in the present as though the dreams were occurring now. Gestalt therapists believe that dreams represented projections of the dreamer; therefore, Perls would have dreamers relive parts of their dreams in the present and have them engage in dialogue with various parts of the dream.

Impasse

An **impasse** occurs when a client attempts to manipulate the environment by playing games or phony roles such as being weak, helpless, stupid, or foolish. When a client moves from external support to internal support, phenomenological energy is freed, and the client feels more mature and able to function independently.

Congruence of Words and Experiences

Perls, like Carl Rogers, believed that the client's speech and experiences should be congruent in order for awareness to occur. Perls would engage in communication with the client's nonverbal body language by asking questions such as the following: "If your body could talk, what would it say?" "What are your eyes expressing now?" "Can you let your left or right hand communicate with me?" In contrast to Rogers, who used reflection mainly based on oral communication, Gestalt therapists tend to communicate empathy by reflecting nonverbal expressions. For example, if a client is expressing sadness a Gestalt therapist may say "What are the tears in your eyes communicating?

Similar to REBT, transactional analysis, and other cognitive-behavioral theories, Gestalt pays attention to clients' language. To illustrate, *it talk*, *you talk*, and *questions* are viewed as impersonal expressions, and Perls would have clients substitute personal pronouns for *it talks* and *you talk*. Perls believed clients could use questions to remain hidden and out of contact with themselves; in addition, he would force clients to take responsibility by having them turn questions into statements.

Many times, Perls would challenge clients who used qualifiers or ambivalent expressions, and he noted that expressions that end in "but" were mostly statements that denied the client's personal autonomy. For example, the statement "I would like to be strong, but I lack power" could be viewed as a way for someone to deny power by using the qualifier "but." Often, clients use qualifiers *maybe*, *I guess*, *who knows*, and *perhaps* to remain ambivalent. Statements with "I can't" may actually mean will not, and clients can use such statements to avoid personal responsibility. Finally, like REBT, there are no "shoulds" or "oughts" in Gestalt therapy. The therapist asks the client to restate "shoulds" as preferences because clients are viewed as autonomous and self-determined (Corey, 2009).

Neurotic Layers

Perls (1969a, b) defined a neurotic disorder as a growth disorder, and he used the analogy of peeling an onion to describe these neurotic layers. The first layer is the **cliché or phony** layer, which is the layer where a client plays the game of noncontact with others. It is not uncommon for clients to assume inauthentic roles such as victim, loser, or helpless person. At this layer, even communication can be stereotypical and routine.

The next layer is the **phobic or role-playing** layer, which is used to avoid emotional pain connected with aspects of the self that clients prefer to deny. The phobic layer involves presenting an impression to others that is a façade, because there is fear that the true self will be rejected.

The third layer is the **impasse** or the place between dependence or environmental support and self-support. Here, the client is essentially stuck in the maturation process. At this point, the client attempts to manipulate the environment as a means to avoid personal responsibility. Often, clients will feel dead and lifeless during this process. It is important for a client to get through this process and to regain contact with the senses (seeing, hearing, feeling, and so on).

The **implosive** layer is the fourth layer, which involves the client's pulling himself or herself together and stripping away roles and imploding. To illustrate, if a client experiences deadness, the client should get into contact and become maximally aware of the experience instead of avoiding it. If the client maintains awareness, implosion will occur, and an authentic self will emerge.

The final layer is the **explosive** one. Once a client makes it to the final process, he or she is capable of experiencing and expressing emotions. When the client explodes, energy moves from pain to joy, and the client becomes authentic and alive.

Breathing and Relaxation

Gestalt therapists use breathing and relaxation exercises very similar to the ones used by behavior therapists. For example, the therapist can use breathing exercises to get a client in touch with his or her feelings. Often, Gestalt therapists will ask a client to show where he or she feels emotions such anxiety, depression, nervousness, and so on. This technique allows the therapist to enter the client's phenomenological world, and it lets the client know that he or she is not alone.

Frustration and Support

Yontef and Simkin (1987) recommend that Gestalt therapy should only be taught to advanced students because it involves a delicate balance between frustrating and supporting the client. In fact, exploring a client's wishes, in contrast to gratifying them, can create frustration. When a client attempts to manipulate a therapist, the therapist can use contact and frustration to decrease that manipulation. The therapist does not have to be purposefully frustrating for a client to experience frustration. That is, if the therapist responds to manipulations without reinforcing or judging such manipulations, it can lead to the client experiencing frustration.

The use of homework assignments is one way therapists establish contact with clients for future sessions. Polster and Polster (1973) encouraged therapists to assign homework that directly relates to the clients' concerns and that can be easily accomplished. In summary, similar to traditional and nontraditional cognitive-behavioral therapy, Gestalt therapy is active and directive, and it involves the use of homework (Polster, 1987).

Therapeutic Process

Gestalt therapy can be practiced as an individual therapy or in groups, with couples, and with families; hence, this therapy has many styles or modalities. The process of Gestalt therapy is primarily affective and experiential. It is the existential encounter between at least two individuals: the client and the therapist. Perls contended that we only use a small portion of our human potential and asserted that this is the reason many clients enter therapy. Because the clients are using only a small portion of their potential, they do not fully experience life and existence; hence, Gestalt therapy has a human potential aspect.

Therapeutic Goals

The goal of Gestalt therapy is awareness, which is viewed as curative in and of itself. Zinker (1991) stated that it is important for clients to gain an awareness of themselves, to gradually accept ownership for experiences, to learn to meet their desires without violating the rights of others, to fully become aware of senses, to move from environmental support to self-support, and to be capable of giving and receiving help from others.

Role of Therapist

The role and function of the Gestalt therapist is to get clients into contact with the obvious, which is an anti-intellectual stance. Often, Perls stated that "one must lose one's mind and come to one's senses." Gestalt therapists employ Level III counseling skills to confront and frustrate clients toward increased awareness. As previously stated, Gestalt therapists point out discrepancies between clients' verbal and nonverbal expressions, and special attention is given to clients' speech – especially speech that denies personal power and responsibility. In summary, Gestalt therapists use frustration and support to move clients toward growth. Also, Gestalt therapists frequently employ Gestalt experiments within the therapeutic process, and it is strongly recommended that clients be prepared for Gestalt therapy. Finally, because clients may not be able to determine the purpose of a given activity, it is important that the therapist prepare them for Gestalt techniques.

Therapeutic Relationship

Very similar to existential and humanistic psychotherapy, Gestalt therapy is based on the I–thou relationship between the client and therapist. This is a person-to-person relationship in which the client and the therapist freely share the mutual awareness and phenomenological perceptions. Even though the therapist employs techniques, exercises, and experiments during psychotherapy, a thorough client–therapist relationship must be established before Gestalt experiments can be implemented. Gestalt therapists attempt to show clients how to discover new aspects of themselves. After the client learns various aspects of himself or herself, he or she can initiate the integration or accommodation of choices that emerge during discovery. Gestalt therapy helps clients to assimilate and accommodate new aspects of themselves. Finally, clients learn to cope with environmental surprises and discover how to maximize the probabilities of getting what is desired (Polster, 1987).

Multicultural Applications and Limitations

Gestalt therapy has many multicultural applications. Many members of minority groups who attempt to be bicultural often have difficulty maintaining parts of their own culture and assimilating aspects of the majority culture. For example, I once counseled a Latino American male who had married a woman from the majority culture. During therapy, he indicated that he felt a strain in attempting to balance the two cultures within his household. So, I had this client role-play various aspects of each culture in empty chairs. Finally, I employed the integrative aspects of Gestalt to break down inner barriers and to help the client become more at ease with both cultures.

Gestalt therapy also has potential multicultural limitations. Specifically, the directive, active, and experimental nature of Gestalt therapy can put some minority clients at risk for premature termination of therapy. Furthermore, the lack of emphasis on cognitive factors could leave some minorities without rationales, meanings, and directions of therapy. If Gestalt therapy is carefully implemented with minority clients, these applications may outweigh the limitations.

Critique

Comprehensiveness: Fritz and Laura Perls borrowed concepts from Gestalt psychology, psychoanalysis, and other theories, but they did not explain how clients developed mental disorders. Some theorists believe that Gestalt therapy is simultaneously simple and complex. For example, Perls did not address developmental issues and provided a relatively simple-to-understand theory that has applications to individuals, groups, families, and couples. Before a student can safely apply Gestalt therapy, however he or she must possess Levels I and II counseling skills (Maples, 1995; Yontef & Simkin, 1989). The existential nature of Gestalt therapy also makes it difficult to practice, because existentialism is a complex philosophy.

Another complex issue involving Gestalt therapy is the hundreds of poorly trained individuals who call themselves "Gestaltists." Actually, Gestalt institutes have not established uniform standards for training despite the fact that scholars, such as Greenberg (1980) and Frew and Spiegler (2008), recommend that Gestalt therapy should be taught only to advanced graduate students. Moreover, some Gestalt institutes offer workshops and training to anyone willing to pay for a weekend seminar. Also, there are courses on Gestalt therapy that are offered across the country for alcohol- and substance-abuse counseling. Many individuals who attend these courses have only a high-school level education. Finally, this writer feels such practice is unethical and that all psychotherapy training should be reserved for graduate students.

Precision and Testability: Gestalt therapy lacks precision and testability. Actually, many of the postulates of Gestalt therapy do not fit together. Moreover, when Perls was developing his theory, he did not encourage the formation of operational definitions. Likewise, the existential nature of Gestalt makes it difficult to operationally test definitions of this therapy.

Parsimony: When compared to the dynamic theories, Gestalt therapy is economical. Perls kept this theory simple by not including inconsequential concepts. Some would argue that Gestalt therapy is too simple to be a complete theory and that it lacks an underlying theory that unifies its techniques.

Empirical Validity: There are hundreds of empirical studies that support the efficacy of Gestalt therapy. For example, Sapp (2004a) reported that Gestalt therapy had a d effect size of .64, and 95% confidence interval around the population d effect size of .2111 for the lower limit and .4118 for the upper limit, and this analysis was based on 375 participants. In addition, Bretz-Joachim, Heekerens, and Schmitz (1994) presented a meta-analysis of 38 studies conducted between 1970 and 1986 on the effectiveness of individual and group Gestalt therapy. These results suggested that Gestalt therapy is just as effective as other forms of psychotherapy. Also, Paivio and Greenberg (1995) employed an experimental design and randomly assigned clients to an experimental Gestalt therapy group using an empty-chair dialogue intervention or an attention-placebo condition. Results indicated that the Gestalt therapy group had greater improvement outcome measures. Moreover, this group maintained treatment gains during a follow-up period. Finally, Gestalt therapy does not have the experimental empirical validity of behavior therapy, and few experimental empirical studies support the efficacy of Gestalt therapy (Frew & Spiegler, 2008; Harman, 1984; Strumpfel, 2004; Strumpfel & Goldman, 2001).

Heuristic Value: During the twenty-first century, it is difficult to ascertain the heuristic value of Gestalt therapy. Gestalt therapy appears not to have as many journal citations as does its cousin, transactional analysis. It is not clear whether Gestalt therapy has just been integrated into other therapies, such as transactional analysis, or if it is declining in its heuristic value.

Applied Value: Even though the journal citations for Gestalt therapy may be declining, it has high applied value. For example, it has multicultural applications, applications in the treatment of certain anxiety disorders, group counseling applications, and marriage and family counseling applications. Finally, certain applications, such as the empty-chair and two-chair techniques, have been integrated into general psychotherapy.

Summary

Gestalt therapy is an affective-experiential here and now approach to psychotherapy. One of its goals is to move from environmental support to self-support. Also, the goal of Gestalt therapy is awareness. Moreover, clients are encouraged to integrate all aspects of themselves. Unlike psychoanalysts, Gestalt therapists do not interpret the behavior of clients. Finally, Gestalt therapists employ experiments to move clients toward growth.

Glossary of Key Terms

Awareness: The key therapeutic process of Gestalt therapy, which is viewed as curative.

Confluence: The blurring of internal and external boundaries.

Confrontation: A common action strategy used to frustrate clients and move them toward personal growth.

Deflection: A defense mechanism used to avoid contact.

Dichotomy: A split in a client's experiences; sometimes mistakenly called a polarity.

Gestalt experiments: Exercises designed to increase a client's awareness.

Impasse: The phenomenological experience of a client feeling stuck.

Polarity: Parts of opposites that complement each other. In contrast, dichotomies are splits of competing parts within a client's phenome-

nological field.
Projection: A defense mechanism in which clients ascribe to others certain aspects of themselves with which they are uncomfortable.
Retroflection: A defense mechanism in which a client does to himself or herself things that he or she would like to do to others.
Unfinished business: Unexpressed affect connected with the past.

Review Questions

1. Some therapists argue that the goal of Gestalt therapy is insight or awareness. Compare and contrast the Gestalt view and psychodynamic view of insight.
2. Field theory explores the interrelatedness of parts. Discuss some possible relationships that field theory may have for Gestalt therapy, existential therapy, and humanistic therapy.
3. Even though Gestalt therapy, Adlerian therapy, and behavior therapy are Level III theories, how are these theories similar and different?

Center for Gestalt Development and Journal

- **Center for Gestalt Development**
  Gestalt Journal
  P.O. Box 990
  Highland, NY 12528-0990
  Telephone: 914-691-7192
  Website:wwwgesta.org
- *International Gestalt Journal*
  P.O. Box 278
  Goalsboro, ME 04607-0278
- *Gestalt Review*
  P.O. Box 515
  South Wellfleet, MA 02263
- *British Gestalt Journal*
  P.O. Box 420
  Bristol, BS99 7PQ
  England

Training Resources

- **Gestalt Institute of Cleveland, Inc.**
  1588 Hazel Drive
  Cleveland, Ohio 44106-1791
  Telephone: 216-421-0468
  Website: www.gestaltcleveland.org
- **Gestalt Therapy Institute of the Pacific**
  1626 Westwood Blvs., Suite 104
  L.A., CA 90024
  Telephone: 310-446-9720
  Website: gestaltherapy.org
- **Association for the Advancement of Gestalt Therapy (AAGT)**
  400 East 58th Street
  New York, NY 10022
  Telephone: 212-486-1581
  Website: www.aagt.org

Chapter 8

MORENO'S PSYCHODRAMA

Chapter Overview

Psychodrama was developed during the 1930s by Jacob C. Moreno (1889–1974). It is mainly applied to groups; however, it can be adapted to individuals and families. Like the role-playing techniques used in Gestalt therapy, with psychodrama, the client is to role play some aspect of his or her problem, and the therapist uses psychodramatic techniques to bring out the client's emotions. Like Adlerian therapy, psychodrama can work with clients from roles in the past, present, and future.

Blatner (2005) claimed that Perls visited one of Moreno's workshops in New York and adapted the empty chair technique and role reversal to Gestalt therapy. In addition, many of the imagery therapies used in behavior therapy were adapted from psychodrama. Moreover, the ego states of transactional analysis can be traced back to psychodrama. Therapists within the area of play therapy will find that this form of therapy naturally involves overlaps with psychodrama. The post-Reichian methods of body therapies were also influenced by psychodrama. In essence, many theories have borrowed techniques from psychodrama.

Biographical Sketch

Throughout history, literature, theatre, and art have been used for therapeutic purposes. Jacob Levy was born in Bucharest, Romania, in 1889 into a Sephardic Jewish family, and he added the name Moreno because it meant teacher. Like Freud and other theorists, Moreno was a physician, and during the 1930s he worked in prisons and advocated group therapy of all kinds. In addition, during the 1930s, Moreno found that psychodrama helped psychotic patients in hospitals.

Moreno founded four journals: *Sociometry*, *Sociatry*, *Group Psychotherapy*, and *The International Journal of Sociometry and Sociatry.* In 1942, he founded the first group psychotherapy association: The International Society of Sociometry and Sociatry. Interestingly, the American Group Psychotherapy, a psychoanalytically oriented journal was founded months later. Moreno's third wife Zerka Toeman Moreno (1971–) was invaluable in helping him promote psychodrama. Moreno's work in role theory and sociometry influenced social psychology and sociology, and he helped found the International Association of Group Psychotherapy. Finally, from the late 1940s until the early 1970s, Moreno popularized his approach until he died in May of 1974.

Key Concepts

As stated earlier, Moreno was one of the orginators of social role theory. Even though most role theorists academically explained role, Moreno stressed practical applications. The word role was derived from roll-up scrolls that early actors used (Blatner, 2005).

Accepting the ideas of humanistic psychology, Moreno viewed **creativity** and **spontaneity** as part of self-actualization. **Warming-up** is an initial stage of group development in which group members slowly become involved and trust develops. Often, the **director** or the **group leader** will provide a brief overview of psychodrama and activities such as music, dancing, and other movements that will be used to warm the atmosphere of the group.

The audience and stage are important concepts of psychodrama. The **audience** consists of the other group members, and the **stage** is where enactments take place (Corey, 2008). Like a play, the **protagonist** is the person who is the focus of an enactment, and **auxillary egos** are other group members who support the protagonist.

During the 1950s and the 1960s, Moreno developed sociometry to measure **tele**, or the two-way flow among group members. For example, roles can be too restrictive or too broad. The goal of good mental health is to balance roles. Psychodrama recognizes that a person can be healthy but locked into a dysfunctional family, relationship, career, or neighborhood.

Therapeutic Process and Goals

The goal of psychodrama is to free group members from past feelings and to use spontaneity, creativity, and role playing to enact or reinact events from the past, present, and future.

Therapeutic Relationship

A director or group leader is aware of the beginning, middle, and ending phases of psychodrama. During the beginning phase, the director encourages group members to get acquainted, decide on certain themes, and select protagonists and other roles for group members. With the middle phase, group members concretely define the situations to be enacted. Group members also serve as auxillary egos for the protagonists. During the ending phase, group members share with protagonists their feelings from enactments. There is a catharsis, therefore, but unlike psychoanalysis and other analytically oriented approaches, the feedback is not analytical but experiential. Moreover, group members gain insights from cathartic experiences.

Although classical psychodrama consists of a director, protagonist, auxillary egos, audience, and a stage, extensive training is required. Psychodramatic techniques can be incorporated into many approaches, however. The following are ten common action strategies used within psychodrama.

Action Strategies

Corey (2008) described the following ten action strategies: self-presentation, role reversal, double technique, soliloquy, the empty chair, replay, mirror technique, future projection, the magic shop, and role training.

With **self-presentation**, the protagonist provides a self-portrait to introduce the situation; essentially, the protagonist talks about his or her problem. **Role reversal** involves the protagonist's taking parts of another personality portrayed during his or her psychodrama, and this allows the protagonist to see himself or herself through the eyes of others. Essentially, the protagonist is able to get outside his or her frame of reference and to enact a side of himself or herself that is rarely revealed to others. Finally, this technique can allow the protagonist to develop empathy for others.

Double technique is where an auxiliary ego stands at the side of the protagonist and speaks for the protagonist. The doubling technique serves as a "voice over" in the world of theatre. **Soliloquy** is a technique by which the protagonist imagines that he or she is alone and speaks his or her thoughts and feelings aloud.

The empty chair was discussed within the Gestalt therapy chapter, but Blatner (2005) claims that Moreno was the originator of this technique, which is sometimes called **auxillary chair**. The empty chair is used when an enactment involves someone who is absent or deceased, and the empty chair represents the absent figure. **Replay** is a technique that has been incorporated into behavior therapy and Gestalt therapy, and it is redoing an action for emphasis and refinement. **The mirror technique** helps the protagonist foster self-reflection by having group members mimic or mirror his or her gestures and words as they occur through an enactment.

Future projection is another technique that has been incorporated into other therapies such as Gestalt therapy, behavior therapy, and Adlerian therapy. This technique allows group members to clarify concerns about the future by having members act out versions of the ways they hope or think the future will turn out.

The magic shop can be used throughout the beginning, middle, and ending phases of group development, and it does not involve having a wish granted. In turn, however a personal quality must be exchanged for the wish. Often the auxillary egos will play the role of gatekeeper, guarding the contents of the magic shop. Essentially, this action strategy allows group members to assess their priorities and to assess their values. **Role training** is called behavioral rehearsal in behavior therapy. With role training, through modeling, members rehearse new interpersonal skills and receive feedback from other group members.

Multicultural Applications and Limitations

Psychodrama can allow minority groups to act out various roles concerning their problems. Like Gestalt therapy, minority groups can learn to integrate cognitive, emotive, and behavioral aspects of themselves through psychodramatic strategies. The active and directive nature of psychodrama, however, can put multicultural clients at risk for premature termination and potential harm from inexperienced therapists.

Critique

Comprehensiveness: Even though psychodrama does not address developmental issues in detail, it does address conscious, unconscious, and preconscious experiences, but not from a psychoanalytical point of view. In comparison to other affective approaches discussed within this text, psychodrama is clearly the most comprehensive, and it is more comprehensive than some behavioral approaches.

Parsimony: In comparison to some nontraditional cognitive-behavioral approaches, psychodrama is parsimonious, but it is not as parsimonious as person-centered therapy, existential therapy, or Gestalt therapy.

Empirical Validity: Kipper and Ritchie (2003) presented a meta-analysis of 25 experimentally designed studies that showed the effectiveness of psychodrama, which was similar and at times better than the effect sizes reported for general group therapy. Specially, they found **an average *d* effect size of .95 for 25 studies**, and these studies were significantly different from zero **$t(280) = 22.30$, $p < .01$**. Moreover, the **99% confidence interval was .847 for the lower limit and 1.061 for the upper limit. This 99% confidence interval contains effect sizes within the large effect size range**. In contrast, the general reported effect size range for group psychotherapy is .50 to .70 (Kipper and Ritchie, 2003). The role reversal technique and the doubling technique were found to be the most effective, but it was difficult to tease out the exact effect of these particular techniques because they are integrative procedures within other forms of psychotherapy. Finally, on-going meta-analytical studies are needed for psychodrama.

Precision and Testability: Psychodrama needs research that tests the psychometric properties of dependent variables. In addition, psychodrama could benefit from operational definitions.

Heuristic Value: It is difficult to determine the heuristic values of psychodrama, but within the area of group psychotherapy, it is commonly cited as a valuable approach to group psychotherapy.

Applied Value: Psychodrama has excellent applied value, and it has been used with hypnosis, guided imagery, body work, spirituality, behavior therapy, gestalt therapy, and transactional analysis. Finally, psychodramatic techniques can be used in a technically eclectic way with other techniques of psychotherapy.

Glossary of Key Terms

Audience: The members within a group who get to explore a particular problem.
Auxiliary ego: A group member who helps the protagonist, or the person who is the subject of a psychodramatic enactment, to explore a role.
Classical psychodrama: Formal psychodrama that requires a director to have specialized training within the intricacies of psychodrama.
Director: The group leader who facilitates an enactment in psychodrama.
Double technique: Auxiliary egos that stand near the protagonist and speak and act for him or her.
Magic shop: A group technique where group members exchange personal qualities for wishes.
Mirror technique: An auxiliary ego assumes the role of the protagonist and mirrors his or her expressions.
Protagonist: The group member who is the participant for group exploration.
Psychodrama: Primarily a group form of psychotherapy that uses the enactment of role playing as a means of psychotherapy.
Role reversal: The protagonist changes roles with other personalities displayed during an enactment.
Soliloquy: The protagonist imagines being alone and speaks aloud his or her feelings and thoughts.
Surplus reality: An enactment that allows the protagonist to replay a role and to change the ending.
Tele: The two-way flow of communication between two people.
Unconscious: A concept that is broader than the psychodynamic notion, and it is the source of spontaneity, creativity, and dissociated affect.
Warm-up phase: The initial phase of group psychodrama that is

designed to help foster trust and group involvement.

Review Questions

1. Describe psychodrama.
2. Describe the theories that psychodrama has influenced.
3. How can psychodrama be classified?
4. Compare and contrast psychodrama with gestalt therapy and behavior therapy.

Societies and Resources

- **American Society for Group Psychotherapy and Psychodrama (ASGPP)**
  301 N. Harrison Street, Suite 508
  Princeton, NJ 08540
  Telephone: 609-452-1339
  Fax: 732-605-7033
  E-mail: asgpp@asgpp.org
  Website: www.asgpp.org
- **Dr. Adam Blatner**
  E-mail: adam@blatner.com
  Website: www.Blatner.com/adam/

  Mrs. Moreno conducts some weekend workshops in Virginia and she can be contacted directly or through Dr. Jeanne Burger via e-mail.
- **Mrs. Zerka Moreno**
  E-mail: tmceline@adelphia.net
- **Dr. Jeanne Burger**
  E-mail: DRJB@mindspring.com

AFTERWORD

COMPARISON OF THEORIES

In this text, three categories of theories were discussed: psychodynamic, affective, and behavioral. The goal of psychodynamic approaches is to integrate clients' conscious and unconscious mentation. In essence, insight occurs when unconscious mentation is brought into conscious awareness. Short-term dynamically oriented psychotherapy and relational psychoanalysis are modifications within the psychodynamic umbrella.

Affective theories include existential psychotherapy, person-centered psychotherapy, Gestalt psychotherapy, and psychodrama. Existential psychotherapy uses Levels I, II, and III counseling skills. In contrast, person-centered psychotherapy uses Levels I and II counseling skills. In contrast, Gestalt therapy employs only Level III counseling skills. Finally, like existential psychotherapy, psychodrama uses Levels I through III counseling skills.

In contrast to theoretical integrationism, this text emphasized technical eclectism. Before one can employ the theories in this text, one must have mastered Levels I and II counseling skills. For example, if one has mastered the prerequisite skills, Gestalt therapy and person-centered therapy could serve as one's primary theoretical orientations without causing syncretism, or the unsystematic form of eclecticism.

Just simply using techniques because they appear to work is not technical eclecticism, and it is unethical to haphazardly select techniques without a theoretical rational and can be harmful to clients. When one has one a theoretical orientation, it is possible to apply techniques from various theories without embracing the theories themselves; this is what is meant by technical eclecticism. The major difficulty with theoretical eclecticism is that it attempts to integrate epistemologically incompatible theories and can create confusion. The major reason technical eclecticism is important is that no single set of techniques can capture the intricacies of human behavior. Finally, this is why the author believes the trend toward multiculturism will continue to influence the area of psychotherapy.

REFERENCES

Abram, J. L. (1983). Cognitive-behavioral strategies to induce and enhance a collaborative set in distressed couples. In A. Freeman, (Ed.). *Cognitive therapy with couples and groups* (pp. 125–155). New York: Plenum.

Abramson, L. Y., Metalsky, G. I., & Alloy, L. B. (1989). Hopelessness depression: A theory-based subtype of depression. *Psychological Review, 96* (2), 358–372.

Agras, W. S., Rossiter, E. M., Arnow, B., Schneider, J. A., Telch, C. F., Raeburn, S. D., et al. (1992). Pharmacologic and cognitive-behavioral treatment for bulimia nervosa: A controlled comparison. *American Journal of Psychiatry, 149,* 82–87.

Allen, J., & Allen, B. (1989). Stroking: Biological underpinnings and direct observations. *Transactional Analysis Journal, 19,* 26–31.

Al-Rashidi, B., & Brickell, J. (1998). *International Journal of Reality Therapy, 17* (2), 4–6.

American Psychiatric Association. (2000). *Diagnostic and statistical manual of mental disorders* (4th ed. Text Revision). Washington, DC: Author.

Anderson, E. M., & Lambert, M. J. (1995). Short-term dynamically oriented psychotherapy: A review and meta-analysis. *Clinical Psychology Review, 15*(6), 503–514.

Anderson, A. K., & Phelps, E. A. (2000). Expression without recognition: Contributions of the human amygdala to emotional communication. *Psychological Science, 11,* 106–111.

Ansbacker, H. L., & Ansbacker, R. R. (Eds.). (1956/1964). *The individual psychology of Alfred Adler: A systematic presentation in selections from his writings.* New York: Harper and Row.

Antonuccio, D. (1995). Psychotherapy for depression: No stronger medicine. *American Psychologist 50* (6), 450–452.

Arlow, J. A. (2002). Psychoanalysis. In R. J. Corsini & D. Wedding (Eds.). *Current psychotherapies* (6th ed., pp. 15–50). Itasca, IL: F. E. Peacock.

Arazoz, D. L. (1981). Negative self-hypnosis. *Journal of Contemporary Psychotherapy, 12,* 45–52.

Austad, C. S. (2009). *Counseling and psychotherapy today: Theory, practice, and research.* Boston: McGraw Hill.

Axelson, J. A. (1990). *Counseling and development in a multicultural society* (2nd ed.). Belmont, CA: Brooks/Cole.

Axelson, J. A. (1993). *Counseling and development in a multicultural society* (3rd ed.). Belmont, CA: Brooks/Cole.

Baldwin, A. C., Critelli, J. W., Stevens, L. C., & Russell, S. (1986). Androgyny and sex role measurement: A personal construct approach. *Journal of Personality and Social Psychology, 51,* 1081–1088.

Balint, M. P., Ornstein, P., & Balint, E. (1972). *Focal psychotherapy: An example of applied psychoanalysis.* London: Tavistock Publications.

Balthazard, C. G., & Woody, E. (1989). Bimodality, dimensionality, and the notion of hypnotic types. *International Journal of Clinical and Experimental Hypnosis, 37,* 70–89.

Bandura, A. (1985). Model of causality in social learning theory. In M. J. Mahoney & A. Freeman (Eds.). *Cognition and psychotherapy* (pp. 25–125). New York: Plenum.

Barabasz, A., & Barabasz, M. (1996). Neurotherapy and alert hypnosis in the treatment of attention deficit/hyperactivity disorder. In I. Kirsch & J. W. Rhue (Eds.). *Casebook of clinical hypnosis* (pp. 271–292). Washington, DC: American Psychological Association.

Barabasz, A., Barabasz, M., Jensen, S., Calvin, S., Trevisan, M., & Warner, D. (1999). Cortical event-related potentials show the structure of hypnotic suggestions is critical. *International Journal of Experimental Hypnosis, 47,* 5–22.

Barber, T. X. (1969). *Hypnosis: A scientific approach.* New York: Van Nostrand Reinhold. (Reprinted 1995, Northvale, NJ: Jason Aronson).

Barber, T. X. (1999). A comprehensive three-dimensional theory of hypnosis. In I. Kirsch, A. Capafons, E. Cardeña, & S. Amigo (Eds.). *Clinical hypnosis and self-regulation: Cognitive-behavioral perspectives* (pp. 3–14). Washington, DC: American Psychological Association.

Barber, T. X. (2000). A deeper understanding of hypnosis: Its secrets, its nature, its essence. *American Journal of Clinical Hypnosis, 42* (3)/42 (4), 208–272.

Bargh, J. A. (1994). The four horsemen of automaticity: Awareness, intention, efficiency, and control in social cognition. In R. S. Wyer and T. K. Srull (Eds.). *Handbook of social cognition* (2nd ed., pp. 1–40). Hillsdale, NJ: Erlbaum.

Bargh, J. A., & Barndollar, K. (1996). Automaticity in action: The unconscious as repository of chronic goals and motives. In P. M. Gollwitzer and J. A. Bargh (Eds.). *The psychology of action: Linking cognition and motivation to behavior,* pp. 457–481. New York: Guilford.

Bargh, J. A., & Gollwitzer, P. M. (1994). Environmental control of goal-oriented action: Automatic and strategic contingencies between situations and behavior. *Nebraska Symposium on Motivation, 41,* 71–124.

Barrett, D. (1990). Deep trance subjects: A schema of two distinct subgroups. In R. G. Kunzendorf (Ed.). *Mental imagery* (pp. 101–112). New York: Plenum Press.

Barrett, D. (1996). Fantasizers and dissociators: Two types of highly hypnotizables, two different imagery styles. In R. G. Kunzendorf, W. P. Spanos, & B. Wallace (Eds.). *Hypnosis and imagination* (pp. 123–135). Amityville, NY: Baywood.

Bartis, S. P., & Zamansky, H. S. (1990). Cognitive strategies in hypnosis: Toward resolving the hypnotic conflict. *International Journal of Clinical and Experimental Hypnosis, 38,* 168–182.

Bartlett, F. C. (1932). *Remembering.* New York: Columbia University Press.

Bauer, G., & Kobos, J. (1993). *Brief therapy: Short-term psychodynamic intervention.* Northvale, NJ: Aronson.
Bauer, S. R., Sapp, M., & Johnson, D. (2000). Group counseling for rural at-risk high school students. *The High School Journal, 83*(2), 41–50.
Beck, A. T. (1976). *Cognitive therapy and the emotional disorders.* New York: International University Press.
Beck, A. T., Freeman, A. (1990). *Cognitive therapy of personality disorders.* New York: Guilford Press.
Becker, J. (1987). *Behavior therapy.* Santa Monica, CA: Association for Advanced Training in Behavioral Sciences.
Beere, D. B. (1992). More on EMDR. *The Behavior Therapist, 15* (8), 179–180.
Bergin, A. E., & Garfield, S. C. (Eds.). (1994). *Handbook of psychotherapy and behavior change* (4th ed.). New York: Wiley.
Binder, J. C. (2004). *Key competencies in brief dynamic psychotherapy.* New York: The Guilford Press.
Bion, W. R. (1967). *Second Thoughts.* London: William Heinemann. (Reprinted London: Karnac Books 1984).
Bird, K. D. (2002). Confidence intervals for effect sizes in analysis of variance. *Educational and Psychological Measurement, 62,* 197–226.
Blackburn, I. M., Eunsun, K. M., & Bishop, S. (1986). *A two-year naturalistic follow-up of depressed patients treated with cognitive therapy, pharmacotherapy, and a combination of both.* Unpublished manuscript. Royal Edinburgh Hospital, Scotland.
Blaine, J., Herman, I., & Hole, A. (1989). Psychotherapy for opiate addicts: Does it help? *Arch Gen Psychiatry, 40*: 639–645.
Blanton, H., & Jaccard, J. (2006). Arbitrary metrics in psychology. *American Psychologist, 61*(1), 27–41.
Blatner, A. (2005). Psychodrama. In R. J. Corsini & D. Wedding (Eds.). *Current psychotherapies* (7th ed.). Belmont, CA: Thompson Brooks/Cole.
Bootzin, R. R., Bower, G. H., Zajonc, R. B., & Hall, E. (1986). *Psychology today: An introduction* (6th ed.). New York: Random House.
Bowlby, J. (1980). *Attachment and loss. Vol. 3. Loss: Sadness and depression.* New York: Basic Books.
Bretz-Joachim, H., Heekerens, H. P., & Schmitz, B. (1994). A meta-analysis of the effectiveness of Gestalt therapy. *Zeitschrift-fur-Klinische-Psychologie, Psychopathologie-und-Psychotherapie, 42*(3), 241–260.
Bugenthal, J. F. T. (Ed.). (1967). *Challenges of humanistic psychology.* New York: McGraw Hill.
Burnett, M. C., & Pulvino, C. J. (1990). Pro-tech, A multimodal group intervention for children with reluctance to use computers. *Elementary School Guidance and Counseling, 24,* 281–288.
Cain, D. J. (1986). Editorial: A call for the "right stuff." *Person-Centered Review, 1*(2), 117–124.
Cain, D. J. (1987). Carl R. Rogers: The man, his vision, his impact. *Person-Centered Review, 2*(3), 283–288.
Cain, D. J. (1990). Further thoughts about nondirective and client-centered therapy. *Person-Centered Review, 5*(1), 89–99.

Cain, D. J. (1993). The uncertain future of client-centered counseling. *Journal of Humanistic Education and Development, 31*(3), 133–138.

Cain, D. J. (2008). Person-centered therapy. In J. Frew & M. D. Spiegler (Eds.). *Contemporary psychotherapies for a diverse world.* Boston: Lahaska Press, Houghton Mifflin Company.

Cautela, J. R. (1967). *The token economy: A review and evaluation.* New York: Plenum Press.

Clark, D. M. (1989). Anxiety states: Panic and generalized anxiety. In K. Hawton, P. M. Salkovskis, J. Kirk, & D. M. Clark (Eds.). *Cognitive-behavior therapy for psychiatric problems: A practical guide* (pp. 52–96). New York: Oxford University Press.

Clarke, K., & Greenberg, L. (1986). Differential effects of the Gestalt two-chair intervention and problem-solving in resolving decisional conflict. *Journal of Counseling Psychology, 33*(1), 11–15.

Coe, W. C., & Sarbin, T. R. (1991). Role theory: Hypnosis from a dramaturgical and narrational perspective. In S. J. Lynn & J. W. Rhue (Eds.). *Theories of hypnosis: Current models and perspectives* (pp. 303–323). New York: Guilford Press.

Cohen, J. (1977). *Statistical power analysis for the behavioral sciences.* New York: Academic Press.

Cohen, J. (1988). *Statistical power analysis for the behavioral sciences.* (3rd ed). New York: Academic Press.

Connery, D. S. (1982). *The inner source: Exploring hypnosis with Dr. Herbert Spiegel.* New York: Holt, Rinehart, and Winston.

Corey, G. (2004). *Theory and practice of group counseling* (4th ed.). Pacific Grove, CA: Brooks/Cole.

Corey, G. (2007). *Theory and practice of group counseling* (5th ed.). Pacific Grove, CA: Brooks/Cole.

Corey, G. (2008). *Theory and practice of group counseling* (7th ed.). Pacific Grove, CA: Brooks/Cole.

Corey, G. (2009). *Theory and practice of group counseling* (8th ed.). Pacific Grove, CA: Brooks/Cole.

Cormier, S., Nurius, P. S., & Osborn, C. (2009). *Interviewing strategies for helpers: Fundamental skills and cognitive behavioral interventions* (6th ed.). Pacific Grove, CA: Brooks/Cole Publishing Company.

Corsini, R. J. (Eds.). (1977). *Current personality theories.* Itasca, IL: F. E. Peacock.

Corsini, R. J., & Wedding, D. (Eds.). (2008). *Current psychotherapies* (8th ed.). Itasca, IL: F. E. Peacock.

Crasilneck, H. B., & Hall, J. A. (1985). *Clinical hypnosis: Principles and application* (2nd ed.). Orlando, FL: Grune and Stratton, Inc.

Crawford, H. J., Kendel, T., & Vendemia, J. M .C. (1998). The nature of hypnotic analgesia: Neurophysiological foundation and evidence. *Contemporary Hypnosis, 15,* 22–23.

Crits-Christoph, P., & Barber, J. (1991). *Handbook of short-term dynamic psychotherapy.* New York: Basic Books.

Cummings, G., & Finch, S. (2005). Inference by eye: Confidence intervals and how to read pictures of data. *American Psychologist, 60*(2), 161–169.

Dasgupta, N., McGhee, D. E., Greenwald, A. G., & Banaji, M. R. (2000). Automatic preference for white Americans: Eliminating the familiarity explanation. *Journal of Experimental Social Psychology, 36* (3), 316–328.

Dattilio, F. M. (1994). Paradoxical intention as a proposed alternative in the treatment of panic disorders. *Journal of Cognitive Psychotherapy, 8* (1), 33.

Davanloo, H. (Ed.). (1979). *Short-term dynamic psychotherapy.* New York: Jason Aronson.

Davidson, P.R., & Parker, K. (2001). Eye movement desensitation and reprocessing (EMDR): a meta-analysis. *Journal of Clinical and Consulting Psychology.* 316. 69(2) 305.

Day, S. X. (2008). *Theory and design in counseling and psychotherapy* (2nd ed.). Boston: Houghton Mufflin.

Day, W. F. (1980). The historical antecedents of contemporary behaviorism, In R. W. Rieber & K. Salzinger (Eds.). *Psychology: Theoretical-historical perspectives* (pp. 203–262). New York: Academic Press.

Day, W. F. (1983). On the difference between radical and methodological behaviorism. *Behaviorism, 11,* 89–102.

Dixon, M., Brunet, A., & Laurence, J. R. (1990). Hypnotizability and automaticity: Toward a parallel distributed processing model of hypnotic responding. *Journal of Abnormal Psychology, 99,* 336–343.

Dixon, M., & Laurence, J. R. (1992). Hypnotic susceptibility and verbal automaticity: Automatic and strategic processing differences in the Stroop color-naming task. *Journal of Abnormal Psychology, 101,* 344–347.

Edmonston, W. F., Jr. (1981). *Hypnosis and relaxation: Modern verification of an old equation.* New York: Wiley.

Edwards, L., & Sapp, M. (2002). Reoperationalizing adaptive regression during hypnosis. *The Australian Journal of Clinical Hypnotherapy and Hypnosis, 23*(2), 115–129.

Elliot, R., Greenberg, L., & Lieter, G. (2004). Research on experiential psychotherapies. In M. Lambert (Ed.). *Bergin & Garfield' handbook on psychotherapy and behavior change* (5th ed.). New York: Wiley.

Ellis, A. (1993). Fundamentals of rational emotive therapy. In W. Dryden & L.K. Hill (Eds.) *Innovations in Rational-Emotive Therapy,* (pp 1-3). Newbury Park, CA: Sage.

Ellis, A., & Dryden, W. (1987). *The practice of rational emotive therapy.* New York: Springer.

Epstein, N. (1982). Cognitive therapy with couples. *American Journal of Family Therapy, 10,* 5–16.

Erickson, M. H. (1944). The method employed to formulate a complex story for the induction of an experimental neurosis in a hypnotic subject. *Journal of General Psychology, 31,* 67–84.

Erickson, M. H. (1958). Hypnosis in painful terminal illness. *American Journal of Clinical Hypnosis, 1,* 117–121.

Erickson, M. H. (1967). *Advanced techniques of hypnosis and therapy.* New York: Grune and Stratton.

Erickson, M. H. (1980). Hypnosis: A general review. In E. L. Rossi (Ed.). *The collect-*

ed papers of Milton H. Erickson on hypnosis (Vol. 3, pp. 13–20). New York: Irvington. (Original work published in 1941.)
Erickson, M. H., & Rossi, E. L. (1979). *Hypnotherapy: An exploratory casebook.* New York: Irvington.
Evanow, Mt. Sapp, M. (1998).
Fairburn, C. G., Jones, R., Peveler, R. C., Hope, R. A., & Doll, H. A. (1991). Three psychological treatment for bulimia nervosa: A comparison trial. *Archives of General Psychiatry, 48,* 463–469.
Fan, X., & Thompson, B. (2001). Confidence intervals about score reliability coefficients, please: An EPM guidelines editorial. *Educational and Psychological Measurement, 61,*(4) 517–531.
Farrell, W., Sapp, M., Johnson, J., & Pollard, D. (1994). Assessing college aspirations among at-risk high school students: A principal component analysis. *The High School Journal, 77* (4), 294–303.
Fish, J. M. (1992). EMDR workshop and openness. *The Behavior Therapist, 15*(8), 180.
Fisher, R. A. (1928). *Statistical methods for research workers* (2nd ed.). London: Olviver and Boyd.
Frank, J. D. (1986). What is psychotherapy? In S. Bloch (Ed.). *An introduction to psychotherapy* (pp. 5–45). New York: Oxford University Press.
Frankl, V. E. (1957). *Psychotherapy and existentialism: Selected papers on logotherapy.* New York: Simon & Schuster.
Frankl, V. E. (1959). *Man's search for meaning: An introduction to logotherapy.* New York: Washington Square Press.
Frankl, V. E. (1963). *Man's search for meaning.* Boston: Beacon.
Frankl, V. E. (1967). *The will to meaning: Foundations and applications of logotherapy.* New York: New American Library.
Frankl, V.E. (1969). *The Will To Meaning.* Boston: Beacon.
Freedman, L. D. (1993). TA tools for self-managing work teams. *Transactional Analysis Journal 23*(2), 104–109.
Freeman, A. (1990). Cognitive therapy. In A. S. Bellack & M. Hersen (Eds.). *Handbook of comparative treatments for adult disorders* (pp. 64–87). New York: Wiley.
Frew, J., & Spiegler, M. D. (2008). *Contemporary psychotherapies for a diverse world.* Boston: Lahaska Press, Houghton Mifflin Company.
Gambrill, D. K. (1994). Concepts and methods of behavioral treatment. In D. Granvold (Ed.). *Cognitive and behavioral treatment: Methods and applications* (pp. 33–57). Pacific Grove, CA: Brooks/Cole.
Garner, D. M., Rockett, W., Davis, R., Garner, M. V., Olmstead, M. P., & Eagle, M. (1993). Comparison of cognitive-behavioral and supportive-expressive therapy for bulimia nervosa. *American Journal of Psychiatry, 150,* 37–46.
Gendlin, E. T. (1986). What comes after traditional psychotherapy research? *American Psychologist, 41,* 131–136.
Germer, C. K. (2005). Mindfulness: What is it: What does it matter? In C. K. Germer, R. D. Siegel, & P. R. Fulton (Eds.). *Mindfulness and psychotherapy* (pp. 3–27. New York: Guilford Press.
Glass, G. V., & Hopkins, K. H. (1996). *Statistical methods in education and psychology*

(3rd ed.). Needham Heights, MA: Allyn Bacon.
Golden, W. L., Dowd, E. T., & Friedberg, F. (1987). *Hypnotherapy: A modern approach.* New York: Pergamon Press.
Granvold, D. K. (Ed.). (1994). *Cognitive and behavioral treatment: Methods and applications.* Pacific Grove, CA: Brooks/Cole Publishing Company.
Grave, J. L. (2004). *The race myth: Why we pretend race exists in America.* New York: Dutton.
Green, B., & Hall, J. (1984). Quantitative methods for literature review. *Annual Review of Psychology, 35,* 37–53.
Greenberg, E. (1989). Healing the borderline. *Gestalt Journal, 12,* 11–56.
Greenberg, L. (1980). An intensive analysis of recurring events from the practice of Gestalt therapy. *Psychotherapy: Therapy, Research and Practice, 17,* 143–152.
Greenberg, L., & Webster, M. (1982). Resolving decisional conflict by Gestalt two-chair dialogue relating process to outcome. *Journal of Counseling Psychology, 29*(5), 468–477.
Greenberg, J. R., & Mitchell, S. A. (1983). *Object relations and psychoanalytic theory.* Cambridge, MA: Harvard University Press.
Guidano, V. F. (1987). *Complexity of the self.* New York: Guilford Press.
Guidano, V. F., & Liotti, G. (1983). *Cognitive processes and emotional disorders.* New York: Guilford Press.
Hamburg, S. R. (2000). Antidepressants are not placebos. *American Psychologist, 55* (7), 761–762.
Hammond, D. C. (1992). *Hypnotic induction and suggestion: An introductory manual.* Des Plaines, IL: American Society of Clinical Hypnosis.
Harman, R. (1984). Gestalt therapy research. *Gestalt Journal, 7,* 61–69.
Hedges, L. (1982). Estimation of effects from a series of independent experimenters. *Psychological Bulletin, 92,* 490–499.
Heimberg, R. G. (1990). Cognitive-behavior therapy (for social phobia). In A. S. Bellack & M. Hersen (Eds.). *Comparative handbook of treatments for adult disorders* (pp. 203–218). New York: Wiley.
Hensel, C. S., Sapp, M., Farrell, W., & Hitchcock, K. (2001). A survey of members of ASCH, SCEH, and Division 30, and if they reported using hypnosis to treat depression. *Sleep and Hypnosis, 3*(4), 152–168.
Herrnstein, R. J., & Murray, C. A. (1994). *The bell curve: Intelligence and class structure in American life.* New York: Free Press.
Hilgard, E. R. (1973). A neodissociation interpretation of pain reaction in hypnosis. *Psychological Review, 80,* 396–411.
Hilgard, E. R. (1994). Neodissociation theory. In S. J. Lynn & J. W. Rhue (Eds.). *Dissociation: Clinical and theoretical perspectives* (pp. 83–104). New York: Guilford Press.
Huddleston, J. E., & Engles, D. W. (1986). Issue related to the use of paradoxical techniques in counseling. *Journal of Counseling and Human Service Professions, 1,* 127–133.
Hull, C. L. (1952). *A behavior system.* New Haven, CT: Yale University Press.
Hunter, J. E., & Schmidt, F. L. (1990). *Methods of meta-analysis: Correcting error in bias*

in research findings. Newbury Park, CA: Sage.

Iverson, G. L. (1994). Will the real behaviorism please stand up? *The Behavior Therapist, 17*(8), 191–194.

Ivey, A. E. (2002). *Intentional interviewing and counseling.* New York: Wadsworth.

Jacobson, E. (1938). *Progressive relaxation.* Chicago: University of Chicago Press.

James, R. K., & Gilliland, B. E. (2003). *Theories and strategies in counseling and psychotherapy* (5th ed.). Boston: Allyn and Bacon.

Joseph, B. (1989). *Psychic equilibrium and psychic change.* London: Routledge.

Kazdin, A. E., & Wilson, G. T. (1978). *Evaluation of behavior therapy: Issues, evidence, and research strategies.* Cambridge, MA: Ballinger.

Kelly, G. (1955). *The psychology of personal constructors* (Vols. 1–2). New York: Norton.

Kendall, P. C. (1992). *Anxiety disorders: Cognitive-behavioral interventions.* Needham Heights, MA: Allyn and Bacon.

Kendall, P. C., & Hammen, C. (1998). *Abnormal psychology: Understanding human problems* (2nd ed.). Boston, MA: Houghton Mifflin.

Keshen, A. (2006). A new look at existentional psychotherapy. *American Journal of Psychotherapy,* 60(3), 385-298

Kihslinger, D., & Sapp, M. (2006). Hypnosis and diabetes: Applications for children, adolescents, and adults. *The Australian Journal of Clinical Hypnotherapy and Hypnosis, 27*(1), 19–27.

King, B. J., & Council, J. R. (1998). Intentionality during hypnosis: An ironic process analysis. *The International Journal of Clinical and Experimental Hypnosis, 45,* 295–312.

Kipper, P. A., & Ritchie, T. D. (2003). The effectiveness of psychodramatic techniques: A meta-analysis. *Group Dynamic, 7,* 111–134.

Kirsch, I. (1997). Hypnotic involuntariness and the automaticity of everyday life. *American Journal of Clinical Hypnosis, 40,* 329–349.

Kirsch, I., Burgess, C. A., & Braffman, W. (1999). Attentional resources in hypnotic responding. *The International Journal of Clinical and Experimental Hypnosis, 47,* 175–191.

Kirsch, I., & Council, J. R. (1992). Situational and personality correlates of suggestibility. In E. Cromm & M. Nash (Eds.). *Contemporary hypnosis research* (pp. 267–292). New York: Guilford Press.

Kirsch, I., & Lynn, S. J. (1995a). The altered state of hypnosis: Changes in the theoretical landscape. *American Psychologist, 50*(10), 846–858.

Kirsch, I., & Lynn, S. J. (1995b). Social-cognitive alternatives to dissociation theories of hypnotic involuntariness. *Review of General Psychology, 2,* 66–80.

Kirsch, I., & Lynn, S. J. (1998). Dissociation theories of hypnosis. *Psychological Bulletin, 123,* 100–115.

Kirsch, I., & Lynn, S. J. (1999). Automaticity in clinical psychology. *American Psychologist, 54,* 504–515.

Kirsch, I., Montgomery, G., & Sapirstein, G. (1995). Hypnosis as an adjunct to cognitive behavioral psychotherapy: A meta-analysis. *Journal of Consulting and Clinical Psychology, 63,* 214–220.

Kirsch, J., & Sapp, M. (2000). Hypnotizability and inattention with college students.

The Australian Journal of Clinical Hypnotherapy and Hypnosis, 21, 13–38.

Kline, R. B. (2004). *Beyond significance testing: Reforming data analysis methods in behavioral research.* Washington, DC: American Psychological Association.

Kohut, H. (1977). *The restoration of the self.* International Universities Press.

Kroger, W. S. (1977). *Clinical and experimental hypnosis in medicine, dentistry, and psychology* (2nd ed.). Philadelphia: J. B. Lippincott Company.

Kroger, W. S., & Fezler, W. D. (1976). *Hypnosis and behavior modification: Imagery conditioning.* Philadelphia: Lippincott.

Lambert, M.J., & Bergin, A.E. (1994). *The Effectiveness of Psychotherapy.* In A.E. Bergin & S.L. Garfeild (Eds.), Handbook of Psychotherapy and Behavior Change (4th ed., pp. 143-189). New York: Wiley.

Lancaster, B. P. (1999). Defining and interpreting suppressor effects: Advantages and limitations. In B. Thompson (Ed.). *Advances in social science methodology,* (Vol. 5, pp. 139–148). Stamford, CT: JAI Press.

Laurence, J. R., & Perry, C. (1983). Hypnotically created pseudomemories among highly hypnotizable subjects. *Science, 222,* 523–524.

Lazarus, A. A. (1976). *Multimodal behavior therapy.* New York: Springer.

Lazarus, A. A. (1980). *Multimodal life history questionnaire.* Champaign, IL: Research Press.

Lazarus, A. A. (1986). Treating agoraphobia: Behavioral/multimodal perspectives. *Psychotherapy in Private Practice, 4,* 11–23.

Lazarus, A. A. (1989a). Brief psychotherapy: The multimodal model. *Psychology – A Journal of Human Behavior, 26*(1), 6–10.

Lazarus, A. A. (1989b). The case of George. In D. Wedding & R. J. Corsini (Eds.). *Case studies in psychotherapy* (pp. 227–238). Itasca, IL: F. E. Peacock.

Lazarus, A. A. (1989c). *The practice of multimodal therapy.* Baltimore: Johns Hopkins University.

Lazarus, A. A. (1992). The multimodal approach to the treatment of depression. *American Journal of Psychotherapy, 46*(1), 50–57.

Lazarus, A. A. (1995). Multimodal therapy. In R. J. Corsini & D. Wedding (Eds.). *Current psychotherapies* (pp. 503–544). Itasca, IL: F. E. Peacock.

Leahy, R. L. (2003). *Cognitive therapy techniques: A practitioner's guide.* New York: Guilford.

Leiper, R., & Maltby, M. (2004). *The psychodynamic approach to therapeutic change.* London: Sage.

Libet, B. (1985). Unconscious cerebral initiative and the role of conscious will in voluntary action. *Behavioral and Brain Sciences, 8,* 529–566.

Linehan, M. M., Dimeff, L., & Reynolds, S. K. (2002). Dialectical behavior therapy versus comprehensive validation therapy plus 12-step for the treatment of opioid dependent women meeting criteria for borderline personality disorder. *Drug and Alcohol Dependence, 67* (1), 13–26.

Linehan, M. (1993). Dialectical behavior therapy for the borderline personality disorder: Theory and method. *Bulletin of the Menninger Clinic, 5*(3), 261–276.

Luborsky, E. B., O'Reilly-Landry, M., & Arlow, J. (2008). Psychoanalysis In R. J. Corsini & D. Wedding (2008). *Current psychotherapies* (8th ed.). Itasca, IL: F. E. Peacock.

Lynn, S. J. (1992). A non-state of hypnotic involuntariness. *Contemporary Hypnosis, 9,*

21–27.

Lynn, S. J., & Kirsch, I. (1993). Cognitive-behavioral hypnotherapy. In J. W. Rhue, S. J. Lynn & I. Kirsch (Eds.). *Handbook of clinical hypnosis,* pp. 439–466.

Lynn, S. J., & Rhue, J. W. (1991). *Theories of hypnosis: Current models and perspectives.* New York: Guilford Press.

Lynn, S. J., & Rhue, J. W. (Eds.). (1994). *Dissociation: Clinical and theoretical perspectives.* New York: Guilford Press.

Malan, D. (1963). *A study of brief psychotherapy.* New York: Plenum.

Malan, D. (1976). *Frontier of brief psychotherapy.* New York: Plenum.

Mann, J. (1973). *Time-limited psychotherapy.* Cambridge, MA: Harvard University Press.

Mann, J., & Goldman, R. (1982). *A casebook in time-limited psychotherapy.* New York: McGraw-Hill.

Maples, M. F. (1995). Gestalt theory. In D. Capuzzi & D. R. Gross (Eds.). *Counseling and psychotherapy: Theories and interventions* (pp. 267–295). Englewood Cliffs, NJ: Merrill.

Marger, M. N. (2000). *Race and ethnic relations: American and global perspectives* (5th ed.). Belmont, CA: Wadsworth/Thomson Learning.

Marger, M. N. (2003). *Race and ethnic relations: American and global perspectives* (6th ed.). Belmont, CA: Wadsworth/Thomson Learning.

Marziali, E., Marmar, C., & Krupnick, J. (1981). Therapeutic alliance scales: Development and relationship to psychotherapy outcome. *American Journal of Psychiatry, 138,* 361–364.

Maslow, A. (1968). *Towards a psychology of being* (2nd ed.). New York: Nostrand.

Maslow, A. (1970). *Motivation and personality* (Rev. ed.). New York: Harper and Row.

Maslow, A. (1971). *The further reaches of human nature.* New York: Viking.

Masson, J. (1984). Freud and the seduction theory. *The Atlantic, 253* (2), 33–60.

May, R., & Yalom, I. D. (1995). Existential psychotherapy. In R. J. Corsini & D. Wedding (Eds.). *Contemporary psychotherapies* (5th ed.). Itasca, IL: F. E. Peacock.

McMillan, M. (2004). T*he Person-centered approach to therapeutic change.* London: Sage.

Meichenbaum, D. (1994). *A clinical handbook/practical therapist manual for assessing and treating adults with post-traumatic stress disorder (PTSD).* Waterloo, Ontario: Institute Press.

Miller, N.E. and Dollard, J. (1941). Social learning and imitation. New Haven: Yale University Press.

Milner, M. (1987). *The suppressed madness of sane men.* London: Routledge.

Milton, J., Polmear, C., & Fabricious, J. (2004). *A short introduction to psychoanalysis.* Thousand Oaks, CA: Sage Publications.

Mitchell, S. A. (1998). The analyst's knowledge and authority. *Psychoanalytic Quarterly, 67,* 1–31.

Munuchin, S. (1974). *Families and family therapy.* New York: Basic Books.

Nash, M. R. (1987). What, if anything, is regressed about hypnotic age regression? A review of the empirical literature. *Psychological Bulletin, 102,* 42–52.

Norman, D. A., & Shallice, T. (1986). Attention to action: Willed and automatic control of behavior. In R. J. Davidson & G. E. Schwartz, *Consciousness and self-regu-*

lation, 4, 1–18. New York: Plenum Press.

Nosek, B. A., & Banaji, M. R. (2003). Understanding and using the implicit association test: I. An improved scoring algorithm. *Journal of Personality and Social Psychology, 85*(2), 197–216.

Opalic, P. (1989). Existential and psychopathological evaluation of group psychotherapy of neurotic and psychotic patients. *International Journal of Group Psychotherapy, 39,* 389–411.

Orne, M. T. (1959). The nature of hypnosis: Artifact and essence. *Journal of Abnormal and Social Psychology, 58,* 277–299.

Orne, M. T. (1979). On the simulating subject as a quasi-control group in hypnosis research: What, why, and how. In E. Fromm & R. E. Shor, (Eds.). *Hypnosis: Developments in research and new perspectives* (2nd ed., pp. 519–565). Chicago, Aldine.

Paivio, S. C., & Greenberg, L. S. (1995). Resolving "unfinished business": Efficacy of experiential therapy using empty-chair dialogue. *Journal of Consulting and Clinical Psychology, 63*(3), 419–425.

Parrot, C. A., & Hawes, J.L. (1991). The application of cognitive therapy to post-traumatic stress disorder. In T.M. Vallis, J.L. Hawes, & P.C. Miller (Eds.), The challange of cognitive therapy: Apllications to non-traditional populations (pp. 85-109). New York: Plenum Press.

Pashler, H. E. (1998). *The psychology of attention.* Cambridge, MA: The MIT Press.

Paul, G. L. (1967). Outcome research in psychotherapy. *Journal of Consulting Psychotherapy, 31,* 109–188.

Pedhazur, E. J. (1997). *Multiple regression in behavioral research: Explanation and prediction* (3rd ed.). Fort Worth, TX: Hartcourt Brace College Publishers.

Pekala, R. J., Kumar, V. K., & Marcano, G. (1995). Hypnotic types: A partial replication concerning phenomenal experience. *Contemporary Hypnosis, 12,* 194–200.

Perls, F. S. (1948). Theory and technique of personality integration. *American Journal of Psychotherapy, 2,* 572–573.

Perls, F. S. (1969a). *Gestalt therapy verbatim.* Moab, UT: Real People Press.

Perls, F. S. (1969b). *In and out of the garbage pail.* Moab, UT: Real People Press.

Perls, F. S. (1970). Four lectures. In J. Fagan & I. Shepard (Eds.). *Gestalt therapy now* (pp. 14–38). Palo Alto, CA: Science and Behavior Books.

Perls, F. S. (1973). *The Gestalt approach.* Palo Alto, CA: Science and Behavior Books.

Perls, F. S., Hefferline, R. F., & Goodman, P. (1951). *Gestalt therapy.* New York: Julian Press.

Polster, E., & Polster, M. (1973). *Gestalt therapy integrated.* New York: Brunner/Mazel.

Polster, M. (1987). Gestalt therapy: Evolution and application. In J. V. Zeig (Ed.). *The evolution of psychotherapy* (pp. 312–325). New York: Brunner/Mazel.

Piaget, J. (1926). *The language and thought of the child.* New York: Harcourt, Brace.

Piccione, C., Hilgard, E. R., & Zimbardo, P. G. (1989). On the degree of stability of measured hypnotizability over a 25-year period. *Journal of Personality and Social Psychology, 56,* 289–295.

Pitsch, E., Sapp, M., & McNeely, R. L. (2001). Effects of locus of control, hypnotizability, transcript type, and gender on vividness of imagination, hypnotic depth, and inner subjective experiences of automaticity. *The Australian Journal of Clinical*

Hypnotherapy and Hypnosis, 22(1), 1–10.
Premack, D. (1959). Toward empirical behavioral laws: In psychological reinforcement. *Psychological Review, 66,* 219–233.
Puk, G. (1994). EMDR: The utility of clinical observation. *The Behavior Therapist, 17*(8), 201.
Radtke, L., Sapp, M., & Farrell, W. C. (1997). Reality therapy: A meta-analysis. *International Journal of Reality Therapy, 17*(1), 4–9.
Raskin, N. J., & Rogers, C. R. (2005). Person-centered therapy. In R. Corsini & D. Wedding (Eds.). *Current psychotherapies* (7th ed.). Belmont, CA: Thomson, Brooks/Cole.
Raskin, N. J., Rogers, C. R., & Witty, M. C. (2008). Person-centered therapy. In R. Corsini & D. Wedding (Eds.). *Current psychotherapies* (8th ed.). Belmont, CA: Thomson, Brooks/Cole.
Ray, W. L., & Oathes, D. (2003). Brain imaging techniques. *International Journal of Clinical and Experimental Hypnosis, 51*(2), 97–104.
Raz, A., & Shapiro, T. (2002). Hypnosis and neuroscience: A cross talk between clinical and cognitive research. *Archives of General Psychiatry, 59,* 85–90.
Rescorla, R. A. (1988). Pavlovian conditioning: It's not what you think it is. *American Psychologist, 43,* 151–160.
Rhue, J. W., Lynn, S. J., & Kirsch, I. (Eds.). (1993). *Handbook of clinical hypnosis.* Washington, DC: American Psychological Association.
Rogers, C. R. (1942). *Counseling and psychotherapy.* Boston: Houghton Mifflin.
Roger, C. R. (1951). *Client-centered therapy: Its current practice, implications, and theory.* Boston: Houghton Mifflin.
Roger, C. R. (1957). The necessary and sufficient conditions of therapeutic personality change. *Journal of Counseling Psychology, 21,* 95–103.
Rogers, C. R. (1961). *On becoming a person.* Boston: Houghton Mifflin.
Rogers, C. R. (1980). *A way of being.* Boston: Houghton Mifflin.
Rogers, C. R. (1983). *Freedom to learn of the '80s.* Columbus, OH: Charles E. Merrill.
Rogers, C. R. (1986). Measuring the self and its changes: A forward step in research. *Archives of Humanistic Psychology,* 1–13.
Rosen, G. M. (1992). A note to EMDR critics: What you didn't see is only part of what you don't get. *The Behavior Therapist, 15*(9), 216.
Rosenfeld, H. (1987). *Impasse and interpretation: Therapeutic and anti-therapeutic factors in psychoanalytic treatment of psychotic, borderline, and neurotic patients.* London: Tavistock Publications, Ltd.
Rosenthal, R. (1984). *Meta-analytic procedures for social research.* Beverly Hills, CA: Sage.
Rosenthal, R., & Rosnow, R. L. (1984). *Understanding behavioral science.* New York: McGraw-Hill.
Rotter, J. B. (1966). Generalized expectancies for internal locus of control reinforcement. *Psychological Monographs, 80,* (1–28, whole No. 609).
Ryckman, R. M. (1998). *Theories of personality* (4th ed.). Pacific Grove, CA: Brooks/Cole.
Sandler, J. (1987). *From safety to superego.* London: Karnac.

Sapp, M. (1990). Psychoeducational correlates of junior high school at-risk students. *The High School Journal, 73*(4), 232–234.
Sapp, M. (1991). Hypnotherapy and test anxiety: Two cognitive-behavioral constructs. *The Australian Journal of Clinical Hypnotherapy and Hypnosis, 12*(1), 25–33.
Sapp, M. (1992a). The effects of hypnosis in reducing test anxiety and improving academic achievement in college students. *The International Journal of Professional Hypnosis, 6*(1), 20–22.
Sapp, M. (1992b). Relaxation and hypnosis in reducing anxiety and stress. *The Australian Journal of Clinical Hypnotherapy and Hypnosis, 13*(2), 39–55.
Sapp, M. (1993). *Test anxiety: Applied research, assessment, and treatment interventions.* Lanham, MD: University Press of America.
Sapp, M. (1994a). Cognitive-behavioral counseling: Applications for African American middle school students who are academically at-risk. *Journal of Instructional Psychology, 21*(2), 161–171.
Sapp, M. (1994b). The effects of guided imagery in reducing the worry and emotionality components of test anxiety. *Journal of Mental Imagery, 18* (3 & 4), 165–180.
Sapp, M. (1995). Hypnosis: Applications for clients with physical disabilities who are seeking supported employment. *The Australian Journal of Clinical Hypnotherapy and Hypnosis, 16*(1), 1–8.
Sapp, M. (1996a). Irrational beliefs that can lead to academic failure for African American middle school students who are academically at-risk. *Journal of Rational-Emotive and Cognitive-Behavior Therapy, 14*(2), 123–134.
Sapp, M. (1996b). Potential negative sequelae of hypnosis. *The Australian Journal of Clinical Hypnotherapy and Hypnosis, 17*(2), 72–77.
Sapp, M. (1996c). Three treatments for reducing the worry and emotionality components of test anxiety with undergraduate and graduate college students: Cognitive-behavioral hypnosis, relaxation therapy, and supportive counseling. *Journal of College Student Development, 37*(1), 79–87.
Sapp, M. (1997a). *Counseling and psychotherapy: Theories, associated research, and issues.* Lanham, MD: University Press of America.
Sapp, M. (1997b). Hypnotizability scales: What are they, and are they useful? *The Australian Journal of Clinical Hypnotherapy and Hypnosis, 17*(11), 25–32.
Sapp, M. (1997c). Order effects for two measures of hypnotizability. *Perceptual and Motor Skills, 85*(3), 1042.
Sapp, M. (1997d). Theories of hypnosis. *The Australian Journal of Clinical Hypnotherapy and Hypnosis, 18,* 43–54.
Sapp, M. (1999). *Test anxiety: Applied research, assessment, and treatment interventions* (2nd ed.). Lanham, MD: University Press of America.
Sapp, M. (2000). *Hypnosis, dissociation, and absorption: Theories, assessment, and treatment.* Springfield, IL: Charles C Thomas Publishers.
Sapp, M. (2002a). *Psychological and educational test scores: What are they?* Springfield, IL: Charles C Thomas Publishers.
Sapp, M. (2002b). Implications of Barber's three dimensional theory of hypnosis. *Sleep and Hypnosis, 4*(2), 70–76.
Sapp, M. (2004a). *Cognitive-behavioral theories of counseling: Traditional and nontradi-*

tional approaches. Springfield, IL: Charles C Thomas Publishers.

Sapp, M. (2004c). Confidence intervals with in hypnosis research. *Sleep and Hypnosis,* 6 (4), 169-176.

Sapp, M. (2004b). Hypnosis: Applications for academically at-risk African American high school student. *Sleep and Hypnosis, 6*(2), 93–99.

Sapp, M. (2008). The effect sizes r and d in hypnosis research. *European Journal of Clinical Hypnosis,* 8(1), 48-59.

Sapp, M. (2006a). Psychological issues with multicultural education. *Multicultural Learning and Teaching, 1*(2), 2.

Sapp, M. (2006b). Counseling At-Risk Youths. *The Counseling Psychologist, 30*(1), 1–10.

Sapp, M. (2006) *Basic psychological measurement, research design, and statistics without math.* Springfield, IL: Charles C Thomas Publisher.

Sapp, M., Durand, H., & Farrell, W. (1995). Measures of actual test anxiety in educationally and economically disadvantaged college students. *College Student Journal, 29*(1), 65–72.

Sapp, M., & Evanow, M. (1998). Hypnotizability: Absorption and dissociation. *The Australian Journal of Clinical Hypnotherapy and Hypnosis, 19*(1), 1–8.

Sapp, M., Farrell, W., & Durand, H. (1995a). The effects of mathematics, reading, and writing tests in producing worry and emotionality test anxiety with economically and educationally disadvantaged college students. *College Student Journal, 29*(1), 122–125.

Sapp, M., Farrell, W., & Durand, H. (1995b). Cognitive-behavioral therapy: Applications for African-American middle school at-risk students. *Journal of Instructional Psychology, 22*(2), 169–177.

Sapp, M., Farrell, W., Hitchcock, K., & Johnson, J. (1999). Attitudes on rape among African American male and female college students. *Journal of Counseling and Development, 77*(2), 204–208.

Sapp, M., Farrell, W., Johnson, J., & Ioannidis, G. (1997). Utilizing the PK Scale of the MMPI-2 to detect posttraumatic stress disorder in college students. *Journal of Clinical Psychology, 53*(8), 1–6.

Sapp, M., Farrell, W., Johnson, J., Kirby, R. S., & Pumphrey, K. (1997). Hypnosis: Applications for rehabilitation counselors. *Journal of Applied Rehabilitation Counseling, 28*(2), 31–37.

Sapp, M., & Hitchcock, K. (2001). Harvard group scale with African American college students. *Sleep and Hypnosis, 3*(3), 111–117.

Sapp, M., & Hitchcock, K. (2003a). Creative imagination, absorption, and dissociation with African American college students. *Sleep and Hypnosis, 5*(2), 90–99.

Sapp, M., & Hitchcock, K. (2003b). Measuring dissociation and hypnotizability with African American college students: A new dissociation scale – the general dissociation scale. *Australian Journal of Clinical Hypnotherapy and Hypnosis, 24*(1), 14–22.

Sapp, M., Ioannidis, G., & Farrell, W. C. (1995). Posttraumatic stress disorder, imaginative involvement, hypnotic susceptibility, anxiety, and depression. *The*

Australian Journal of Clinical Hypnotherapy and Hypnosis, 16(2), 75–87.

Sapp, M., McNeely, R. L., & Torres, J. B. (1998). Death and dying of aged African Americans. *Journal of Human Behavior in the Social Environment, 1*(2/3), 229–315.

Sapp, M., Torres J. B., & McNeely, R. L. (2007). Dying a "good" death, the desire to die, and rational-emotive behavior therapy: Focus on aged African Americans and Hispanics/Latinos: Focus on aged African Americans and Latinos. In L. A. See (Eds.). *Human behavior in the social environment from an African American perspective.* pp. 695–713 (2nd ed.). Binghamton, NY: Haworth Press.

Sapp, M., McNeely, R. L., & Torres, J. B. (2007). Hypnotherapy: A useful modality for serving African American and Latino Clients and Patients. In L. A. See (Eds.). *Human behavior in the social environment from an African American perspective.* pp. 677–693 (2nd ed.). Binghamton, NY: Haworth Press.

Sapp, M., Obiakor, F. E., Gregas, A., & Scholze, S. (2007). Mahalanobis Distance: A multivariate measure of effect in hypnosis research. *Sleep and Hypnosis 9*(2), 67–70.

Sarason, I. G. (1984). Stress, anxiety, and cognitive interference: Reactions to test. *Journal of Personality and Social Psychology, 46,* 929–938.

Sarbin, T. R. (1998). Hypnosis as a conversation: "Believed in imaginings" revisited. *Contemporary Hypnosis, 14,* 203–215.

Sarbin, T. R. (1999). *Believed-in imaginings: The narrative construction of reality* (pp. 15–30). Washington, DC: American Psychological Association.

Sarbin, T. R., & Coe, W. C. (1972). *A social hypnosis psychological analysis of influence communication.* New York: Holt, Rinehart, & Winston.

Scholze, S., & Sapp, M. (2006). Understanding test anxiety and the multicultural learner. *Multicultural Learning and Teaching, 1*(2), 12–23.

Segal, H. (1981) *The work of Hanna Segal: A Kleinian approach to clinical practice.* London: Jason Aronson.

Seligman, M. E. P. (1975). *Helplessness: On depression, development, and death.* San Francisco: W. H. Freeman.

Shapiro, F. (1989). Efficacy of the eye movement of desensitization procedure in the treatment of traumatic memories. *Journal of Traumatic Stress, 2,* 199–223.

Shapiro, F. (1991). Eye movement desensitization and reprocessing procedure: From EMD to EMD/R – A new treatment model for anxiety and related traumata. *The Behavior Therapist, 12,* 133–135.

Shapiro, F. (1994). EMDR: In the eye of a paradigm shift. *The Behavior Therapist, 17*(7), 153–155.

Shapiro, F. (2001). *Eye movement desensitization and reprocessing: Basic principles, protocols, and procedures* (2nd ed.). New York: Guilford Press.

Sharf, R. S. (2004). *Theories of psychotherapy and counseling: Concepts and cases* (3rd ed.). Pacific Grove, CA: Thomson Brooks/Cole.

Sharf, R. S. (2008). *Theories of psychotherapy and counseling: Concepts and cases* (4th ed.). Pacific Grove, CA: Thomson Brooks/Cole.

Sharf, R. S. (2009). *Applying career development theory to counseling* (5th ed.). Pacific Grove, CA: Thomson Brooks/Cole.

Sheehan, P. W., & McConkey, U. M. (1982). *Hypnosis and experience: The exploration of phenomena and process.* Hillsdale, NJ: Erlbaum.

Shor, R. E. (1959). Hypnosis and concept of the generalized reality orientation. *American Journal of Psychotherapy, 13,* 582–602.

Siegel, S. (1983). Classical conditioning, drug tolerance and drug dependence. In Y. Israel & F. B. Smart (Eds.). *Research advances in alcohol and drug problems* (pp. 207–246). New York: Plenum.

Siegel, S. (1984). Pavlovian conditioning and heroin overdose: Report by overdose victims. *Bulletin of Psychonomic Society, 22,* 428–430.

Sifneos, P. (1972). *Short-term psychotherapy and emotional crisis.* Cambridge, MA: Harvard University Press.

Sifneos, P. (1979). *Short-term dynamic psychotherapy: Evaluation and technique.* New York: Plenum Press.

Silver, S.M., Rogers, S. & Russell, M. (2008). Eye movement desensitization and reprocessing (EMDR) in treatment of war veterans. *Journal of Clinical Psychology,* 64 (8), 947-957.

Skinner, B. F. (1974). *About behaviorism.* New York: Knopf.

Skinner, B. F. (1987). Whatever happened to psychology as the science of behavior? *American Psychology, 42*(8), 780–786.

Skinner, B. F. (1988a). The operant side of behavior therapy. *Journal of Behavior Therapy and Experimental Psychiatry, 19,* 171–179.

Skinner, B. F. (1988b). Reply to Harnard. In A. C. Catania & S. Harnard (Eds.). *The selection of behavior: The operant behaviorism of B. F. Skinner: Comments and consequences* (pp. 468–473). Cambridge: Cambridge University Press.

Sloane, R. B., Staples, F. R., Cristol, A. H., Yorkston, N. J., & Whippler, K. (1975). *Psychotherapy versus behavior therapy.* Cambridge, MA: Harvard University Press.

Smith, C. L., Sapp, M., Farrell, W., & Johnson, J. H. (1998). Psychoeducational correlates of achievement for high school seniors at a private school: The relationship among locus of control, esteem, academic achievement, and academic self-esteem. *The High School Journal, 81*(3), 161–167.

Smith, M. L., Glass, G. V., & Miller, T. I. (1980). *The benefits of psychotherapy.* Baltimore: Johns Hopkins Press.

Smithson, M. (2001). Correct confidence intervals for various regression effect sizes and parameters: The importance of noncentralized distributions in computing intervals. *Educational and Psychological Measurement, 61,* 605–632.

Smithson, M. (2003). *Confidence intervals.* Thousand Oaks, CA: Sage Publications.

Symth, L. (1999). *Overcoming post-traumatic stress disorder: A cognitive-behavioral exposure-based protocol for the treatment for PTSD and the other anxiety disorders.* Oakland, CA: New Harbinger Publication.

Spanos, N. P. (1986). Hypnotic behavior: A social psychological interpretation of amnesia, analgesia and "trance logic." *Behavioral and Brain Sciences, 9,* 489–497.

Spanos, N. P. (1991). A sociocognitive approach to hypnosis. In S. J. Lynn & J. W. Rhue (Eds.). *Theories of hypnosis: Current models and perspectives* (pp. 324–361). New York: Guilford Press.

Spanos, N. P. (1997). *Multiple identities and false memories: A sociocognitive perspective.* Washington, DC: American Psychological Association.

Spanos, N. P., & Chaves, J. F. (Eds.). (1989). *Hypnosis: The cognitive-behavioral perspective.* Buffalo, NY: Prometheus Books.

Spiegel, H., & Connery, D. J. (1982). *The inner source: Exploring hypnosis with Dr. Herbert Spiegel.* New York: Holt, Rinehart, and Winston.

Spiegler, M. D., & Guevremont, D. C. (2003). *Contemporary behavior therapy* (4th ed.). Belmont, CA: Wadsworth.

Spielberger, C. D., & Vagg, P. R. (Eds.). (1995). *Test anxiety: Theory, assessment, and treatment.* Washington, DC: Taylor and Francis.

Stampfl, T. G., & Levis, D. J. (1967). Essentials of implosive therapy: A learning-theory-based psychodynamic behavior therapy. *Journal of Abnormal Psychology, 72,* 496–503.

Steiger, J. H., & Fouladi, R. T. (1997). Noncentrality interval estimation and the evaluation of statistical models. In L. Harlow, S. Malaik, & J. H. Steiger (Eds.). *What if there were no significance tests?* (pp. 222–257). Hillside, NJ: Lawrence Erlbaum Associates.

Stern, D. (2004). *The present moment in psychotherapy and everyday life.* New York: Norton.

Stevens, J. P. (1980). Power of the multivariate analysis of variance tests. *Psychological Bulletin, 88,* 728–737.

Stevens, J. P. (1984). Outliers and influential data points in regression analysis. *Psychological Bulletin, 95,* 334–344.

Stevens, J. P. (1999). *Intermediate statistics: A modern approach.* Mahwah, NJ: Lawrence Erlbaum Associates.

Stevens, J. P. (2002). *Applied multivariate statistics for the social sciences* (4th ed.). Mahwah, NJ: Lawrence Erlbaum.

Stevens, M. J., & Morris, S. J. (1995). A format for case conceptualization. *Counselor Education and Supervision, 35,* 82–94.

Strumpfel, U. (2004). Research on Gestalt therapy. *International Gestalt Journal, 27,* 9–54.

Strumfel, U., & Goldman, R. (2001). Contacting Gestalt therapy. In D. Cain & J. Seeman (Eds.). *Humanistic psychotherapies: Handbook on research and practice.* Washington: American Psychological Association.

Sue, D. W., & Sue, D. (1990). *Counseling and the culturally different* (2nd ed.). New York: John Wiley and Sons.

Suinn, R. M. (2001). The terrible twos – anger and anxiety: Hazardous to your health. *American Psychologist, 56* (1), 27–36.

Suinn, R. M., & Richardson, F. (1971). Anxiety management training: A nonspecific behavior therapy program for anxiety control. *Behavior Therapy, 2,* 498–510.

Sweet, A. A. (1995). Clinical notebook: A theoretical perspective on the clinical use of EMDR. *The Behavior Therapist, 18*(1), 5.

Tellegen, A., & Atkinson, G. (1974). Openness to absorbing and self-altering experiences ("absorption"), a trait related to hypnotic susceptibility. *Journal of Abnormal Psychology, 83,* 268–277.

Thompson, B. (1992). Two and one-half decades of leadership in measurement and evaluation. *Journal of Counseling and Development, 70,* 434–438.

Thompson, B. (2002). "Statistical," "practical," and "clinical:" How many kind of significance do counselors need to consider? *Journal of Counseling and Development, 80,* 64–71.

Thorne, G. (1992). *Carl Rogers.* Newbury Park, CA: Sage.

Van Den Hout, M., & Merckelbach, H. (1991). Classical conditioning: Still going strong. *Behavioral Psychotherapy, 19,* 59–79.

Van Deurzen-Smith, E. (1988). *Existential Counselling in Practice.* London: Sage.

Vogt, W. P. (1999). *Dictionary of statistics and methodology: A nontechnical guide for the social sciences.* Thousand Oaks, CA: Sage Publications.

Wagstaff, G. F. (1981). *Hypnosis, compliance and belief.* New York: St. Martin's Press.

Wagstaff, G. F. (1991). Compliance, belief, and semantic in hypnosis: A nonstate sociocognitive perspective. In S. J. Lynn & J. W. Rhue (Eds.). *Theories of hypnosis: Current models and perspectives* (pp. 362–396). New York: Guilford Press.

Wallace, W. A. (1993). *Theories of personality.* Needham Heights, MA: Allyn and Bacon.

Wang, Z., & Thompson, B. (2007). Is the Pearson r^2 biased, and if so, what is the best correction formula? *Journal of Experimental Education, 75*(2), 109–125.

Watson, J. B. (1930). *Behaviorism* (Rev. ed.). New York: Norton.

Wegner, D., & Wheatly, T. (1999). Apparent mental causation: Sources of the experience of will. *American Psychologist, 54,* 480–492.

Wester, W. C. (1987). *Clinical hypnosis: A case management approach.* Cincinnati, OH: Behavior Science Center, Inc. Publications.

Wiener, N. (1948). *Cybernetics.* New York: Wiley.

Winnicott, D. W. (1958). *Collected papers: Through pediatrics to psychoanalysis.* London: Tavistock Publications.

Winnicott, D. W. (1965). *The Family and Individual Development.* London: Tavistock Publications.

Wilson, S. C., & Barber, T. X. (1981/1983). The fantasy-prone personality: Implications for understanding imagery, hypnosis, and parapsychological phenomena. In A. A. Sheikh (Ed.). *Imagery: Current theory, research, and applications* (pp. 340–387). New York: Wiley.

Wilson, T. G. (1989). Behavior Therapy. In R. J. Corsini & D. Wedding (Eds.). *Current psychotherapies* (4th ed., pp. 241–284). Itasca, IL: F. E. Peacock Publishers, Inc.

Wolf, F. M. (1986). *Meta-analysis: Quantitative methods for research synthesis.* Beverly Hills, CA: Sage.

Wolpe, J. (1958). *Psychotherapy by reciprocal inhibition.* Stanford, CA: Stanford University Press.

Wolpe, J. (1973). *The practice of behavior therapy.* New York: Pergamon Press.

Wolpe, J. (1982). *The practice of behavior therapy.* (3rd ed.). New York: Pergamon Press.

Wolpe, J. (1997). Commentary on "Beyond the Efficacy Ceiling": Responses to an irrelevant subtitle. *Behavior Therapy, 28*(4), 613–615.

Woody, E., & Bowers, K. S. (1994). A frontal assault on dissociated control. In S. J. Lynn & J. W. Rhue (Eds.). *Dissociation: Clinical, theoretical and research perspectives* (pp. 52–79). New York: Guilford Press.

Woody, E., & Farvolden, P. (1998). Dissociation in hypnosis and frontal executive function. *American Journal of Clinical Hypnosis, 40,* 206–216.

Woody, E., & Sadler, P. (1998). On reintegrating dissociated theories: Comment on Kirsh and Lynn. *Psychological Bulletin, 123,* 192–197.

Yalom, I. D., & Lieberman, M. A. (1991). Bereavement and heightened existential awareness. *Psychiatry, 54,* 334–345.

Yontef, G. M., & Simkin, J. S. (1987). Gestalt therapy. In R. J. Corsini & D. Wedding (Eds.). *Current psychotherapies* (2nd ed.). Itasca, IL: F. R. Peacock.

Yontef, G. M., & Simkin, J. S. (1988). Gestalt therapy. In R. J. Corsini & D. Wedding (Eds.). *Current psychotherapies* (3rd ed.). Itasca, IL: F. R. Peacock.

Yontef, G. M., & Simkin, J. S. (1989). Gestalt therapy. In R. J. Corsini & D. Wedding (Eds.). *Current psychotherapies* (4th ed.). Itasca, IL: F. R. Peacock.

Young, J. E. (1990). *Cognitive therapy for personality disorders: A schema focused approach.* Sarasota, FL: Professional Resources Exchange.

Zeig, J. (1980). *Teaching seminar with Milton Erickson, M.D.* New York: Brunner/Mazel.

Zinker, J. (1991). Creative process in Gestalt therapy: The therapist as artist. *Gestalt Journal, 14,* 71–88.

AUTHOR INDEX

C

D

E

F

G

SUBJECT INDEX